Pixar's Boy Stories

Pixar's Boy Stories

Masculinity in a Postmodern Age

Shannon R. Wooden
Ken Gillam

ROWMAN & LITTLEFIELD
Lanham • Boulder • New York • Toronto • Plymouth, UK

Published by Rowman & Littlefield
4501 Forbes Boulevard, Suite 200, Lanham, Maryland 20706
www.rowman.com

Unit A, Whitacre Mews, 26-34 Stannary Street, London SE11 4AB

Copyright © 2014 by Rowman & Littlefield
First paperback edition 2016

British Library Cataloguing in Publication Information Available

Library of Congress Cataloging-in-Publication Data
The hardback edition of this book was previously catalogued by the Library of Congress as follows:

Wooden, Shannon R.
Pixar's boy stories : masculinity in a postmodern age / Shannon R. Wooden, Ken Gillam.
pages cm
Includes bibliographical references and index.
1. Masculinity in motion pictures. 2. Men in motion pictures. 3. Animated films–History and criticism. 4. Pixar (Firm) I. Gillam, Ken. II. Title.
PN1995.9.M34W66 2014
791.43'65211–dc23
2013046686

ISBN 978-1-4422-3358-4 (cloth : alk. paper)
ISBN 978-1-4422-7565-2 (pbk. : alk. paper)
ISBN 978-1-4422-3359-1 (ebook)

∞™ The paper used in this publication meets the minimum requirements of American National Standard for Information Sciences Permanence of Paper for Printed Library Materials, ANSI/NISO Z39.48-1992.

Printed in the United States of America

Contents

Introduction

A Feminist Approach to Boy Culture

It is an exciting time to be feminists and parents in America. Our daughter, if we had one, could be spending her childhood amid a growing and powerful sisterhood of American women: voting for female candidates in her school's mock elections, cheering on the 2012 American Olympic team in what was widely dubbed "The Year of the Woman," competing in her very own girls-only road races and triathlons, and learning in girls-only science camps and media workshops with openly feminist (or at least actively pro-girl) teachers. We would be invited to take our daughter to work, to learn with her at local women's arts and history events, even to walk a mile in women's shoes, taking back the night for her and her girlfriends. Select media, provided we carefully chose and screened, from documentary films to advertising campaigns to gender-specific psychology and self-help books, could tell her what a complex soul she has inside her, what a rich history she has behind her, and what a promising future ahead, as a powerful, smart young woman, beautiful on the inside, where it counts.

Granted, if we had a daughter, we would also have to help her navigate thong underwear marketing directed at tween girls, the relentless standards of thinness, and, tragically, the climate of sexual violence that hangs over high school and college cultures, especially when boys and girls and alcohol converge. We would have to dig up old Wonder Woman comics and nourish a healthy scorn toward macho action flicks whose female sidekicks seem to have failed to evolve even at the glacial pace of the rest of American society. We would still have to be vigilant about the numerous negative messages assaulting our child as she learns what being a woman in our culture has meant and anticipates what it might someday mean, taking care to check our own insidious biases and resist perpetuating the mixed and flawed messages we ourselves still sometimes blindly consume. As parents of a daughter, we might be even more determined to break glass ceilings, even more outraged at the persistent wage gap between men and women, even more aghast at Rihanna videos than we already are, just as feminists and parents.

In this imperfect and exciting time, though, we would have help: an emerging, and effective, feminist discourse is teaching us how to talk to and for our girls. As parents of a daughter, we would have an enthusiastic if not univocal American community in our corner, encouraging us to consciously and deliberately help our child develop into a strong person, ready to dream her big dreams and enjoy previously unthinkable opportunities now widely available. If examples of the media's exploitative relationship to women still abound and even yet outnumber the positive and healthy representations we need—and this is true, as social media sites and advocacy groups like Miss Representation continually remind us—the very existence of organizations like this and the innumerable internet conversations its members begin every day suggest that an important conversation is well underway. That Barack Obama, arguably the least sexist president in history, would thoughtlessly and inappropriately praise the physical appearance of the California attorney general in 2013 is only half the story; the way the internet blew up in blogs, editorials, and social media the very next day reveals an unprecedented fluency with gender discourse and a freedom in exercising it that marks real progress and warrants real optimism. We can all agree that there is more work to do for women in early twenty-first-century American culture—and globally, of course, much remains to be done to make the world safer, freer, and fairer for women and girls—but it is just as evident, if more willfully hopeful, that a productive conversation has at least begun to shape our cultural imagination.

No longer restricted to academics and political activists, this discourse about women and girls is taking place across a wide swath of media. Scholarly articles in academic journals join with everything from blogs, message boards, and websites to satiric memes and parodic tweets to examine and critique the roles and representations of women in contemporary culture. This chorus of disparate voices, from different walks of life and various levels of theoretical sophistication, is itself a testament to feminist thought in more ways than one: besides scrutinizing social constructions of gender, feminism has long been dedicated to giving voice to the previously silenced. That girls themselves can talk about the world they live in—even, ironically, offering spirited defenses of their decision to shun the word *feminist*—could be celebrated as one of feminism's greatest achievements. Further, it would seem, a feminist discourse has enthusiastically crossed the divide between pedagogy and popular culture in terms of locating its subject matter, as cultural critics like Paulo Friere and Henry Giorux have long encouraged.

Friere and Giroux see critiquing popular culture as an urgent intellectual endeavor, revelatory of "some of the most pressing problems confronting . . . society," and comprising a crucial "part of a wider struggle for democracy."[1] Giroux argues that the media in particular is "a substantial, if not the primary educational force in regulating the meanings, values, and tastes that offer up and legitimate particular subject positions."[2] Similarly, borrowing language from Louis Althusser, Stanley Aronowitz argues that mass media should be considered a "public school system," working alongside formal educational institutions as a "chief ideological state apparatus," that which maintains the "social imaginary, the place where kids situate themselves in their emotional life."[3] As if in direct response to such exhortations, current feminist discourse both within and beyond the academy takes as a commonplace the notion that popular culture's representations of women have a direct and meaningful influence on shaping the identities of girls. The discourse that political and academic feminisms have created is thus critically situated, even when cultural theories are not explicitly brought to bear.

This current conversation likewise benefits from its intellectual and theoretical roots in gender studies, which continue to give it shape and rigor. The basic truisms of gender theory—that gender identity is socially constructed, built of numerous performed behaviors, and policed from within—have pervaded the popular discourse so that even the most accessible cultural analyses may yet be incisive and insightful. Humorous blogs that circulate in social media every spring, for example, send up the women's-magazine phrase "bikini body" by reminding women that such a phrase governs a particular set of behaviors and that any of us with a body could don a bikini if we chose. Judith Butler might include such a behavior as a "cultural performance," among a number of "signifying gestures through which gender is established"[4]; alongside the bloggers' exhortation to women to decorate their bodies with bikinis if they wish to, regardless of age, weight, or fitness level, thus logically creating a "bikini body" but obviously violating the disciplinary spirit of the phrase, Butler might note that women monitor and judge one another through "the compulsory frames set by the various forces that police the social appearance of gender."[5] Gayle Rubin might echo the bloggers' implicit or explicit critique of a society that trains women to primarily value their bodies as visually pleasurable to others; Sandra Bartky might lament that women still over-identify with their bodies, finding their erotic pleasure through their own objectification. At any rate, even nonacademic writing enjoyed by thousands of nonacademic readers reflects the theoretical constructs of academic feminism.

The analytical humor, or humorous analysis, of "bikini body" texts exemplifies also the practical aims of feminist discourse: unlike earlier models of textual analysis, feminism has sought to affect lived cultural practice. Recognizing, with cultural critics like Giroux, that messages in popular texts are ideological "teaching machines,"[6] feminists have targeted texts as widely diverse as advertising's images of women's bodies, the political rhetoric of so-called women's issues, institutional structures that impede women's success in the workplace, and the narratives charted for female characters in books, film, and television, endeavoring not only to record the world but also to change it.

A particular target of this conversation has been the reductive stereotypes of women relentlessly promoted by the Disney Princess films and branding. Disney, with its extensive cultural reach, "wields enormous influence pedagogically," as feminist scholars before us, like those in Elizabeth Bell et al.'s excellent critical collection *From Mouse to Mermaid: The Politics of Film, Gender, and Culture,* have noted.[7] Jack Zipes says, following Sandra Gilbert and Susan Gubar, that the "classic 'sexist' narrative" of films like *Snow White* consistently denies women the right to "chart their own lives," instead "reinforc[ing] nineteenth-century patriarchal notions . . . about the domestication of women," rendering their heroines "pale and pathetic . . . [and] helpless."[8] These critical observations about the princesses are nearly a generation old now, but their rhetorical daughters and granddaughters are still speaking, not just about the films but also about the vast cornucopia of merchandise, and not only from the academy but also in popular or journalistic books like Peggy Orenstein's *Cinderella Ate My Daughter* and in social media texts generated from (and shared across) a million cell phones and personal computers.[9] One needn't look far to find complaints about the residual sexism in Disney, lamentations of the dearth of female leads in Disney/Pixar, or criticism of other reductive representations of girls in mainstream, mass-marketed cultural output.

Such voices, scholarly and otherwise, are having an effect on the culture they monitor, even if their progress seems at times maddeningly slow. As of this writing, there is still no definitive news of a Wonder Woman feature film in the works, for instance, despite male comic book heroes' seeming to grace movie screens all summer every summer, but when Disney revealed its boys' and girls' Marvel Avengers shirts in the spring of 2013—the boys' shirts said, "I'm A Hero," while the girls' said, "I Need a Hero"—the internet outcry and online petition, according to Miss Representation, compelled the company within days to pull the shirts from Disney Store shelves and online catalogs. Though there's obviously more work to do, in other words, the effects of the crescendoing feminist discourse on the manufacture of cultural texts and products are indisputably beginning to materialize.

In narrative cinema, too, changes are slowly taking place. Pixar's Scottish archer and rebel Merida, in 2012's *Brave,* and Disney's ambitious restaurateur Tiana, from 2009's *The Princess and the Frog,* respond, if imperfectly, to the ongoing critique of the Disney princesses, offering new versions of the traditional fairy tale heroine that reflect some reconsideration of the historically flawed narrative trajectories (if not the chronically idealized body shapes) of previous generations' leading ladies. Tiana still gets married, but perhaps on her own terms and with her dream of running a successful business intact. Merida successfully resists arranged marriage, not just changing her own future but also challenging her kingdom's traditional views, by demonstrating a strong voice, will, and body; though a girl, she is outspoken within her family and physically capable, even of surviving in the wilderness. Though some criticized the film for either political or cinematic shortcomings—Merida was too little too late, or a good character in a flawed film—many feminists and parents hailed *Brave* as a refreshing change. If we were parents of a daughter, we too might appreciate its having given us an animated heroine we don't mind our child emulating, the others teaching her egregiously skewed messages about how women should be valued.

TOWARD A CRITICAL DISCOURSE OF BOYHOOD

Alas, we are not parents of a daughter. We have two rowdy, beautiful, brilliant boys. As feminists and parents, though, we still need to interrogate the constructions of gender that influence and shape them, as we seek to understand everything we can about the culture that contributes to their upbringing with or without our consent. Yet the conversation that has authorized voices of outrage to rise up against cultural oppression, exploitation, and unhealthy stereotyping of women and girls has given us little to say to our sons. Ken Corbett argues that though "masculinity has finally become a site of inquiry, a problem, the way femininity has been regarded for nearly a century . . . still, the normative narrative of masculinity has yet to be reset."[10] Consider, for instance, the most common responses to *Brave:* cheering its revolutionary representations of "gender," critics largely ignored (or enjoyed!) the fact that its boys and men populate a spectrum that stretches only from animal to imbecile, providing comic relief but little else to its ostensible girl-power message. We have built the discourse to encourage our girls to be self-possessed and tough, like Merida, but there is no one to authorize our objection to the uninterrupted masculine buffoonery of the same film. On the contrary, such male idiocy is widely received with delight.

If we had a girl, in other words, the rich and complex ongoing cultural discourse, rooted in theory and flowering into the popular imagination, could help us think through the films, fashions, and other artifacts that colored her world; our parenting would benefit from a cultural awareness informed by forty years of theory and activism. When we talk about boys, on the other hand, there's hardly a critical discourse in which to participate. Like contemporary race scholars such as Richard Dyer have observed about whiteness, masculinity is the "invisible" gender, the "unremarkable" identity against which other identities are illuminated.[11] Though nearly every review we've seen of *Brave*—dozens of them—refers to its protagonist's gender, for example, and many explicitly consider her interpretation of femininity in pedagogical relation to young female viewers, virtually no one mentions that Lightning McQueen, Buzz Lightyear, and James P. Sullivan are male, and virtually no one has discussed whether these representations of maleness might too have ramifications for boy viewers learning how to define themselves as men. As we discuss throughout this book, boy culture needs examination too. Indeed, *Brave's* depiction of men as buffoonish thugs, amid its supposedly bold stride forward toward gender equality in children's film, reveals one contemporary attitude toward masculinity that merits some serious attention.

Feminists have noticed at least that the overwhelming majority of Pixar's main characters are male, calling Pixar a "boys' club" in which models of femininity are too few and too far between. In the popular conversation about Pixar's gender record, though, few of those *criticizing* that fact actually also *critique* the films' representations of masculinity or femininity. Instead, one finds a lot of *counting*: the problem seems to be, simply, that there are too many boys in leading roles and too few girls. This superficial complaint contributes little to the conversation besides a general feeling that boys and men are kind of in the way, that it's just not fair that so many of them hold the positions they do. Clamoring for arithmetic equality does not equal critical rigor, enumeration is no substitute for what Bell et al. describe as a necessary "system or vocabulary" for critically approaching Disney,[12] and superficial comparisons are not the theoretically sound conclusions of academic gender studies at all. In fact, counting as criticism assumes the a priori power of the masculine without problematizing the underlying structures on which it is built, without interrogating the definitions and rubrics by which a male character may be judged, and without even examining the surface elements of his character's development or plot trajectory. By his very presence, in other words, we assume the imperviousness of a male protagonist's patriarchal power and do nothing to inquire into (a) whether such an assumption is valid anymore (or ever was), (b) at what cost said power is granted, or (c) how such power might be ethically and productively refigured for our current age. In huge ways, feminism is past this: forty years after Title IX, our understanding of gender and social justice has evolved far beyond the simplistically quantifiable, to include analysis of how complex discursive constructs of power may be built, maintained, altered, or dismantled. Male bodies, though, are still largely read as simple metonyms of power, regardless of whether such power is available or illusory, or in either event, enabling or damaging.

Often, in American popular culture, patriarchy and traditional masculinity do still seem to rule. Countless texts celebrate the traits of physical might, aggression, emotional reserve, and authority and/or dominance over women, suggesting that the type of masculinity R. W. Connell and others describe as "hegemonic" yet prevails.[13] As a descriptive phrase, Connell and Messerschmidt argue that hegemonic masculinity is at least potentially fluid, as hegemonies can evolve,[14] but even the most uncritical assumption of masculine power in mainstream cultural texts is easily enough supported by scads of textual evidence: live-action superhero films, for instance, however they develop the tortured backstory of their (increasingly anti-)heroes, seldom question masculine might or right, seldom seek solutions apart from violent conquest, and seldom elevate "alternative" masculinities to the levels of power occupied by the hegemonic males. By turning our focus to boys, we don't mean to ignore this reality. Neither would we suggest that feminism's work in girl culture is finished or that anywhere in what we sometimes call a "postfeminist" world, feminism is no longer needed.[15] But we do believe that the landscape is changing for masculinity, that it needs to change, and that it is time to borrow from feminism the practices of theoretically informed cultural interrogation so effectively used to examine, illuminate, and productively change the world for women and girls. In this book, we train the critical lenses of gender studies onto the constructions of boys in children's film, investigating the culture of boyhood and the cinematic pedagogies that reinforce it, and striving to contribute to a critical discourse too often lacking productive explorations of masculinity. It is a good thing that the voices—male and female alike—that today rise to critique gender inequity are no longer limited to the political fringe or to the academy. It remains necessary, however, to continue developing and interrogating theories of gendered selves to keep pace with the changing cultural landscape. In the Pixar films, we find culturally influential representations of boyhood that nonetheless cling to flawed historical models of masculinity. By critically examining these representations and the culture to which they contribute, we hope to make our own small contribution to a richer and more just future.

Hanna Rosin sounds a somewhat frantic alarm about the current state of masculinity with the title of her recent book *The End of Men (and the Rise of Women)*, and she is not alone in announcing the ways men have become "disposable" in a world increasingly full of opportunities for women. Catchy title phrases like *Boys Adrift*, *The War Against Boys*, and *The Richer Sex* suggest a growing anxiety about a postfeminist future for men and boys.[16] Critics and scholars from a variety of disciplines, from education to history to sociology to psychotherapy, for a decade have been describing a "boy crisis," citing rising numbers of young male victims or perpetrators of crime, bullying and other forms of violence; increases in boys' rates of depression, substance abuse, and other mental illnesses; and subsequent decreases in academic, professional, and economic performance by boys and men. There is no consensus on the nature or causes of the problem(s), and opinions are at times stridently in opposition to one another: a surprising number of people still disbelieve or deny that a "crisis" for boys exists at all. Though the data are complex and at times very differently interpreted,[17] boys are still far more likely than girls to get into trouble, to get bullied, to do drugs, to be assigned to special education classes, and to devalue their educational opportunities—including dropping out—and studies are unequivocal about the particular challenges facing boys of color.

But however necessary they are beginning to seem, conversations about boys have proven to be more difficult than one might think. Several strains of masculinist discourse have emerged since the onset of the modern feminist movement, but the attempt to meaningfully extend them to popular conversations about men and boys is fraught with pitfalls and obstruction. Widely variant in foundational paradigm, and surprisingly—even angrily—divisive, those concerned with men and boys both face and create obstacles to a productive, widespread cultural critique. Though current academic scholarship in "masculinity studies" weds sociology, history, and cultural theory to establish a theoretical paradigm heavily indebted to feminism, offering critiques like Michael Kimmel's of *masculinity* as a social and historical construct, this approach represents only one pole on a continuum. On the other side, the continuum stretches all the way to arch-conservative, misogynistic "men's rights" groups who purport to represent a relatively monolithic category of *men* in a battle of the sexes whereby they've lost jobs, child custody, and other real and symbolic expressions of power. In between lies everything from anti-feminism to evolutionary theory to psychotherapy to biomedical psychology, and paradigmatic disagreements not only on the solution(s) to the problem(s) but also on the cause(s). These ranging rhetorics can be nearly unnavigable: the American Men's Studies Association, the Male Studies Foundation, and various "men's rights" associations, coalitions, and advocacy groups are all based on very different intellectual foundations, for instance, despite their similar names, and sometimes the very same people who are hailed as gurus by some are vilified as monsters by others.[18]

Perhaps the most fundamental problem, as Susan Faludi notes, is that "crises" in masculinity, however defined, are often understood and/or rhetorically presented as being *about* women on some level.[19] Some advocates for boys have even directly blamed feminism for their current plight. Christina Hoff Sommers's *The War Against Boys: How Misguided Feminism Is Harming Our Young Men* (2000) is among the most famous articulations of the pro-boy argument that blames boys' failures to thrive on the "feminization" of our educational institutions. Despite a 2013 revision of her book that revises the title to blame "misguided *policies*" rather than "*feminism*," and despite the author's having articulated "regrets" for her initial titular blame of feminism, Sommers's case for boys still defends them from a number of "politically correct" or, in the 2013 revision, "boy-averse" policies put in place to level the educational playing field for girls. Sommers argues that things like minimizing violent and aggressive games allowable at school and zero-tolerance policies for violence punish boys "who will, after all, be boys," with rough-and-tumble, aggressive natures that cannot be suppressed.[20] If one's line of reasoning leads to the conclusion that policies designed to help girls must be undone in an effort to help boys, it is understandable that advocates for girls would be unwilling to engage or that an unproductive fight over fairness would be its primary result, which of course gets us nowhere nearer to a productive critical discourse of boyhood.

In less pointed conversations as well, speaking for boys can inspire odd—even hostile—binaries and defensiveness. Even when feminism is neither blamed nor even mentioned, advocacy for boys often initiates a sort of competition between males or females for who has it worse in American society. A telling example begins with a 2012 opinion piece by David Brooks in the *New York Times*.[21] Brooks uses the conceit of Shakespeare's Prince Hal to illustrate the difficulties faced by "rambunctious," immature boys in American schools. Citing reputable—and disconcerting—statistics, Brooks does not blame feminism; indeed, he hardly mentions girls or women at all and hypothetically includes some of them among individuals who don't well fit the specs of the current model student. What he does do is describe how the rowdy but lovable Hal might end up suffering from modern institutions (and medicalization) of education, and calls, if generically, for pedagogical ingenuity that might actually make a difference in the lives of children or could at least influence public opinion about educational design. His argument, though, seems to have fallen on some of the selectively deaf either/or antagonists to a productive conversation about the boy question. Informally, in the message board after the online article, "MKG" from New Jersey articulates a forceful but fairly common, and ostensibly feminist, refusal to even entertain the question: "When there are more female CEOs than male CEOs, then we can begin to worry about this so-called boys' crisis," he or she writes. Feminist blogger Soraya Chemaly more formally typifies the obstructionist tendency to hijack boy questions and mire them in arguments about the state of the world for women. In her *Huffington Post* op-ed, days after Brooks's article, Chemaly steadfastly refuses to engage with the data Brooks cites, on the grounds that whatever boys' struggles, women have always had it worse: "Brooks' description of boys' woes in school sounds like girls' and women's experiences *in all of life* after the age of five," she says. "Take the situation faced by boys in school, gender reverse it and exponentially explode it and you might get a hint of what it is like for women in the U.S. workplace."[22] Such arguments, of course, illogically punish children for the apparent sins of their fathers, but, moreover, they are explicit in their attempts to filibuster the conversation about boy culture in twenty-first-century America.

We agree with what psychotherapists Dan Kindlon and Michael Thompson say in their book *Raising Cain: Protecting the Emotional Life of Boys*: "As right as the concern for girls is, we are disturbed by the dialogue when it seems to pit boys against girls in the quest for fairness."[23] Besides, the very structure of this straw-man argument indicates a thought error: gender critique cannot be an either/or conversation without reinforcing the very essentialist binary that feminists and queer theorists have been troubling for decades. Kimmel points out that Sommers's argument, even in its well-intentioned effort to effect positive change, cites the "natural" aggression and physicality of boys and thus fails to interrogate the "ideology of masculinity" instead of just assuming how boys (essentially) are and what, then, they (naturally) suffer from. One consequence of this error, as Kimmel says, is that it gives up, acquiescing to the notion that boys can't be any better than stereotypes of their "boy-savage" if not quite "feral" natures.[24] Persisting in naturalizing the "boys will be boys" nonsense of the past may authorize violence and competition and resist the potential for boys to develop their nurturing and loving aspects, aspects that should be readily available to all people: "Are we not also hard-wired," Kimmel says, "for compassion, nurture, and love?"[25] From the field of psychoanalysis, Corbett identifies another danger of such essentialism, namely its normalization of a "culturally ordered" masculine template and consequent underestimation of the "spectrum of masculine bodies and minds."[26] This alone is a problem, enabling exclusion and abuse for countless boys whose self-concepts fall outside these narrow cultural norms. Corbett is emphatic: "We can no longer presume that masculinity develops within a psychically specific heteronormative . . . story."[27]

Even more basically, such an essentialist binary is theoretically unsound and thus can't sustain a critical dialogue. Feminism has long assumed that gender is not an essential, "coherent and stable" identity. Butler criticizes such a construction of "woman" as "an unwitting regulation and reification of gender relations," and argues that "such a reification [is] precisely contrary to feminist aims."[28] Yet both sides of the "men's crisis" debates seem to revert to second-wave essentialist binaries without a second thought: boys suffer because of girls, or boys suffer because they're boys, or boys suffer in comparison to girls, or girls still have it worse than boys, with each claim paying little regard to the questions it's begging. Essentialist assumptions of women, says Butler, have presumed essentialist views of men, historically coexisting with the equally "fictive" logical "shortcut" of believing "that the oppression of women has some singular form discernible in the universal or hegemonic structure of patriarchy."[29] But a monolithic construct of masculinity, left uninterrogated, is as false as one for femininity and must comprise as much of a trap for individual people as "femininity" has been. To dismantle systematic challenges facing children and to liberate boys and girls alike from the restrictive models of gender that shape so much of their identities, this conversation has to be both/and—interrogating the spectrum of identities and social performances. Oversimplifying to a retrograde theory of gendered identity undoubtedly causes more problems than it solves.

Finally, though, the biggest obstacle to a productive critical discourse about representations of masculinity in culture, a conversation that could inform our consumption of the cultural texts that shape American boys as we have learned to more critically consume the culture of girlhood, seems to be the sense that it's unnecessary. Kindlon and Thompson attest that one of their first challenges, as they began their work with boys, "was to convince skeptical parents and educators," who tend to see men's power and prestige in society as a guarantee of boys' future success and "to diminish the importance of any problems they might experience in childhood."[30] Chemaly's response to Brooks indicates an angrier version of this same skepticism: boys don't deserve to have a critical discourse, she implies, because they already bear the mantle of privilege. Attacking concepts like the "male standard" and "boy entitlement" to argue that boys will be fine over the long haul, Chemaly takes Brooks to task for failing to note "boys' unbounded confidence or life for Henry after school where Henry will probably get a job in a higher-paying male-dominated sector."[31] In so doing, Chemaly unwittingly exemplifies what Kindlon and Thomspon observe as a common "tendency to presume that a boy is self-reliant, confident, and successful, not emotional and needy. People often see in boys signs of strength where there are none, and they ignore often mountainous evidence that they are hurting."[32]

It is true enough that boys do still have many cultural models to emulate (a lack of which, historically, feminists have rightly lamented for girls) and, according to recent educational statistics, little being demonstrably taken away, even as girls succeed. But as Kindlon and Thompson have learned, from a combined thirty-five years of experience, "boys suffer deeply as a result of the destructive emotional training our culture imposes upon them, . . . many of them are in crisis, and . . . all of them need help."[33] For the majority of boys and young men, the "power" on display may do more harm than good.

A BOY CULTURE IN CRISIS

Beyond the illogic of blaming millennial boys for their forebears' privilege is the fact that American power has always been the hallmark of class as well as gender and as such has always been concentrated in the hands of a small few. Patriarchal privilege never did trickle down with particular generosity for most individual men, even in the most unambiguously patriarchal periods in American history, and "hegemonic masculinity" has been the privilege of the

minority.[34] Furthermore, without blaming feminism for the failures of masculinity to adapt, it is undeniable that at the current moment, even this (in-
consistent) landscape must be changing for boys and men as it changes for
girls and women. If boys ever did expect the power of patriarchy to trickle
down evenly, irrespective of the lines of class, in other words, they have even
less reason to expect it to anymore. While we celebrate and perpetuate the
emerging rhetoric(s) of girl culture (and continue to critique it with vigilance
and rigor, as is appropriate), we need also to acknowledge the fact that this
new, popularized feminist rhetoric isn't working to change the conversation
for boys in equally exuberant ways, despite the eroding historical structures
of masculine identity. "Girl power" may be an exciting, even compelling
rhetorical concept before it's a full-blown social success story, but "boy
power" is finding fewer and fewer socially appropriate expressions, engen-
dering more confusion or fear than celebration.

Again, this inequity isn't the fault of those who advocate for girls and
women, whose work is still needed and appreciated, and if we were parents
of a daughter we would probably be even more grateful for their tireless
effort than we already are. But it is bizarrely antithetical to early iterations of
third-wave academic feminism and its foundational belief in gender identity
as cultural construct, which could lead us all into freedom from social prescription and its many discontents. Kimmel says we have traditionally struggled to understand masculinity as a gender identity, built across our cultural
history, because "we haven't known what questions to ask."[35] Thanks to
feminism, we do, now, have some idea of what these questions are, but most
of us still aren't asking them.

It should come as no surprise to anyone who's been active in theory-
based conversations about women and girls that masculine identity is taught,
performed, and disciplined, and it should be obvious that cultural representations of boys might influence actual boys. If we find unhealthy representations and troubling messages in mainstream American media—that "public
school" for maintaining ideological hegemony—it is reasonable to fear their
having adverse influence on our children. Lyn Mikel Brown et al., in *Packaging Boyhood*, argue that "media and marketing are far more insidious and
pervasive" than politics, education, or other forces, in shaping masculinity.[36]
If lacking a lightning rod like Barbie or the Disney princesses, boy culture
has always been just as deeply immersed in popular media as girl culture, and
the media tutorials on how to grow into adult male identity have been far too
monolithic and far too stagnant. As feminists have worked to revise the
scripts for girls, the cultural definitions of masculinity have "remained relatively inelastic, while the world around has changed fundamentally," according to Kimmel, "and we are not preparing young boys for the world they are
about to enter."[37]

We fail to prepare boys, in part, by juxtaposing the erosion of patriarchal privilege—the world, moving toward equality, that "[boys] are about to enter"—with the reification and celebration of a macho ideal, an exaggeration of that very eroding power. It seems reasonable to speculate that boys are thus facing a kind of subcultural identity crisis, receiving mixed, even paradoxical, messages of gender ideals and norms, as a postfeminist society allows (and/or demands) respect and cooperation from men while boys' toys, shows, clothes—even, sometimes, the tutelage of friends, coaches, and parents—reinforce an outdated and "politically incorrect" manhood.[38] Brown et al. examine an impressive body of cultural artifacts from action figures to pajamas that, though they saturate boy culture and are readily evident to anyone looking, nonetheless overwhelm when collected in a single volume. From Toys"R"Us catalogs to Nick TV commercials to disdainful "loser" t-shirts to animated action films and shows, boy culture's texts tend to draw masculinity as relentlessly competitive, aggressive, violent, and emotionally restrictive, a "parody of manhood" that constructs "a version of power that entices boys into a world of absolute control, dominance over others, and stunted emotional development."[39] Boys are taught to be independent, fearless "winners"; boys are taught to be the first-person shooter, the tough guy with swagger, the superhero with a sharp tongue.[40] But while "boys who can approximate this version of manhood might have more power in the world . . . it's not a world that serves twenty-first century reality very well."[41] Being hyperbolic, of course, it's not an ideal that anyone can actually attain, and few can even hope to approximate.

The anecdote of the Newtown, Connecticut, elementary student who wanted to use his ninja skills to protect his friends from the school shooter in December 2012—who, adorably, sounds like just about every little boy we know—may poignantly exemplify the fruits of boy culture. Certainly, standing up for one's friends is noble, and maybe all children to some degree believe themselves invincible. But understanding that one's strength and bravery must be proven by violence in the face of violence, that "being on the side of justice is an excuse for aggression," is a five-year-old's superheroic dream that doesn't get much displaced on the way to a mature American manhood that bases political opinion on the macho falsehood that "the only way to stop a bad guy with a gun is to be a good guy with a gun."[42] It is a tragic irony that the same culture that taught that brave child how to imagine himself a heroic fighter for good is the very same culture that teaches other boys to shoot up schools in their anger and despair and professes that it is unmanly to opt for nonviolence (or gun control). The dangerous culture of boyhood becomes most urgently visible in troubled boys' too-frequent explosive reactions, the increasingly common face of the outcast acting out, but our desire to exempt those extremely disturbed boys from prevalent social norms is naïve. Jessie Klein, in *The Bully Society*, argues that though they may be depicted as falling far outside of social norms, school shooters typically "affirm[ ], rather than reject[ ] . . . the hypermasculine values" of their schools and communities.[43] We can hardly praise the heroic but inherently violent fantasies of some without considering the full spectrum on which they appear.

The hypermasculinity of boy culture is also notoriously homophobic and rigorously policed for same-sex intimacies or any behaviors—including emotional display or even kindness and consideration—that could indicate a chink in a boy's masculine armor.[44] The danger of a boy culture steeped in "hegemonic masculinity" is not just that boys are restricted, limited, or victimized by artificial yet persistent models of identity but that they are "socialized to do harm to others" and to shy away from gestures of affection or respect.[45] The same culture that authorizes a rhetoric of violence to prove manhood and bravery may thus also enable other horrific eruptions of violent conquest like sexual assault. In a TED talk on masculinity in children's film, Colin Stokes notes that though scholars have studied the impact that boys' violent cultural narratives have on girls, and that culture is beginning to teach girls how to "protect themselves from the patriarchy," we haven't paid much attention to what the same narratives do to boys, despite the obvious and urgent connection between those two potential influences.[46] Certainly the media's reinforcement of a singularly narrow model of manhood has dramatic implications for the way boys learn to think of women and of themselves as citizens in a complex and diverse world. If the ideological pedagogies of both the media and actual educational institutions enforce an aggressive, competitive framework for judging manhood, "violence as a requisite of masculinity,"[47] and we continue to present women as narrative rewards, Stokes implies, perhaps we ought to feign less surprise when they perform masculinity in aggressive and competitive ways and behave as if women are props in the performance, a form of social capital. "Who are these guys?" Stokes asks of the hypothetical sexual assailants responsible for staggering numbers of sexual violence against women. "What are they learning? What are they failing to learn?"[48] In isolation, any one of the numerous occurrences of mass violence or sexual assault to hit the media in recent years might be traceable to a small, specifically unhealthy subculture, an individual person's neurochemical illness or sociopathology, or a damaged child's particularly horrible upbringing, but in their sheer numbers and striking parallels, these incidents must call attention to the cultural landscape from which they emerge.

In contemporary boy culture, boys use the language of violence even to forge friendly relationships with one another: in *Guyland,* Kimmel describes hazing rituals as acts of violence to which boys willingly submit in order to become men in one another's eyes by showing neither fear nor pain. When we assume the boys who commit dramatic acts of violence are wholly delinquent, entirely outside the norms of society, we fail to understand the structures of boy culture and the spectrum of male behaviors alike in kind if, mercifully, not degree. Kimmel is emphatic: "There is no way around it: Most young men who engage in acts of violence—or who watch them and do nothing, or who joke about them with their friends—fully subscribe to traditional ideologies about masculinity. . . . If anything, they are overconforming to the hyperbolic expressions of masculinity that still inform American culture."[49] Certainly, individual boys have idiosyncratic problems, but the ideas of masculinity that yet hold sway in our culture are themselves deeply problematic.

According to Kindlon and Thompson, what boys' acts of violence may reveal is an "exercise [of] emotional ignorance."[50] What we don't give boys is the psychological equipment to sort through the myriad emotions they, like any children, experience; on the contrary, the aggressive and competitive models of boyhood and manhood in their media actively shut down the development of a vocabulary with which to understand and communicate feelings, creating an epidemic of "emotional illiteracy."[51] Even very young boys, Kindlon and Thompson argue, are redirected from their complex individual emotional landscapes "toward silence, solitude, and distrust," and that even at a young age, such emotional illiteracy shows through their inconsiderate treatment of others.[52] Without a working vocabulary with which to understand the complexity of his inner self, "a boy meets the pressures of adolescence and that singularly cruel peer culture with the only responses he has learned and practiced—and that he knows are socially acceptable—the typical 'manly' responses of anger, aggression, and emotional withdrawal."[53] Most boys, mercifully, don't shoot or rape their peers, but individual psychological problems are regrettably common conclusions of this identity-building structure presumed to be rooted in (or evidence of) the male body. Simply put, stunted emotional development plus the relentlessness of a competitive, aggressive boy culture equals staggering rates of depression, substance abuse, and suicide, much more frequently experienced by boys than girls.[54]

Where does this inner turmoil come from? What is the "singularly cruel peer culture" Kindlon and Thompson describe? Much of Giroux's work in cultural criticism has pointedly to do with education, as he exhorts schools themselves to acknowledge the pedagogical influence of extracurricular culture on the identities of their students and even the assumptions on which their curricula are based. Education cannot stand outside culture, Giroux argues, "because it always presupposes a particular view of citizenship, culture, and society."[55] Furthermore, though, as Klein argues, "what occurs in schools themselves"—the ideological constructs that create social and cultural norms within school, yet still presumed to exist outside the curriculum—may be what "causes so many students to become anxious, depressed, and motivated by rage."[56] Connell and Messerschmidt claim that "gender is made in schools and neighborhoods through peer group structures,"[57] and Klein, similarly, sees American schools as a microcosm of oversimplified, anti-progressive American values (like patriarchy, competition, and economic inequality). For boys, before entering the postfeminist world of changing power distribution, childhood institutions may provide an appealing, if simplistic taxonomy of power, an illusion that uncomplicated patriarchal authority still exists. High school, and earlier, becomes a testing ground for these immature ideas of power, "pressure cookers where ruthless competition and other hypermasculinity imperatives are expressed in extreme form,"[58] "the central terrain where gender identity is tested and demonstrated."[59] Boys rank, socially, by their possession of certain types of "capital"—including money, yes, but also body type, talent in certain peer-sanctioned activities (like athletics), and access to the most socially important information.[60] The result is a "bully society" based on a value system of homophobia, classism, sexism, and violence, echoing and perpetuating the "zero-sum game" of American culture beyond high school, where one "can win only if someone else loses, rise only by ensuring that someone else falls."[61]

American boy culture's failure to revise its criteria for masculine success ensures that many boys—most of them, by definition—will fail to measure up. Though it may seem like it defines the norm, "hegemonic," say Connell and Messerschmidt, is "not assumed to be normal in the statistical sense; only a minority of men might enact it."[62] The rest occupy a spectrum of "alternative masculinities" that range from "complicit" to "marginalized" to directly "oppositional."[63] In extreme cases, this failure might result in violence or, more commonly, in emotional distress. In popular media, though, a new option between success story and "loser" does seem to be emerging: the "cool, slacker dude" that gives boys a "saving-face alternative" to failure.[64] Sometimes called a "beta," or even "omega" male, to distinguish him from the "alpha male" typically understood to occupy the top of the social pyramid, this character is distinct from masculine underachievers as old as the ill-fated Don Quixote, in that he remains "unbothered by his inability to live up to the masculine ideal,"[65] neither ambitiously trying to climb the illusory ladder nor angrily trying to dismantle it. Exemplified to Brown et al. by a number of Will Farrell characters, this character also tends to occupy a leading role, rather than a peripheral one like the Shakespearean fool and his descendants. The contemporary beta or omega male seems happy enough in his apathy, organizing into groups of like-minded guy friends, all unconsciously objecting to the relentless success measures of masculinity. They populate numerous humorous marketing campaigns: Rosin cites a television spot advertising a pickup truck that features a group of men nagged into a stupor by the idea of girlfriend—no women ever appear in the ad—but commercials for everything from beer to cell phones similarly celebrate the type. Frequently characterized not only by professional and romantic apathy but also by substance abuse, the character pervades television and film as well, in characters from Seth Rogan's Ben Stone in *Knocked Up* (2007), the lovable loser who implausibly ends up co-parenting with the professional power-house played by Kathryn Heigl, to the stoner trio of Comedy Central's *Work-aholics.* Underachievement has begun to appear a desirable option for men who fail to conform to the "ridiculous" masculine norms that elsewhere prevail.[66]

Though it may seem a leap at first, we posit that—or at least seriously wonder if—substance abuse in these texts is analogously endorsed by the frantic rush to medicalize boyhood. If the leads of *Pineapple Express, Our Idiot Brother,* and a dozen other omega-male stories are perpetually stoned or drunk, we may reasonably assume that they've *learned* to self-medicate as an alternative to the success models they cannot attain. When we look for the juvenile sources of that lesson, we find not only adolescences full of illegal substances but also a flurry of prescription drugs, given with the consent, or even enthusiasm, of parents. We freely acknowledge ADHD as a legitimate condition for which many children may benefit from drug regimens in con-cert with other forms of therapies, and we don't consider ourselves qualified to speak with authority on our suspicion that such a condition is sometimes conveniently diagnosed or overprescribed, though we are clearly not alone in that suspicion.[67] In any case, we are shocked by the rhetorical nonchalance with which contemporary American culture tells roughly one in ten of our children—and nearly three times as many boys as girls—that they're dis-eased or medically "disordered," formalizing a "frantic new version of the old view of a boy as someone who needs 'fixing.'" Kindlon and Thompson argue that "in this fix-frenzied spirit of the times," ADD/ADHD can become an default explanation for any boys who struggle with self-discipline and impulse control that incites a "willingness—even an eagerness, on the part of some adults—to medicate boys, not just to make them clinically 'better,' but to make them *better boys.*"[68] If in childhood, we increasingly promote phar-maceuticals as reasonable solutions to social and environmental difficulties, it stands to reason that adult men might incorporate chemical solutions into their responses to social failure.

Though an apparent alternative to traditional masculine success, the emergence of drugged "beta" or "omega" male leads does nothing to disman-tle the structure on which masculine power has been built; on the contrary, if paradoxically, such a subject position reinforces it. As Adorno and Hork-heimer, Gauntlett, and others have argued, the complicity of the underprivi-leged in their own domination and the enjoyment with which audiences receive (and embody) the disenfranchised subject position depend on an acceptance of the very set of assumptions that renders them powerless. More simply put, if the structures of power against which the "loser" is apathetical-ly revolting actually began to crumble because of his revolution, the humor would fail—the loser would become a winner in a social text difficult for its viewers to comprehend. The emotional honesty and intimacies between friends allowed by these "lovable loser" texts, rather than signifying, or enabling, a kind of "queer" revolution from the trappings of heteronormative masculinity as Judith Halberstam hopes,[69] may actually even more forcefully exclude such traits from dominant masculine performances by tying them to "loser" male identities.

Even the most innocuous of children's media mimic the simplistic, hegemonic masculine hierarchies that define boy culture and demonstrate an uncomplicated pecking order of winners and losers and thus reinforce the structures that enable the bully society. The 2010 film *Alpha and Omega* may be the most laughably obvious example, with the lowest-ranked male marked as such in the very title of the film, his natural loser status a crucial plot point in the narrative. There may be some evidence slowly accumulating of a growing complexity in the depiction of masculine identity in children's animated films, however, given examples like *Shrek* and *Rango*. One might reasonably make a case for cinematic characters drawn from books, like Harry Potter and Percy Jackson, who begin as smart, talented outcasts (even, in Percy Jackson's case, with ADHD, which he utilizes as a kind of extrasensory power) but on their respective narrative journeys both find inner strength and learn to rely on the cooperation of trusted friends, including girls and women, and to work through their complex feelings of fear, sadness, and abandonment. Still, for every one of these characters, it seems, there are a million simple iterations of the alpha (*The Teenage Mutant Ninja Turtles*), and omegas (*Spongebob Squarepants*), with little of interest in between. And within the monolithic Disney world, the anomalous Phineas and Ferb stand nearly alone as brilliant, odd, friendly, and happy boys for whom the bully society is an ironic punch line and girls are still (if quietly lovestruck) buddies, active and capable in their own right. Disney's film and television offerings are more typically populated with dumb younger brothers, vaudevillian sidekicks, and dissolute cads as love interests. Even in the be-yourself universe of *High School Musical,* the most successful high school boys aim to play sports at state universities while the female leads are headed to the Ivies. With the incomparable cultural reach of Disney, "hold[ing] such sway over American society," such consistency is troubling.[70]

PIXAR AND BOY CULTURE

Into this world of "crisis" and static masculine roles, the Pixar films seem like a breath of fresh air for parents of little boys. Disney, distributor of Pixar's feature films from the very beginning, has long been creatively involved with the animation studio's products, even before buying Pixar in

2006. But the films that have come out of Pixar seem to tell a very different story of masculinity than that promoted by Disney's other products. With twelve of thirteen films featuring a leading male character, there is some quantifiable merit for the feminist complaint that Pixar is a "boys club," but its membership includes a different sort of boy from the uncomplicated alpha or lovable loser. If their protagonists are also toys or monsters or cars or bugs, the Pixar films tell stories of action and adventure, exciting enough to protect their young male fans from the panoptical discipline of the "boy police" at least through second grade or so (and we can personally attest that even this early boys learn from one another not to confess their fondness for *My Little Pony*).[71] For boys, Pixar's men embody speed, they display super-human strength, and if they can't fly, at least they fall with style. At the same time, as we've argued previously, for concerned parents, they are well situated between the alpha and omega poles: neither excessively violent action heroes nor apathetic male slackers, they are extraordinary yet humble, dynamic yet approachable, forceful yet funny.[72] At the end of the day they each learn to love their friends, nurture children, and support their communities, as they each come to recognize that love is really all you need.

Nearly all of Pixar's women, admittedly, play supporting roles, but they too are interesting characters who at very least represent a variety of successful female types. As feminists and parents who are also academics, we're happy to gently disturb, if not wholly dismantle, the common complaint of female disenfranchisement in the Pixar universe. Neither hypersexualized nor beelining for the altar, Pixar's women are not given as prizes at the end of masculine success stories, as Stokes observes in other boy-oriented narratives (though, admittedly, particularly in *Cars*, this trope lurks just under the surface in the film's depiction of "Piston Cup" racing culture). Granted, they seldom pass the Bechdel test,[73] and there are probably too few of them to satisfy girl viewers looking for someone with whom to identify, but they are also not cookie-cutter women, featuring different skills, interests, desires, and walks of life. Pixar's women are smart, strong, and capable, often even professional. Sally may end up as Lightning's girlfriend, but she's doing fine without a man when he shows up, having chosen to relocate to Radiator Springs after a successful, but stressful, white-collar career in California. Outside Andy's playroom, Jessie is Woody's co-star, not his love interest, and her broken heart has nothing to do with Woody or any other male peer. The young Elastigirl is a rival to Mr. Incredible before she becomes his wife and an adroit colleague afterward. Holly Shiftwell's professional role is different from but not inferior to Finn McMissile's, and she can even step in as "field agent" in a pinch, after Finn's cover is blown. Colette, in *Ratatouille*, is not only a professional woman but also one painfully aware of the inequalities for women in the world of haute cuisine. Even *Monsters Inc.*, whose most visible female character is a three-year-old child, features a female undercover agent, Roz, investigating the corruption at Waternoose's plant. *A Bug's Life*, though it does rewrite a natural matriarchy to feature its male protagonist, also presents feminine strength as inborn. The stay-at-home women in the *Toy Story* trilogy—Bo Peep, Mrs. Potato Head, and Barbie— may exemplify domesticity, more or less, but Pixar elsewhere does a pretty good job of diversifying and empowering its female types. By nearly any measure, Pixar has a more progressive track record with women than Disney does and certainly more than most contemporary action films even aspire to.

At very least, Pixar's women are more fully drawn than most of Disney's men, those "cardboard" princes of the fairy tale films largely "flat depictions of masculinity and . . . broad caricature[s] of the 'hollow crowns' of masculine power and authority."[74] More importantly, though, as we have said previously, these comparative conversations are simplistic and unproductive: neither our descriptions of Pixar's strong women nor others' complaints about their relatively small amount of screen time ought to stand in for more rigorous analysis of gender representations in the texts. Such criticism as yet is scarce. Bell et al. position their collection against Disney's tendency to "successfully invite[ ] mass audiences to set aside critical faculties," its cultural products having been historically treated as off-limits to criticism, partly because of the nostalgic fondness they engender, and Pixar seems to be so far enjoying a similarly Teflon existence. Numerous articles explore the revolutionary computer animation for which the studio is famous, and scholars outside film and literature have used individual films to exemplify economic, archaeological, psychotherapeutic, philosophical, and educational theories. Still, only a miniscule amount of academic literary or cultural criticism interrogates the films' representations of age, race, fat, class, consumerism, or the environment, and even less mentions the films' constructions of gender. To date, only one book-length work, Keith Booker's *Hidden Messages in Disney and Pixar,* deals specifically with Pixar.[75] In embarking on this work, though confessing our own pleasure with the texts as feminists and parents of sons, we nonetheless need to "break the spell," to "intervene" in Disney's otherwise-unchallenged constructions of the very categories we use to shape our own identities and those of our children.[76]

Said spell is cast not only by the films' technologically masterful animation and entertaining characters, but also by their feel-good narratives of love and friendship. Indeed, the lack of attention to Pixar's gender-norming may be precisely because the films *aren't* sensational in their depiction of femininity or masculinity. Even with all those male protagonists, the films are not overtly sexist, and even with all that action, they are seldom explicitly violent, often displacing aggression into verbal taunts or onto nonhuman characters. But as Brown et al. note, the power of the everyday may be insidiously influential in shaping particular narrative scripts for young minds, largely because they go unchallenged, while more graphically, shockingly violent or sexist cultural texts "actually 'deflect' attention away" from those that "don't reach the level of shock and awe that lands them on talk shows and the news."[77] Moreover, cinema may be uniquely suited for perpetuating messages about gender in particular. Citing Teresa de Lauretis, Bell et al. argue that "the technology of cinema constructs gender, controlling the field of social meaning, creating representations that we negotiate and inhabit."[78] Even further, as Booker notes, children's film is particularly important because of the "unusually long lives" of films watched over and over on DVD to become "integral parts of children's worlds."[79] The combination of these elements—the innocuousness of Pixar's depictions, plus cinema's combined visual and narrative tools, the endless repetition of favorite films in a child's life, and a dash of animation's ability to exaggerate the natural—could, hypothetically, wield extraordinary influence in creating new ways of thinking about gendered identities, as Halberstam has argued. Contrarily, though, these features might just converge as a perfect storm in terms of maintaining traditional notions of gender. In either case, we believe that Disney's representational world, powerfully "pedagogical as a hegemonic practice," demands critique, and we hope that such a critique may contribute to a richer understanding of "the politics of everyday life."[80]

Gender critics like those in *From Mouse to Mermaid* have laid the groundwork for this analysis, first, by acknowledging Disney's power to reinforce gender models and then by examining Disney's women. Giroux sees the princess model of femininity as "one of the most controversial issues in Disney animated films."[81] Having been "mythologized" for decades as the "memorable icons" of the Disney oeuvre, the editors claim, the princesses have also been read as reductive, stereotypically beautiful models of domestic femininity.[82] Zipes explains how the lives of the princesses are framed "through a male discourse that pits women against women in competition for male approval of their beauty," and how their stories teach that "the house . . . [is] where the good girl remain[s]."[83] Karen Brooks reads *The Little Mermaid* as saying, "Have an extreme makeover and the world will love you."[84] Dozens of other articles and dissertations contribute examinations of the iconic princesses, nearly all critical of their persistent traditionalism and often lumping them together in an implicit structuralist critique: the problem with, say, Cinderella is not that she happens to occupy a particularly oppressive narrative moment or that she's just a traditional girl at heart but that she's one of an endlessly repeated type of feminine performance, and a restrictive one at that. As late as 1989's *The Little Mermaid*, Zipes says, Disney films depict women as "helpless ornaments in need of protection," and Giroux includes *Beauty and the Beast*'s Belle and Pocahontas among their "retrograde gender roles."[85] Each princess story tells essentially the same tale over and over, reiterating "static" and "androcentric" hierarchies, changing little from decade to decade.[86]

The Disney princes fare just as poorly in terms of their complexity or progressiveness, having always been relatively hollow signifiers, one-dimensional placeholders of power in a patriarchal system unchanged, it would seem, from medieval times. And they have fared even worse in the criticism, with virtually no sustained gender analysis of the princes ever, though Zipes does argue that the princess films ironically "perpetuate a male myth," even more than a female stereotype, and Brooks says the depictions of the fairy tale males are "narrow and often aggressive."[87] Zipes's argument focuses on class, for the most part, seeing *Snow White*'s prince as Walt Disney's view of himself "as lord and master over his company, reaping the fruit of others' labors," while the dwarves depict a humble and determined ethic of work.[88] A small handful of articles on Disney's *Pinocchio, Tarzan,* and *Davy Crockett* comprise the bulk of the criticism on male leads, but they too focus on things other than protagonists' gender identity. Claudia Card ties masculinity to ethics in her reading of Disney's *Pinocchio* becoming a particularly American cultural tale, as the "sanitized" animated version changes the original text's message about developing one's moral agency, to "a macho exercise in heroics," wherein its young protagonist learns that being "real" means "follow[ing] orders," and "avoid[ing] humiliation by pleasing one's father."[89]

Susan Jeffords "The Curse of Masculinity: Disney's *Beauty and the Beast*" is one notable exception among the criticism, and one we used in our previous work on Pixar. Considering the 1991 film as the utterance of a particular historical moment, Jeffords examines the Americanization—and, specifically, the Reagan-era Americanization—of *Beauty and the Beast*, arguing (as Card does) from changes between the Disney version and the source material. Less akin to his eighteenth-century fairy tale ancestor than to his early 1990s cinematic brothers, like Schwarzenegger's "kindergarten cop" John Kimble, Jeffords argues, men who "retroactively [gave] feelings" to their 1980s antecedents, Disney's beast begins not as a nobleman with a wicked fairy's spell already cast on him, but as a selfish, spoiled, childish prince who refuses to help an old beggar woman. The film's plot, focusing on Beast's journey instead of Belle's, thus transforms from a female-centered fairy tale about the power of goodness and kindness into a masculine bildungsroman of sorts, as Belle nurtures the "childish Beast into a loving man."[90] Initially exemplifying the "hardened . . . domineering man of the '80s," Beast becomes "the New Man . . . considerate, loving, and self-sacrificing."[91] Of course, such a plot still places women in the service of men, suggesting that while "no one can be free until men are released from the curse of living under the burdens of traditional masculinities," women like Belle must be available to teach men the lessons necessary to grant such release.[92] But the journey into a "new" model of sensitivity and compassion from one of traditional patriarchal detachment still seems to correspond to the changing world of feminism.

We followed Jeffords's example in our previous article, using her "New Man" model to explain how three of the Pixar films—*Cars*, *The Incredibles*, and the original *Toy Story*—narratively fashion postfeminist men out of traditional "alpha male" types. Across the films' similar plot structures and their narratives of negotiation through various constructs of (hegemonic masculine) power and (feminist) communality and compassion, we demonstrate that Lightning, Mr. Incredible, and Buzz Lightyear all develop a gentler ethic of manhood. Each of these characters, having begun his respective film believing himself an "alpha" superstar or superhero, learns to find joy and satisfaction in a community, cherishing his friends and/or nurturing children. Lightning grows when he learns to respect not only his elders but also his own privilege, contributing materially to the economy and the dignity of the dying Radiator Springs and lending his youthful vigor to the damaged King. Buzz likewise reorients to the playroom community and learns that to care for his child is his most important job. Mr. Incredible, the only natural father in the three films, learns to engage as a dad and a husband, finding a new well of strength in his relational role rather than doggedly holding on to the individualistic power of his past.

These observations hold beyond the three films we looked at in our previous article, ranging only a little in the conspicuousness of their celebrations of (direct or surrogate) fathering. Just as Buzz and Woody take care of Andy in *Toy Story*, Mike and Sulley parent Boo in *Monsters, Inc.* and Mr. Frederickson becomes a substitute step-(grand)dad to Russell in *Up*. Even WALL-E nurtures the fruit of his beloved EVE's abdominal cavity. This trope reminds us that the films are not just for children but for parents who hold the purse strings, and in this context they seem aimed precisely at fathers who grew up watching Michael Gross's Steven Keaton on *Family Ties*, or grandfathers who learned manhood from Alan Alda's Hawkeye on *M*A*S*H*. These narrative gestures—even the new Buzz Lightyear and his father the Emperor Zurg are reunited at the end of *Toy Story 2* for a game of catch, after a send-up of the Oedipally conflicted *Star Wars* trilogy—reward postfeminist dads and the families who love them. This is a social good, even if it's also genius marketing, making parents who take their kids to the movies feel good about being the kind of parents who take their kids to the movies, that ice cream cone at the end of *Up* a kind of reward for all of us who didn't skip our sons' Wildnerness Explorer Scout badge ceremony. *Finding Nemo* is so much about fathering that one critic even thinks it's about mothering. Defining "cultural mothering" as the nurturing behavior overwhelmingly performed by women even in very recent American history, Suzan Brydon argues that Marlin, like the hermaphroditic clownfish he is, "enacts motherhood," not fatherhood as conventionally understood.[93]

Besides Brydon's piece, though, and our previous work, nothing focuses specifically on Pixar's depictions of masculinity; certainly nothing yet published has entirely upset the feel-good conclusions we came to in 2008. But as Bell et al. strive to "enable oppositional readings" of Disney's products,[94] we too have come to value more counterintuitive critical approaches to Pixar, and in this book we challenge our own earlier responses, admittedly born of our parental approbation and fondness for the texts. When we study the texts for what they assume but don't say, when we reset the ends of our historical timelines of masculinity and examining the films' play with historical time, when we situate the films' value systems within the complex culture of contemporary boyhood to which they actually contribute, we may make visible that which has been hidden in plain sight. By asking how the villains are brought to be seen as villainous, charting what the films consistently reward, and identifying which social behaviors are permitted and which disallowed, we may articulate the films' underlying truisms, so "everyday," so normalized in our culture that not even as parents who are also feminists and academics did we notice them at first, or even after several subsequent viewings.

Our first counterintuitive gesture is to situate masculinity within history, to make the gender historically "visible" and to explore the ways in which contemporary representations of masculinity reiterate and/or revise older models. Chapters 1 and 2 revisit the notion of the domesticated man that guided our previous work but take a longer view of the history of manhood. From this new vantage point, we can see the films' obvious nostalgia less as carving out a postfeminist opportunity for men than conservatively reifying an antiquated model of manhood, namely a "greatest generation"—or earlier—brand of physical strength, silence, and conformity. Well-suited to a postfeminist society's demands for male domesticity, engaged parenting, and community orientation, the values that inform this archetype are hardly negative on the whole, but, not unproblematic even in its original historical moment, such a type may be even less suitable as a response to the contemporary "crisis" moment of boyhood.

In the first chapter, we begin by considering *Toy Story* against the backdrop of Kimmel's and Faludi's works on midcentury American masculinity, fatherhood, and celebrity. In the wake of the Great Depression and WWII, Kimmel argues, the markers of "self-made" masculinity had, for many, eroded, creating a midcentury male cultural identity characterized by anxiety and conformity. A cultural celebration of familial patriarchy responded almost frantically to the fear of "gender failure," and the homesteader cowboy became a model of manhood both segregated from the feminine space of the home and safe from contingency on economic success.[95] As the second world war ended and the space race began, Faludi argues, the ideal of the American man evolved from the socially minded, hardworking WWII troop on the ground, to a celebrity masculinity, the offspring of the WWII "flyboy" transfigured into the astronaut. This solo-alpha type, dominant through the later decades of the twentieth century, may appear now as if it has always been, and it is against this type, typically, that forward-looking comparisons (like Jeffords's and ours) are made. With a fuller view of the early to midcentury historical backdrop, though, invited by the very iconography of *Toy Story,* we can situate Woody and Buzz's rivalry in an earlier historical moment. Woody, that representative of 1950s television's nostalgia for America's homesteader past, goes head to head with the astronaut that figuratively replaced him as the idealized male type at midcentury, the film thus privileging something far older than a broadening of masculinity for a postfeminist age.

On the face of it, this nostalgic gesture may seem appealing, particularly to the innumerable fathers in the audiences of Pixar films. But in the same gesture that honors Woody, *Toy Story* disciplines the ambitious, self-aggrandizing standout represented by Buzz Lightyear, stripping him of any dreams of his own excellence and requiring him to reinvent himself as a caregiver. In the reformed Buzz's message to *Toy Story 2*'s Woody, facing his own celebrity status, these same parameters are even more sharply drawn: the domestic space of the playroom and its associated domestic duties provide the only option for masculine satisfaction. In our contemporary moment of "boy crisis," and with four decades of feminism behind us, such a message may be read as far more restrictive than empowering, a lesson of obedience and conformity as compelling—or compulsory—as it would have been for women a generation ago.

As with all our chapters, an argument about one film becomes far more persuasive with the inclusion of evidence from numerous others. The privileging of the conformist, domestic male we identify in *Toy Story* is echoed by the indirect pedagogies of *Cars* and *Finding Nemo* but even more explicitly in the direct instructions given to the young Dash of *The Incredibles* and to *A Bug's Life*'s Flik. Both of these characters are told unambiguously to conform, to "fit in," to "get back in line, like everybody else." These films collectively suggest something further unsettling in our contemporary age of boy crisis: active, ambitious boys either lose (Dash must come in second or be disallowed from competing at all; Lightning McQueen only earns his longed-for Piston Cup between the two *Cars* films, when no one is looking), or get excessively punished (Flik is exiled for a well-intentioned accident; Nemo is threatened with death after showing off his strength and bravery for his new school friends). In the climate of skyrocketing medicalization of boyhood, the cultural view of boys' "toxicity," the epidemic of boys' emotional illiteracy, and the visible dangers of exiling the outcasts, such a push for conformity and silent cooperation to uninterrogated social norms is disconcerting, to say the least.

Since we argue that "alpha" or celebrity males—even rough-and-tumble, high energy, show-off boys—are narratively disciplined into conformity, whether "new men" or "greatest generation" types, it may seem paradoxical that in the next two chapters we claim that the films simultaneously celebrate a traditional "alpha" masculine type. But as we explain in chapter 2, films like *The Incredibles* demonstrate how a certain male body, even as it's controlled or disciplined, may be simultaneously held up as the unassailable standard of manly virtue and success, essentializing masculinity and authorizing a hegemonic masculine performance. If Mr. Incredible needs self-control and a more open mind, broadened so as to include an acceptance of his domestic roles and a newfound respect for his wife and children, he still occupies the *right* body to house male success. It is Syndrome who, small and inauthentically "super," ultimately lacks the appropriate capital to advance on the hierarchy of masculinities. It is Syndrome, too, whom the film punishes, not only foiling his ambitions but actually thrusting him into a jet engine for a particularly brutal demise.

Furthermore, the films' tendency to essentialize masculinity, rooting male success in the athletic "alpha" body, may also be considered amid the historical set pieces that sound a nostalgic call to conformity, especially when we consider how often the films associate the brawny body with manual labor. Ruth Oldenziel explains how the early twentieth century paradoxically celebrated—even fetishized—blue-collar brawn as changes in industrial production divided shop floor knowledge from an increasingly academic engineering profession and thus lowered manual workers' actual authority and power. James P. Sullivan, in *Monsters Inc.* and *Monsters University*, also exemplifies this authorization of traditional "body capital" and a nostalgia for shop floor honor. Contrasted with the one-eyed, skinny-limbed performer (and, in the prequel, scholar), Mike, and the metaphorically inauthentic chameleon, Randall, Sulley's big, blue, and blue-collared masculine body transcends even species variety to reinforce the ideal male physical type.

This essentializing of masculinity in a particular body type may reinforce the ideological structures of the bully society by insisting on, and privileging, physical definitions of manliness to which most boys fall short, and perpetuating what Klein calls "the jock cult."[96] Alpha in their brawny bodies, Pixar's men are often measured in a competitive environment that predictably excludes, exiles, and punishes characters who don't fit the idealized masculine model. As we discuss in chapter 3, the geek-uprising plot of *Monsters University* does not even marginally threaten the hierarchy that allows it to mercilessly bully Mike, the supposed protagonist of the film who, instead of reaching his dream, gets decisively situated in his "natural" status, beneath the RΩRs, the JθX, and his own best friend. The glorification of athleticism is most evident in *Cars* and *Cars 2*, where the stocky, speedy Lightning is not only the utmost alpha male but also the very symbol of America's global authority (contrasted to the bumpkin abroad, Mater). His American steel, honored along its patriarchal lineage in the first film when set to go head-to-head with an evenly matched foe, is visually contrasted in the sequel to the sleek, delicate European Formula cars, a contrast that, reinforced by Lightning's unlikely successes in the World Grand Prix, validates not only his athletic body but also a view of American superiority that then enables the film's surprising xenophobia and unapologetically discriminatory treatment of others. Besides the fast but metrosexual European racecars, the rightness of Lightning's body is contrasted to the wrongness of the disabled, weak, and unfashionable Lemons, and as he and the narrative figuratively vanquish each foe, the film reiterates this value structure whereby violence becomes an appropriate response to those that seem "naturally" inferior. Furthermore, aligning Lightning's body with "big oil" (and simultaneously queering biofuel), the film also masculinizes the sequel's anti-environmental message.

In the fourth chapter, we counter-intuitively examine what Pixar does value by studying what it doesn't and find that what Pixar chooses to vilify is remarkably consistent across the films. Oldenziel's historical context, a period when changes in industrial production materially and rhetorically pitted the idea of the blue-collar worker against the middle-class and rising engineer, may inform not only Pixar's nostalgia for "real-man" brawn but also a clear condemnation of the ostensibly fraudulent masculinity performed by the engineer, technophile, or intellectual. It is beyond ironic that the "fraternity of geeks" who created the innovative technologies of Pixar would be hard on talented inventors,[97] regardless of how Klein says the bully society "nerd-bashes" high academic achievers.[98] But what becomes visible from the historical vantage point of the early twentieth century shop floor is that the films' nostalgic celebration of the brawny male body is continually reinforced by their cruel but consistent punishment of smart boys and men. Indeed, none of the films allow for a techno-geek to achieve masculine success; technology itself appears as the very antithesis to authentic masculinity. Structurally, visually, and descriptively, Pixar bullies the very nerds it creates. Furthermore, if cognizant of the spectrum of "intensities" frequently experienced by gifted children, we can see that Pixar aptly characterizes its misunderstood and under-nurtured gifted boys if only to vilify and exile them. Educational psychologists have noted the particular challenges that intellectual, emotional, and creative intensities might pose for gifted boys, whose talents and interests fall far from the hegemonic "boy code." Like Buddy Pine, whose extraordinary inventive ability dangerously blends with an exaggerated sense of justice, perfectionism, and emotional extremes, these boys can suffer alienation, isolation, and other emotional problems. *Toy Story*'s failure to acknowledge that the complementary constructive and destructive impulses of Sid Phillips are quite common among gifted kids, puts him, with a surprising amount of other extraordinary boys, on a path toward underachievement.

Of course, an essential masculine body (and average intellect) does not suffice to ensure a boy's status in contemporary boy culture, either. The power of wealth and the sign value of particular commodified products are hallmarks of the bully society as well. Historians of masculinity link men's participation in a consumerist economy to changes in production that shifted men's sense of social worth from the labor of his hands to the consumer space once seen as largely feminine, and indeed, some edgy, popular adult films like *Fight Club* have gotten critical attention for their treatment of the postmodern consumerist male as a fraught, and miserable, identity. Such an approach initially may seem entirely irrelevant to the Pixar canon, with all its messages of authenticity and love. Yet right in the middle of the *Toy Story* trilogy is a film almost entirely about shopping, recalling Disney's mega-corporate status and reminding us of Disney's role in "determining the role of consumerism in American life."[99] Facing obsolescence—and confronting the vulnerability of their alpha bodies—*Toy Story 2*'s protagonists get a makeover and some retail therapy, indicating that some masculinities can be bought and worn, what Faludi calls "ornamental masculinity." Even the film most obviously critiquing consumer culture, *WALL-E*, assumes the metonymic relationship between self and stuff. Further, noting the fetishization of the commodity in the films retrospectively enriches our previous chapter's critique of Sid Phillips as villain, as breaking *stuff* becomes coded as sociopathic. In chapter 5, we suggest that, even as they superficially encourage their characters to embrace an ostensibly more authentic, and important, emotional life, they ironically teach potentially damaging lessons about determining one's identity and worth with a marketplace mentality.

An interrogation of villainy makes another stripe of Pixar's conservative nostalgia abundantly clear: the so-called "family values" so often perceived as under attack by the progressive energies of feminism. In chapter 6, we challenge the apparently progressive family structures Pixar puts forth with its numerous single and surrogate dads, positing that all these ostensibly postfeminist celebrations of fatherhood simultaneously indicate little progress for women. As is made most obvious in the epic *Toy Story 3*, bullying is a symptom long before it is a cause of social evil; throughout the films, Pixar's bully villains are themselves victims, specifically of absent or neglectful parental figures. Buddy becomes Syndrome only after being denied Mr. Incredible's nurture; the Prospector in *Toy Story 2* is angry about the figurative orphanage—the dime store shelf—where he spent his early days. Sid, for all his gifts and flaws, also enjoys far too much unsupervised play. The biggest bully in the bunch, Lotso Huggin' Bear, has never gotten over being abandoned by his little girl, spending his whole life in the institutional setting of daycare. Daycare is chaotic, terrifying, and dangerous, so it stands to reason that nearly all of the successful mothers or mother figures in the entire Pixar canon stay at home or do part-time caretaking work. The idyllic two-parent nurturing home where Andy's toys end up in *Toy Story 3* directly contrasts to horrors of Sunnyside, after all, suggesting that postmodern parental failures may be specifically postfeminist failures. Tracing the changing spectatorial position of the adult over the evolution of the fairy tale into animated feature films, we posit that Pixar's messages resonate with adults on multiple levels simultaneously, perpetuating a conservative model of motherhood and a sharp critique of the way we parent our boys.

Giroux and Roger Simon insist that "when we engage [in] a critical consideration of particular cultural forms . . . we must begin with an acknowledgement and exploration of how we—our contradictory and multiple selves . . .are implicated in the meanings and pleasures we ascribe to these forms."[100] The chapters in this book stem from our great fondness for the Pixar films, as feminists and parents, and an appreciation of the many positive messages they aim to convey. At the same time, we must consider that the ideological structures on which these films are built—particularly those persistent yet unhealthy traditional standards of male value—might complicate or even undermine the messages we think we and our sons are receiving. In several instances, it took us multiple viewings to become aware of the ideological structures: we were shocked, on a few occasions, to see what had been for months (or years) invisible to us, even in plain sight. Such is ideology. Finally, regardless of whether one concludes that Pixar's model of masculinity is more retrograde than it appears—or, contrarily, that Pixar is teaching a progressive new narrative of American boy culture—critics, feminists, and parents need to view its output with much more scrutiny than we are currently doing. We offer this book as a contribution to a conversation about boy culture in media that we hope continues and, as feminism has done, makes a difference in the world for our boys.

NOTES

1. Paulo Friere and Henry A. Giroux, "Pedagogy, Popular Culture, and Public Life: An Introduction," in *Popular Culture, Schooling and Everyday Life,* eds. Henry A. Giroux and Roger Simon (New York: Bergin & Garvey, 1989), viii, xii.

2. Henry A Giroux, *The Mouse That Roared: Disney and the End of Innocence* (Plymouth, England: Rowman & Littlefield, 1999), 2.

3. Stanley Aronowitz, *The Politics of Identity* (New York: Routledge, 1992), quoted in *From Mouse to Mermaid: The Politics of Film, Gender, and Culture,* ed. Elizabeth Bell, Lynda Haas, and Laura Sells (Bloomington: Indiana University Press, 2008), 7.

4. Judith Butler, *Gender Trouble: Feminism and the Subversion of Identity,* 2nd ed. (New York: Routledge, 1990), viii.

5. Butler, *Gender Trouble,* 33.

6. Giroux, *The Mouse That Roared,* 84.

7. Henry A. Giroux, "Memory and Pedagogy in the 'Wonderful World of Disney': Beyond the Politics of Innocence" in *From Mouse to Mermaid,* ed. Elizabeth Bell, Lynda Haas, and Laura Sells (Bloomington: Indiana University Press, 2008), 45.

8. Jack Zipes, "Breaking the Disney Spell," in *From Mouse to Mermaid,* ed. Elizabeth Bell, Lynda Haas, and Laura Sells (Bloomington: Indiana University Press, 2008), 36–37.

9. Peggy Orenstein, *Cinderella Ate My Daughter: Dispatches from the Frontlines of the New Girlie-Girl Culture* (New York: HarperCollins, 2011).

10. Ken Corbett, *Boyhoods: Rethinking Masculinities* (New Haven, CT: Yale University Press, 2009), 8. We must acknowledge the signs of change noted by a few current gender scholars. Judith Halberstam's delightfully optimistic *The Queer Art of Failure* describes the unique opportunities of animated film to rewrite the normative scripts of gender, (Durham: Duke University Press, 2011), and R. W. Connell and James Messerschmidt similarly see the structures of hegemonic masculinity as changing, offering "tremendous multiplicity of social construction" ("Hegemonic Masculinity: Rethinking the Concept" [*Gender & Society* 19, no. 6 (2005)]). We share their hopefulness but agree with Michael Messner, Michael Kimmel, and many others that the nonacademic mainstream culture is very, very behind. See Kimmel, *Guyland: The Perilous World Where Boys Become Men* (New York: HarperCollins, 2008), especially chapter 7, "Boys and their Toys: Guyland's Media," and Messner's *Power at Play: Sports and the Problem of Masculinity* (Boston: Beacon Press, 1992).

11. Richard Dyer, *White: Essays on Race and Culture* (London: Routledge, 1997), 3.

12. Bell et al., *From Mouse to Mermaid,* 3.

13. Connell and Messerschmidt, "Hegemonic Masculinity," 832.

14. Connell and Messerschmidt, "Hegemonic Masculinity," 835.

15. The only real consensus on "postfeminism" is that there's no real consensus on postfeminism. Stèphanie Genz and Benjamin A. Brabon's excellent introduction to *Postfeminism: Cultural Texts and Theories* explains the dozens of interpretations of the hotly contested term. When we use the term in this book, we often qualify it, in part to suggest that feminism's having evolved to a "post" status is more impression than reality. Certainly, we do not use the *post* prefix to indicate that the work of feminism is over, either by completion or demise; though feminism has been a successful, if multifaceted social movement, there is much more work to do. At the same time, we do see the current moment as host to a broad but silent assumption of the most fundamental principles of early feminism. To many of our peers and our millennial-generation students, the right to professional and legal equality for women goes without saying, and many, even without identifying as "feminist," strongly hold the convictions that women (and men, theoretically), can choose from a variety of gender performances. In this respect, our "postfeminist" world is one in which girls and young women simply expect the same rights, privileges, and opportunities as their brothers. When we use the term to describe the current moment, this is the attitude we intend to imply. We see postfeminism not as a social reality, as a death-knell to feminism, or as a specific fourth-wave direction for feminist theory and practice, but as a familiar attitude among young people and, for our purposes, one that often displaces traditional notions of masculinity. Life "post" early feminism could break down barriers for men and women alike, but, as we argue, our society's ostensibly "postfeminist" gestures are often less progressive than they at first appear.

16. Hanna Rosin, *The End of Men and the Rise of Women* (New York: Riverhead Books, 2012); Leonard Sax, *Boys Adrift: The Five Factors Driving the Growing Epidemic of Unmotivated Boys and Underachieving Young Men* (New York: Basic Books, 2007); Christina Hoff Sommers, *The War Against Boys: How Misguided Policies Are Harming Our Young Men* (New York: Simon & Schuster, 2000); and Liza Mundy, *The Richer Sex: How the New Majority of Female Breadwinners Is Transforming Our Culture* (New York: Free Press, 2013).

17. Conventional wisdom increasingly presumes that boys are suffering in school, even when those repeating the claim beg the question in their endeavors to speculate solutions. When amid the clamor, evidence is cited to support the truism, it usually comes more from semester grades and college graduation rates than test scores. Test score data, in fact, seem to generally support the opposite point: the National Science Foundation, for instance, has found that though a gender gap is eroding that has traditionally favored boys on standardized tests in math, girls' and boys' performances on the tests are actually about the same (Tamar Lewin,

"Math Scores Show No Gap for Girls, Study Finds," *New York Times,* 25 July 2008, www.nytimes.com/2008/07/25/education/25math.html [30 October 2013]); similarly, think tank Education Sector analyzed federally collected data in 2006 to the conclusion that boys' test scores are actually fine, "better than ever," and that the so-called "crisis" had been "greatly overstated" (Jay Mathews, "Study Casts Doubt on the 'Boy Crisis,'" *Washington Post,* 26 June 2006, www.washingtonpost.com/wp-dyn/content/article/2006/06/25/AR2006062501047.html [30 October 2013]). This information suggests that only comparisons with thriving girls make successful boys appear less so: Sara Mead, senior fellow at Education Sector, claims, "The real story is not bad news about boys doing worse; it's good news about girls doing better" ("The Evidence Suggests Otherwise: The Truth about Boys and Girls," *Education Sector,* June 2006, www.educationsector.org/sites/default/files/publications/ESO_BoysAndGirls.pdf, 3 [30 October 2013]). Thomas Mortenson, senior scholar at the Pell Institute for the Study of Opportunity in Higher Education, says "boys are about where they were 30 years ago, but the girls are just on a tear, doing much, much better" (quoted in Lewin, "At Colleges, Women are Leaving Men in the Dust," *New York Times,* 9 July 2006, A1, www.nytimes.com/2006/07/09/education/09college.html [30 October 2013]). Still, boys' "treading water" in a changing world is hardly equivalent to "better than ever" (Sarah D. Sparks, "Report Points to Widening Gap in Boys' Educational Attainment," *Education Week,* 17 May 2011, http://blogs.edweek.org/edweek/inside-school-research/2011/05/report_boys_college_readiness.html [30 October 2013]). Moreover, as Kimmel explains, boys' struggles in school are not measurable by the single criteria of test scores ("A War Against Boys?" *Tikkun,* November–December 2000, www.tikkun.org/nextgen/a-war-against-boys [30 October 2013]). Boys' grades are worse from the early grades forward, indicates a recent study by faculty at the University of Georgia, and "in every subject," but those grades do not correlate to their test scores" (Christopher Cornwell, David B. Mustard, and Jessica Van Parys, "Noncognitive Skills and the Gender Disparities in Test Scores and Teacher Assessments: Evidence from Primary School," *Journal of Human Resources* 48, no. 1 [Winter 2013]: 238). Further, Kimmel and many others have noted that boys are far more likely to be marked with other measures of failure: they drop out or flunk in much higher numbers than girls; they are far more likely to be suspended or to get into fights; and they are far more often assigned to special education classes or medicated for ADHD (Kimmel, "Solving the 'Boy Crisis' in Schools," *Huffington Post,* 30 April 2013, www.huffingtonpost.com/michael-kimmel/solving-the-boy-crisis-in_b_3126379.html [30 October 2013]). See also Kimmel, *Manhood in America: A Cultural History,* 3rd ed. (New York: Oxford University Press, 2012), 268, and the National Center for Educational Statistics cited at pbs.org, "Understanding and Raising Boys," www.pbs.org/parents/raisingboys/school.html [30 October 2013]). Dan Kindlon and Michael Thompson include substance abuse, suicide, and homicide among the disproportionately male tragedies of American childhood (*Raising Cain: Protecting the Emotional Life of Boys* [New York: Ballantine Books, 1999], 6).

18. In 1998, Messner analyzed the rhetorics of men's rights organizations, arguing that as early as the late 1970s, men's liberation had split into the "conservative and moderate wings," on the one hand, which "became an anti-feminist men's rights movement" and a progressive, "profeminist" movement on the other, which abandoned "sex role theory" as its foundation ("The Limits of 'The Male Sex Role': An Analysis of the Men's Liberation and Men's Rights Movements' Discourse," *Gender & Society* 12, no. 3 [June 1998]: 255). More recently, Jennifer Epstein described the differences between academic "men's studies" and "male studies" in her account of the establishment of the Foundation for Male Studies ("Male Studies vs. Men's Studies," *Inside Higher Ed,* April 2010, www.insidehighered.com/news/2010/04/08/males [30 October 2013]). Two of the foundation's three directors are medical doctors, so perhaps not surprisingly its focus is much more on the biology of maleness than the social construction of masculinity. To muddy the waters, though, the foundation's board of advisors includes both Christina Hoff Sommers, a former ethics professor who frequently spars with Kimmel over same-sex schools and other potential educational reforms (see n. 20, below), and Warren Farrell, a polarizing figure who has said both that the American family suffers from our "matriarchal" society, and, through a concept he calls "date fraud," that women often say "no" (to sexual activity) when they actually mean "yes," putting men at "risk" of rejection (*The Myth of Male Power: Why Men Are the Disposable Sex* [New York: Simon and Schuster, 1993]).

19. Susan Faludi, *Stiffed: The Betrayal of the American Man* (New York: Harper Perennial, 2000), 7–9.

20. Sommers, it seems to us, has some interesting suggestions about alternative education formats that might better suit some boys: her "The Boys at the Back" begins with the University of Georgia study and describes apparently successful projects to reengage boys in learning (*New York Times*, 2 February 2013, SR1, http://opinionator.blogs.nytimes.com/2013/02/02/the-boys-at-the-back [30 October 2013]). Philosophically, she says, her goal is "fairness," and with that we certainly agree. The difficulty with Sommers's position becomes more evident in immediate contrast to Kimmel, for instance, in a 2000 *Think Tank* conversation between the two, where they wrangle over Sommers's use of words like *natural* and *universal* to describe the high-energy and "rough-and-tumble" play of boys ("Is There a War Against Boys?" *PBS*, 29 July 2000, www.pbs.org/thinktank/transcript893.html [30 October 2013]). Kimmel insists that such rhetoric is self-defeating and discriminatory to many boys—and girls—who fall outside those lines, but Sommers argues that efforts (like Kimmel's) to see masculinity as constructed instead of embodied result in a "feminization" of boys. In 2013, they faced off again, and while Sommers claims to have "softened" her tone, Kimmel still criticizes her "stereotypical thinking" (Kimmel and Sommers, "Do Boys Face More Sexism Than Girls?" *Huffington Post*, 20 February 2013, www.huffingtonpost.com/michael-kimmel/lets-talk-boys_b_2645801.html [30 October 2013]).

21. David Brooks, "Honor Code," *New York Times*, 5 July 2012, A23, www.nytimes.com/2012/07/06/opinion/honor-code.html (30 October 2013).

22. Soraya Chemaly, "'Boy Crisis' in Education Is a Microcosm of Women's Lives," *Huffington Post*, 9 July 2012, www.huffingtonpost.com/soraya-chemaly/boy-crisis-in-education_b_1655282.html (10 June 2013).

23. Kindlon and Thompson, *Raising Cain,* 23.

24. Kenneth B. Kidd, *Making American Boys: Boyology and the Feral Tale* (Minneapolis: University of Minnesota Press, 2004), 16, 182.

25. Kimmel "A War Against Boys?" n.p.

26. Corbett, *Boyhoods,* 8–9.

27. Corbett, *Boyhoods*, 10.

28. Butler, *Gender Trouble,* 5.

29. Butler, *Gender Trouble,* 4.

30. Kindlon and Thompson, *Raising Cain,* 5–6.

31. Chemaly, "'Boy Crisis' in Education," n.p.

32. Kindlon and Thompson, *Raising Cain,* 6.

33. Kindlon and Thompson, *Raising Cain,* 5.

34. Connell and Messerschmidt, "Hegemonic Masculinity," 832.

35. Michael Kimmel, *Manhood in America*, 2.

36. Lyn Brown, Sharon Lamb, and Mark Tappan, *Packaging Boyhood: Saving Our Sons from Superheroes, Slackers, and Other Media Stereotypes* (New York: St. Martin's Press, 2009), x.

37. Kimmel quoted in *Think Tank,* "Is There a War Against Boys?"

38. Kimmel, *Manhood in America,* 6.

39. Brown et al., *Packaging Boyhood*, xi–xii.

40. Brown et al., *Packaging Boyhood*, 3–8, 255.

41. Brown et al., *Packaging Boyhood*, xii.

42. Wayne LaPierre, *National Rifle Association*, 21 December 2012, http://home.nra.org/pdf/Transcript_PDF.pdf (30 October 2013), 5. See also Angela Stroud, "Good Guys with Guns: Hegemonic Masculinity and Concealed Handguns," *Gender and Society* 26, no. 2 (April 2012).

43. Jessie Klein, *The Bully Society: School Shootings and the Crisis of Bullying in America's Schools* (New York: New York University Press, 2012), 16. See also Kimmel, *Manhood in America,* 270.

44. Kimmel, *Guyland*; see also Kimmel, "Masculinity as Homophobia: Fear, Shame, and Silence in the Construction of Gender Identity," in *The Masculinities Reader,* ed. Stephen Whitehead and Frank Barrett (Cambridge: Polity, 2001).

45. Brown et al., *Packaging Boyhood*, 15; Connell and Messerschmidt, "Hegemonic Masculinity," 832.

46. Colin Stokes, "How Movies Teach Manhood," *TED: Ideas Worth Spreading*, November 2012, www.ted.com/talks/colin_stokes_how_movies_teach_manhood.html (30 October 2013).

47. Klein, *The Bully Society*, 63.

48. Stokes, "How Movies Teach Manhood," n.p.

49. Kimmel, *Guyland*, 59.

50. Kindlon and Thompson, *Raising Cain*, 6.

51. Kindlon and Thompson, *Raising Cain*, 6.

52. Kindlon and Thompson, *Raising Cain*, 4.

53. Kindlon and Thompson, *Raising Cain*, 4–5.

54. Kindlon and Thompson, *Raising Cain*, 6.

55. Giroux, *The Mouse That Roared*, 21.

56. Klein, *The Bully Society*, 3.

57. Connell and Messerschmidt, "Hegemonic Masculinity," 839.

58. Klein, *The Bully Society*, 6.

59. Kimmel, *Manhood in America*, 270.

60. Klein, *The Bully Society*, 12.

61. Klein, *The Bully Society*, 155.

62. Connell and Messerschmidt, "Hegemonic Masculinity," 832.

63. R. W. Connell, *Masculinities* (Berkeley: University of California Press, 1995), quoted in Klein, *The Bully Society*, 47–48.

64. Brown et al., *Packaging Boyhood*, xii, 5.

65. Jessica Grose, "Omega Males and the Women Who Hate them," *Slate*, 18 March 2010, www.slate.com/articles/double_x/doublex/2010/03/omega_males_and_the_women_who_hate_them.html (1 November 2013).

66. Brown et al., *Packaging Boyhood*, 7.

67. Alan Schwarz and Sarah Cohen, responding to 2011–2012 data collected by the National Survey of Children's Health, cite pediatric neurologist Dr. William Graf, CDC director Dr. Thomas Frieden, Harvard Medical School professor Dr. Jerome Groopman, child psychiatrist Dr. Ned Hallowell, and others. The experts suggest that the staggering rise in diagnoses may indicate a "dangerous" tendency to use prescription medication as what Hallowell calls "mental steroids." ("A.D.H.D Seen in 11% of U. S. Children as Diagnoses Rise," *New York Times*, 1 April 2013, www.nytimes.com/services/xml/rss/yahoo/myyahoo/2013/04/01/health/more-diagnoses-of-hyperactivity-causing-concern.xml [26 September 2013]).

68. Kindlon and Thompson, *Raising Cain*, 44. Emphasis in original.

69. Halberstam posits that the "Pixarvolt" genre—a collection of films from Pixar, DreamWorks, and other contemporary animation studios—could "actually . . . produce new meanings of male and female" through the sheer "weirdness" of animated bodies (*The Queer Art of Failure*, 48–49). In a rich, enthusiastic, and compelling argument about the innate "queerness" of childhood, Halberstam argues that new developments in CGI technology make possible the subversion of children's films' traditionally heteronormative pedagogies and the potential for connections between "alternative forms of embodiment and desire . . . [and] the struggle against corporate domination" (29). As much as we enjoy Halberstam's optimistic readings of several "Pixarvolt" films, like *Chicken Run*, though, we don't see Pixar's use of nonhuman characters as presenting very many "new forms of being and offer us different ways of thinking about being, relation, reproduction, and ideology" (42).

70. Giroux, *The Mouse That Roared*, 12.

71. "Boy police" is a phrase used by Kimmel in *Guyland*, by Klein in *The Bully Society*, and by others. The *My Little Pony* example comes from personal observation, but according to Orenstein, a study at Creighton University found that boys will generally play with anything—nearly half of the subjects, aged 5–13, chose "girl" toys—unless they know someone is watching (*Cinderella Ate My Daughter*, 21).

72. Ken Gillam and Shannon R. Wooden. "Post Princess Models of Gender: The New Man in Disney/Pixar," *Journal of Popular Film and Television* 36, no. 1 (2008): 2–8.

73. Named for cartoonist Alison Bechdel, most famous for the *Dykes to Watch Out For* comic strip, the Bechdel test for feminism in films and literature is comprised of three parts: whether the text features more than one woman, whether the two women speak to one another, and whether they speak to one another about something other than a man. Originating from one of her 1985 comic strips, it's sometimes called the "Mo Movie Measure," after one of her recurring characters, and is widely cited in popular and social media.

74. Bell et al., *From Mouse to Mermaid*, 10.

75. Keith Booker, *Disney, Pixar, and the Hidden Messages of Children's Films* (Westport, CT: Greenwood, 2010). Booker's chapter on Pixar, "Magic Goes High Tech," moves through the films chronologically from *Toy Story* to *Up*, providing lively and detailed descriptions of each film. Citing their generally "sentimental" endings (84), Booker notes the ironic tension between the films' narratives and their merchandising strategies and the films' tendencies to "effectively defuse[ ]" the potential political and/or economic critique that their narratives may raise. "Very much in the tradition of Disney's children's films," Booker argues, the Pixar films tell stories of authenticity, commodification, and "heartwarming" action, as we discuss elsewhere in this book (86).

76. Zipes, "Breaking the Disney Spell," 40; Bell et al., *From Mouse to Mermaid*, 2–3.

77. Brown et al., *Packaging Boyhood*, 2.

78. Bell et al., *From Mouse to Mermaid*, 10.

79. Booker, *Disney, Pixar*, xxii.

80. Henry A. Giroux and Roger Simon, eds., *Popular Culture, Schooling and Everyday Life* (New York: Bergin & Garvey, 1989), 3.

81. Giroux, *The Mouse That Roared*, 98.

82. Bell et al., *From Mouse to Mermaid*, 10.

83. Zipes, "Breaking the Disney Spell," 36.

84. Karen Brooks, *Consuming Innocence: Popular Culture and Our Children* (Brisbane: University of Queensland Press, 2010), 183.

85. Zipes, "Breaking the Disney Spell," 37; Giroux, *The Mouse That Roared*, 86, 101.

86. Patrick D. Murphy, "'The Whole Wide World Was Scrubbed Clean': The Androcentric Animation of Denatured Disney," in *From Mouse to Mermaid*, ed. Elizabeth Bell, Lynda Haas, and Laura Sells (Bloomington: Indiana University Press, 2008), 126.

87. Zipes, "Breaking the Disney Spell," 37; Brooks, *Consuming Innocence*, 176.

88. Zipes, "Breaking the Disney Spell," 37.

89. Claudia Card, "Pinocchio," in *From Mouse to Mermaid*, ed. Elizabeth Bell, Lynda Haas, and Laura Sells (Bloomington: Indiana University Press, 2008), 63, 66–67.

90. Susan Jeffords, "The Curse of Masculinity: Disney's *Beauty and the Beast*," in *From Mouse to Mermaid*, ed. Elizabeth Bell, Lynda Haas, and Laura Sells (Bloomington: Indiana University Press, 2008), 169.

91. Jeffords, "The Curse of Masculinity," 170.

92. Jeffords, "The Curse of Masculinity," 171.

93. Suzan Brydon, "Men at the Heart of Mothering: Finding Mother in *Finding Nemo*," *Journal of Gender Studies* 18, no. 2 (June 2009): 137.

94. Bell et al., *From Mouse to Mermaid*, 3

95. Kimmel, *Manhood in America*, 171.

96. Klein, *The Bully Society*, 25.

97. David A Price, *The Pixar Touch* (New York: Vintage Books, 2008), 25.

98. Klein, *The Bully Society*, 31.

99. Giroux, *The Mouse That Roared*, 10.

100. Giroux and Simon, *Popular Culture, Schooling and Everyday Life*, 19.

Chapter One

Postfeminist Nostalgia for Pre-Sputnik Cowboys

The Disney spell—that visual and narrative pleasure that has tended to render the films immune from critical analysis—is cast across nostalgic narratives that operate on multiple levels simultaneously, conjuring both the simpler days of viewers' childhoods and an idealized social past. In Keith Booker's analysis, the Disney films' depictions of individual characters' maturation processes parallel society's ugly march toward modernity from historical moments nostalgically drawn to signify innocence and charm, suggesting that the past, both social and individual, "is always a better time than the present."[1] Such nostalgic "ideology of enchantment," as Giroux has argued, effaces historical inequities and injustices and allows even films with fairly overt sexist, racist, or colonialist content to appear "wholesome," even "huggable."[2]

Pixar's reputation for revolutionarily innovative animation might seem sufficient to exempt its films from this observation. For all its cultural reach—the familiar characters, the ubiquitous merchandising, the continuous sequels—Pixar is perhaps most renowned for its cutting-edge technologies, and the vast majority of criticism and scholarship on Pixar has to do with its technical artistry. The effects of Pixar's computer animation techniques are indeed often breathtaking: *Finding Nemo*'s flowing underwater scenes, the light bouncing off of *Cars'* speeding racers, each blade of grass blowing in the Scottish breeze of *Brave,* all add a considerable level of pleasure to the viewing experience and set Pixar apart from its predecessors and most of its contemporaries. Booker reminds us that early Disney, too, was revolutionary in terms of animation, its nostalgic plots asynchronous with its innovations in art and entertainment. *Dumbo*, he offers, "leav[es] little doubt that at least some of Disney's animators of the time saw themselves as participating in a cutting-edge aesthetic endeavor."[3] Like early Disney, Pixar changed the game, presenting "an entirely new form to feature film"[4] ; like early Disney, we'd argue, Pixar's forward-looking technology is asynchronous with its rather backward-longing stories.

Certain narrative components across the Pixar *oeuvre*—namely setting— though much less often the focus of critical comment, may similarly insulate the films from the declarations of Disney's nostalgia, traditionalism, even "conservative" view of history, of economics, and of family values.[5] Usually set in a simulacrum of the present rather than the faux-medieval landscape of the Disney fairy tales, Pixar's stories may seem narratively, as well as technologically, modern, coincident with the values or issues of their moment of production rather than championing an outdated version of the American past. Upon closer scrutiny, we can see Pixar's tendency toward the same conservative nostalgia that has long characterized Disney's wonderful world—a similarity that stands to reason, given the influence of Disney's writers over Pixar's early stories,[6] but should nonetheless open the films to the same sorts of interrogations that the Disney films have undergone.

The films' nostalgia is easy to see even if it has not been extensively analyzed. Their plots frequently evoke, or even flash back to, some poignant version of the past, and even their contemporary settings are populated by vintage décor, art, and artifacts, visually celebrating an earlier moment and gently lamenting of the passage of time. Though only *The Incredibles* is actually set in an identifiable historical moment, if from a speculative version of American history, just two of the thirteen films resist conspicuously looking backward. These, *A Bug's Life* and *Finding Nemo,* are also the only two animal stories, told largely outside of human social time. *Monsters Inc.,* whose not-quite-human inhabitants populate a society decidedly more human than animal, occupies an alternative universe with a decidedly retro vibe, conveyed by a 1960s-esque animated credit sequence, public-service-style television advertising, and a blue-collar boys-club labor model, as well as cosmetic details like font and architecture. *Cars* and *Cars 2*, though NAS-CAR-modern on the surface, unambiguously advocate a simpler "Route 66" American heyday, celebrating the small-town world of cruising and drive-in soda shops. *Up*, likewise modern in its immediate moment, unapologetically honors an individual past through its famously touching passage-of-time montage, detailing Carl's life with Ellie. Moreover, through black-and-white cinema and the pictures of midcentury children adoringly following the adventures of their celebrity hero, the film honors a simpler, midcentury childhood rendered even more affecting by contrast to the isolated and acquisitive urban "scouting" in which Russell is involved decades later. The present's claims to progress, it seems, include its willingness to tear down an old man's house with little regard for his welfare and to send a lonely child door-to-door looking for a father figure. Even *WALL-E*, set far in the future, anchors its story's heart in the ambiguous past of *Hello, Dolly!*, a 1969 film based on a 1964 musical based on a 1938 play, set in 1895, establishing an idealized, if inexact time much earlier than either the film's setting or the present moment of the film's release. And *Ratatouille*, the odd film out by nearly every measure, hinges on a food critic's Proustian recollection of his own childhood. The three *Toy Story* films, set more or less in the modern day, describe the passage of time with similar poignancy to *Up*, as Andy ages across the trilogy and his playful childhood innocence gives way to adulthood (a growth process made even more tragic in Jessie's Sarah-McLaughlin-enabled memory montage, in *Toy Story 2*), and, like *Monsters Inc., Cars*, and *WALL-E*, the films' present settings showcase markers of the past, in the form of vintage toys. Across the films, and with few exceptions, the past is present and privileged.

Again, this nostalgia should not surprise us, given Pixar's close relationship with Disney, that "immense nostalgia machine" that has always worked to hold "antiquated views of society *still*."[7] Nor, perhaps, should such a motif of yearning in texts targeted at children concern us, since, arguably, a maturation plot necessarily beginning in a representation of the past is both naturally suited to childhood tales and easily analogous to social progress. But this traditional flavor is not without pedagogical consequences, and as Giroux and others have modeled, it may inform concepts whose traditional interpretations have outlived their usefulness. For Booker, Disney's nostalgia is always aligned with an idea of authenticity, the past or its childhood analogue housing "a constellation of images involving the natural, the real, and the authentic."[8] Embedded in the nostalgic past of the Disney plots, in other words, is the sense of a "true, real, authentic, natural, original identity," too often lost or obscured in the process of maturation or the analogous progression into modernity.[9] Oddly anti-capitalistic for such a profitable corporate brand, Booker notes, this notion of authenticity undergirds a powerful (if vaguely feudal) model of identity, whereby one's true identity appears as fixed and discoverable rather than fluid and potentially alterable.

For feminist scholars, the idea of identity being "authentic" and "fixed" in a social past is a familiar foe, and Booker himself points out that Disney's continuous depiction of a "true" (feminine) self is disturbing, particularly when that supposed "authenticity" is disclosed through heteronormative romance and/or domesticity, "singing and doing housework."[10] But the fixity, sources, and locations of identity are not concepts that tend to generate much attention in conversations about men or male characters. Even now, most conversations about gender identity focus on women, and even now, many self-proclaimed men's rights or male studies scholars seem to presume, even while seeking to recover or protect, an uninterrogated idea of manhood. Most commonly, maleness remains invisible, so we read plots about male selves in ostensibly non-gendered ways and fail to understand "authenticity" as a loaded, even socially prescriptive concept. In *Toy Story*, for instance, Booker indeed sees Buzz's journey as moving him toward the discovery of his authentic self—a supposedly "natural" way of *being*[11] —but even he doesn't argue that said authenticity inheres in a specifically *male* self, naturalizing and reifying a particular model of *manhood*. A quick scan of critical articles, popular reviews, and fan writing about all the Pixar films though 2011 reveals that the male protagonists' gender simply goes without saying (saving those who have simply lamented what it's not). This absence of gender awareness over the first two decades of Pixar becomes even clearer when contrasted to writing about 2012's *Brave*, which nearly always lists Merida's gender among the very first descriptors and nearly always addresses whether she's being depicted in (or successfully rebelling against) gender stereotypes historically presumed to be innate.

But if Pixar shares Disney's nostalgic conservatism and its silent claims to authenticity, its representations of maleness merit attention. Such attention reveals that the films' invisibly gendered plots engage with some of the central—and difficult—features of contemporary boy culture: characters must navigate bullying, competition, self-control, the fragilities of same-sex friendship, the social dangers of emotional literacy and display, risky performances of bravery, and various paths to masculine self-worth. Situated nostalgically in relation to an idealized if ambiguous history, these factors in the development of male identity must be considered across the films' broader ideological timelines. Neither innate nor fixed aspects of "authentic" masculinity, and yet crucial to contemporary boyhood, these concepts have emerged from historical and cultural sources that may or may not render them healthy and appropriate now.

The pleasure factor—the "Disney spell"—may be largely what blinds viewers and critics alike to particular elements of the films, and the invisibility of maleness further limits what we see about the films' visual and narrative constructions of gender. Further, though the postmodern ahistoricity of the Disney princesses seems to cause no confusion in terms of seeing older models of femininity as contemporarily relevant, Pixar's almost-present settings might misdirect us from seeing its representations of gender as historical constructs. Details like Andy's mom's flowered capris and ballet flats in *Toy Story,* for instance, may root viewers in the present moment of the film's production (ironically, the late 1980s' nostalgia for the 1960s), blinding us to any sort of significant social historical context. Sid's bullying, Woody's domesticity, Buzz's ego in other words, are seen less as aspects of masculinity in the 1990s than of a type of masculinity that presumes ahistoricity, an "authenticity" that needs no cultural ancestry and carries no particular cultural significance. A few critics have begun to sketch a timeline of Disney's masculinities. To Zipes, Disney has always told a history of masculinity, even the princess tales being reiterations of old-fashioned feudal patriarchy.[12] Coming-of-age stories like *Pinocchio*, argues Claudia Card, reflect the civilizing of boys as akin to the civilization of "humanity" in the 1940s society, the inherent masculinity of the plot suggesting that "becoming human [is] a triumph of masculine order."[13] At a few moments, Disney scholars have noted glimmers of alternative templates for boys and men: Brian Attebery has examined lesser-known Disney live-action science fiction films for the ways they seem to document changes in gender coding between the 1960s and the 1980s, and Susan Jeffords' reading of 1990's *Beauty and the Beast* has influenced our previous work with its sense of a "New Man" postfeminist emotional wholeness for men, emerging from the alpha-male type that dominated the popular culture of 1980s.[14] In view of this historical scholarship, *Toy Story* may represent one iteration, a 1990s one, in a long historical account of Disney masculinities. Moreover, Pixar's complexly nostalgic plots and staging invite us back further than their present-moment details suggest, as the modernity of the moment masks a hodgepodge of historical moments from across the twentieth century.

THE COWBOY AND THE SPACE RANGER

The inhabitants of Andy's playroom in the original *Toy Story* span at least two generations, even before *Toy Story 2* fills in the midcentury history of "Woody's Roundup Gang." From the beginning of the trilogy, the family not-quite-heirloom Sheriff Woody doll coexists with toys from the 1950s (Slinkie Dog [1952]), the 1960s (Rock-'em-Sock-'em Robots [1964]), and the 1970s (Speak 'N Spell [1978]), as well as that late-1970s and early 1980s cultural phenomenon, the pizza arcade, and the late-1980s flowered capris and minivan that signify Andy's mother. When a "space ranger" with his own television cartoon arrives on the scene (a toy-marketing strategy characteristic of the late 1980s, as Stephen Kline details[15]), his presence momentarily threatens, but does not modernize, a cross-generational playroom dynamic. Rather than catapulting them all into a feminist or postfeminist reality, that is—rather than bringing the modern to bear on the past—he is the one changed. Indeed, everything he represents ends up being wrong. The plot, handing the keys of wisdom to the oldest of the toys, thus encourages us to examine the world to which it fondly glances—not the world it occupies—as the source of its values.

Of course, ideas of masculinity have always resulted from complex social tensions—economic, domestic, and cultural, as well as historical. If we look backward, to explore what type of manhood Woody might represent, we find that the decades represented by the toys in Andy's room comprise a complicated span for American masculine identity. Kimmel's excellent account of the twentieth-century's evolving masculine ideals, *Manhood in America,* explains how, between the Great Depression and WWII, masculinity suffered a kind of emasculation wrought by years of unemployment and a changing world of work.[16] The American ideal of the "self-made" man, celebrated throughout the late nineteenth and early twentieth centuries, was "unmade" in the early decades of the twentieth century by men's inability to financially provide, to attain demonstrable measures wealth, or to stand out in an increasingly corporate economic machine. War, though bringing some celebratory cultural narratives for men, also brought "shell-shock" and a singularly unhelpful notion of emotional stoicism, further contributing to a difficult moment for American manhood. The 1950s, says Kimmel, contrary to the idyllic pastiche we imagine, mark an "era of anxiety and fear, during which ideas of normality were enforced with a desperate passion. . . . The trappings of gender failure were all around us."[17]

This anxious cultural moment, not surprisingly, produced its own nostalgic responses. If 1990s cultural examples of masculinity can be traced to the 1950s, so too may 1950s texts betray their much older roots. Disney, already a powerful cultural force in the mid-twentieth century, provided cultural models, idealistically restored from history, that proved both pleasurable and pedagogical for American men. In 1955, Fess Parker appeared for Disney as Davy Crockett over three weeks of *Disneyland* (later *Walt Disney Presents),* later edited into the feature-length *Davy Crockett: King of the Wild Frontier*; the same series presented *Daniel Boone* in four episodes in 1961–1962, followed up by Fess Parker again, this time as Daniel Boone, in a six-season television series (1964–1970). Susan Faludi points to these exceedingly similar vehicles to illustrate a crucial moment in the cultural development of American manhood, one that simultaneously celebrated two surprisingly distinct and equally heroic models of masculinity from the past and began to efface the differences between them. Though folklorists have not forgotten, of course, and biographies still record the dissimilarities between Daniel Boone and Davy Crockett, the parallels between these two 1950s Disney texts certainly began to blur the two historical figures in the general cultural memory. Featuring the same actor, the same hat, the same gun, and very similar opening credits, the texts did little to preserve or celebrate the two actual men's quite different performances of manhood. Soon, says Faludi, "Davy Crockett would eclipse Daniel Boone for good" in the cultural imagination.[18]

Largely self-constructed, having authored (and exaggerated) his autobiography through what Henry Allen calls "legendary . . . brags" and tall tales, Crockett's story essentially begins with his running away at thirteen and progresses through increasingly iconic isolation and derring-do. Crockett allegedly identified himself as "fresh from the backwoods, half-horse and half-alligator, a little touched with the snapping turtle; [a man who] can wade the Mississippi, leap the Ohio, ride upon a streak of lightning."[19] He was married, he had children, but it is not for his domestic duties that he is typically memorialized. Instead, as Allen says, "Crockett matched the modern definition of celebrity—famous for being famous . . . and [modeled] a kind of American manhood . . . one that depends on believing it can always survive walking alone down whatever mean streets—can pack up and head West as a last resort."[20] The 1955 film version of *Davy Crockett* introduces the hero from the very first line of the theme song as "the man who knew no fear," the man who in the first scene actually kills a bear with a hunting knife, much to the acclaim of the men around him. Crockett, says Faludi, exemplifies "the prevailing American image of masculinity" even today, "[a] man controlling his environment . . . [who] is expected to prove himself not by being part of society but by being untouched by it."[21] Certainly, this individualistic "alpha" model has persisted into much later twentieth- and twenty-first-century culture, from the Marlboro Man to Batman to Jason Bourne, as "the very paradigm of modern masculinity," if it owes as much to 1950s frontier nostalgia as to actual (presumed essential) frontier masculinity.[22]

In fact, a longer view of cultural history reveals something more complicated about the 1950s Fess Parker palimpsest onto American folkloric masculinity. Before Parker became both heroes almost indistinguishably, it wasn't necessarily the Crockett model that held sway in the popular imagination. From "the nation's earliest frontier days," Faludi argues, "the man in the community was valued as much as the loner in control, homely society as much as heroic detachment."[23] Daniel Boone's history and lore made him an equally compelling but quite different alternative masculine archetype to Crockett. Like Crockett, Boone's frontier bravery and skill made him one of the first and most lasting folk heroes of American culture, but Boone's exploits are generally contextualized within his reputation as a husband, father, and homesteader. Married for fifty-six years and a natural or surrogate parent to dozens of children, Boone's actual legacy is markedly different from his Disney double's. To be sure, aspects of his heroism might be seen as violent and imperialistic by modern standards—conquering Native Americans, for instance—Boone's reputation was one of pioneer and protector, frontiersman and family man, rather than the isolated celebrity type of Davy Crockett. Biographer John Faragher calls him "a hero . . . of a new, democratic type, a man who did not tower above the people but rather exemplified [them]."[24] According to Faludi, his risky, even violent feats of bravery and strength only had value for Boone if they "meant something for the future of his family and society."[25] Even in his television show, Daniel Boone's adventures were more pointedly ethical and/or in service to others than they were grandstanding.

Still, Disney's visual conflation of Davy Crockett and Daniel Boone—both in coonskin caps, for instance, though the real Boone refused to wear them, and more inseparably, both in the person of Fess Parker—not only reflected but also influenced a paradigmatic shift in American attitudes toward masculinity that transpired over the mid-twentieth century, as Faludi explains. Expressed by Disney and other cultural texts, nostalgia for an idealized brand of manhood, born on the American frontier, one that uncoupled masculine success from the real-world woes of the midcentury economy and the horrors of the Second World War, made 1950s popular culture a comfortable second historical home for the Crockett and Boone archetypes. The TV cowboy momentarily held two desires in tension; he could be both the strong, silent type like John Wayne and still a kind of father figure, paralleling TV fathers like Ward Cleaver but without risking emasculation that could come with overly engaged parenting. But the tension did not last. As Disney elided differences between Boone and Crockett, not just by costuming them nearly identically but by similarly celebrating them for individual greatness—each was the title character and star of his own show, after all—the phenomenon Kimmel calls the "cult of the cowboy," fueled by characters like the Lone Ranger, increasingly privileged the rugged individualism, isolation, and bravado of Crockett. The cowboy type began to emerge as a "manly hero" more than "quiet team player," celebrating a manhood that society perceived to be lost more than honoring the one that remained. The frontier was gone; modern capitalism had "transformed a nation" into hired employees, corporate "cogs," and "middle class conformity" who sought an escapist fantasy.[26]

For a time, at least, there seems to have been some effort to resist this rise of the Crockett cowboy as the dominant male ideal, the "two fisted loner who would not get tied down by domestic responsibility."[27] Famed journalist Ernie Pyle and cartoonist Bill Mauldin endeavored to exalt and reward the duty-bound, community-minded figure of the WWII grunt with his own honored place in culture, celebrating in him the homesteader characteristics of Daniel Boone and his ilk. The "band of brothers" who faced the particular horrors on the battlegrounds of the Second World War, Pyle and Mauldin demonstrated, displayed their heroism not by standing out as individuals but by being faithful, "anonymous" team members who collectively strove to "successfully complet[e] the mission their fathers and their fathers' fathers had laid out for them," says Faludi.[28] In his coverage of the war, Pyle celebrated this persona—man as dedicated family member, a literal and figurative brother and son, a person whose objective was entirely communal, who "proved his virility . . . by being quietly *useful*"—and hoped it would maintain after the war as a model of masculine identity.[29] This celebration was reinforced by none other than Eisenhower, who called the "G.I. Joe" the "one truly heroic figure in the war," whose "devotion to duty and indomitable courage . . . will live in our hearts as long as we admire those qualities in men."[30] Pyle, as Faludi describes, "by lionizing the grunt . . . inadvertently became an architect of what many hoped postwar manhood would become."[31]

The Prospector, in *Toy Story 2*, however, gives us "two words" for what happened next: "Sput-nik." World War II, as Faludi notes, marked "not the coronation of this sort of masculinity but its last gasp."[32] The tension between celebrity and the homesteader, Crockett and Boone still held together within the figure of the cowboy, was undone by the astronaut. Pyle had loathed the showy heroism of the fighter pilots, but the model of manhood enthusiastically embraced by post-WWII culture descended not from his beloved grunt but of this very "flyboy."[33] John F. Kennedy rhetorically attempted to share the glory of the astronaut among the tens of thousands of workers supporting the space program, claiming that "it will be an entire nation" that goes to the moon, but over the next several years, the social institutions that had apparently promised to reward common man's anonymous, patriotic loyalties with masculine honor, converted into a competitive, consumerist, and increasingly mass-mediated world, where success was increasingly based on being one of "the handful of men plucked arbitrarily from the anonymous crowd and elevated onto the new pedestal of mass media."[34] This model—the celebrity grandson of Davy Crockett, with all his fantastic exploits and social detachment—seems to be the one that has persisted; though battered by feminism, civil rights, and an increasingly global economy, and though clearly not representative of the vast majority of actual men, *this* model of manhood is the one that contemporary society assumes to be either essential or unproblematically "traditional."

YOU ARE A T-O-Y!

Judith Halberstam optimistically explores the ways that the nonhuman bodies in animated films might afford an escape from traditional gender models, a "deconstruction of ideas of a timeless and natural humanity."[35] The Pixar films and others like them, a subgenre she calls "Pixarvolt," depend on the "weirdness of bodies, sexualities, and genders."[36] But, as Halberstam herself acknowledges, animation can be an "ambivalent mode of representation," as readily enabling caricature as revolution.[37] Though her optimism is perhaps warranted by numerous non-Pixar films, and by her readings of *Finding Nemo*'s Dory as epistemologically othered and Marlin as a "parent, but not a father," it seems that most of Pixar's worlds—worlds of cars, toys, and monsters—are populated not by queer but by hyperbolically embodied masculine typology. As in the bodies of Barbie and G.I. Joe, freedom from the limitations of the actual human form makes possible the ridiculous exaggerations of physical gender markers. The two male characters in *Toy Story*, rivals for Andy's affection and, arguably, protagonist status, become the very embodiment of rival masculine types. As physical iterations of Boone and Crockett in their midcentury manifestations—the television cowboy and the astronaut—Buzz and Woody are overtly allegorical for the changing face of American manhood.

Sheriff Woody, like Fess Parker playing Daniel Boone, is historically overdetermined as both Wild West/homesteader lawman from a frontier age, and 1950s television patriarch, and in this conflated role embodies precisely what Kimmel describes as the early/midcentury middle-class masculine mindset: an other-directed "family provider." Woody's responsibilities in the playroom community involve taking charge, but moreover, taking care: keeping the others safe and informed (e.g., holding seminars on things like "what to do when you, or part of you gets swallowed"); giving direction (e.g., encouraging them all to find moving buddies in anticipation of the family's upcoming move); and providing emotional support and comfort (e.g., the assurance that "no one's getting replaced," even with Andy's birthday party on the horizon).

What threatens Woody's prominence in the present of the first film is birthday gift Buzz Lightyear, a perfect analogy to what kills his show at the cliffhanger moment in the cultural history wrought by the second film: enthusiasm for the astronaut over the cowboy. In the historical context mapped by Kimmel and Faludi, the sheriff and his show's being rendered obsolete by emblems of the space race can furthermore be seen as signifying the supplanting of one male ideal—of ethical, contributing communal leader—for another, that rooted in the cult of individual masculine celebrity. The "flyboy," Buzz Lightyear, enters the world of the film (and the playroom) in full, egocentric view of his celebrity identity and proves (illegitimately, but unwittingly so) his supremacy over the others, first and foremost, by his ability to fly. "Falling with style," he convinces the others of his "flyboy" *bona fides* and establishes himself as both superior and stylish. Equipped with gadgets and an exaggerated sense of his own cosmic importance—though his responsibilities are ostensibly communal, in that he's supposed to save the planet from the evil Emperor Zurg—Buzz possesses no sense of a "band of brothers" or team on which he selflessly serves, and he commands the helpful denizens of the playroom as if they're servants who happen to have the tape he needs to fix his ship.

We have argued that Buzz's nostalgic journey is toward postfeminist fatherhood, learning how to allow himself the joy of participating in a community and family.[38] But when viewed through the nostalgia invited by the cowboy/astronaut rivalry, Buzz's trajectory seems not necessarily progressive into postfeminist "New Man" territory but may actually be regressive to early twentieth-century masculine values: an evocation of Pyle's exclamation, "goddamn the big shots," more than the encouragement of a postfeminist sensitive man. Not only does Buzz need to learn to care for a child, but he also must stop being "the" Buzz Lightyear, becoming instead a generic "t-o-y." He needs not only to learn to love and be loved in return (like Beast does, according to Jeffords), but also to stop showing off, to quit condescending to others, and to accept the fact that he is not now and never will be on a mission to save the planet. He needs to realize that his flyboy persona is fraudulent and to embrace instead the role of homesteader, team player, anonymous grunt. In Booker's terms, this is Buzz's journey to authenticity: he must realize the "true self" of his toyhood and begin to perform the behaviors that this authentic identity compels. Even so, the gentle pleasures of Pixar might make this seem unworthy of attention or concern. Since his natural role is apparently just to love others, one could argue that *Toy Story* offers a rich and joyous celebration of parenthood—or, more generically, simple empathy and generosity—as the most authentic of human experiences, a celebration that audience members, parents, and feminists would all happily join. But if we imagine Buzz as the embodiment of an "authentic" *masculinity,* particularly in view of feminist discourse, the celebration becomes as disturbing as Booker's take on Snow White: you can't be an astronaut, the film tells him, and the only way you can ever be fulfilled is to stay home and love children.

This picture of supposedly "authentic" masculine fulfillment also reinforces what Dan Kindlon and Michael Thompson call "a fortress of solitude."[39] Amid his caretaking duties, Woody seems unable to seek assurance himself, to confront his feelings of jealousy, worthlessness, and the fear of being unloved. Bo Peep does reach out, gently, but when Woody is not being the sheriff, just like the adolescents Kindlon and Thompson describe, he can only stew, sulk, and act out in a violent manner. Finally, his narrative breakthrough is nothing more than a confession of honest emotions. Tough-guy Buzz devolves from his astounding confidence (even believing himself crashed on a strange planet, he is both unafraid and quick to anger) to a full-on drunken depression after learning he's a toy, slurring, "Don't you get it?!? I AM Mrs. Nesbitt!" and surrendering himself to dismemberment at the hands of Sid Phillips, but even in this dramatic decline into self-loathing he fails to demonstrate fluency in what must be an extremely complex snarl of emotions, presumably ranging from disillusionment and disappointment to shame and fear. In neither case do *Toy Story*'s men seem emotionally healthy, even if they have learned to be nurturing. As Kindlon and Thompson note is very common to boys, Woody and Buzz know how to be stoic, how to get angry, and how to lash out, but "these are not visions of manhood that celebrate emotional introspection."[40]

The second film likewise rewards the paternalistic homesteader over the self-centered celebrity flyboy, if even more complexly, as Woody himself is tempted away from his supposedly essential, natural masculine role. Even more explicitly than that of the original film, the plot of *Toy Story 2* situates this shift in a specific midcentury historical moment, with the cancellation of *Woody's Roundup* in the wake of the space race paralleling Buzz's interloping on his turf in Andy's room. *Toy Story 2* further replicates that midcentury moment and its rival versions of idealized American manhood, ironically, by elevating Woody to celebrity status, likening "the" Buzz Lightyear of the first film with "a real" Sheriff Woody doll in the second. The film renders Sheriff Woody not an authentic homesteader type after all, but a famous character who starred in a popular show. Though in the plots of his television show's episodes, Woody's leadership style still reflects a Daniel Boone archetype (putting out a fire, saving animals, and so on), and though the film honors the value system of the lost show simply by associating its cancellation with profound sadness and loss instead of, say, cultural enthusiasm for a new, modern vision of the universe, when Woody learns about the show's history he begins to see himself differently.

The strange existential landscape of the film suggests that "a real" Sheriff Woody is both role and actor. Though Woody has no memories of the show (and, as Jessie teaches us, toys do retain memories), and though the actual star of the show is a puppet rather than a doll, Woody finds his new identity as well-fitting as custom foam packing material. The ontological oddness doesn't faze him at all. In fact, faced with a wall of merchandise, he identifies not only with the puppet and the character but also with each and every piece of memorabilia, syntactically blending the self with the hallmarks of celebrity identity ("I was a yo-yo!" he insists, when Buzz and the gang arrive to rescue him). If Disney films take us on narrative journeys to protagonists' authentic selves, Woody's authentic identity would seem to be a media-constructed celebrity, a flyboy.

Though for a short while Woody still wants to go home to Andy, in the identity crisis that ensues, he temporarily loses sight of the satisfaction he once had (authentically) performing that caretaking role in the community of Andy's room. What narratively presents as divided loyalties (between his old friends and his new ones, between Andy and all the children in Japan) can just as easily be seen as the appeal of being a superstar on an international scale instead of just a guy dutifully and thanklessly serving his small community. Still, though, this identity cannot shake the "authentic" paternalism of his playroom homesteader role. As Booker says about Marlin, even an ostensibly natural role is trumped by the pull of domesticity. In *Finding Nemo*, Booker notes, Pixar seems to break the Disney pattern whereby a protagonist follows a narrative arc to a discovery of his innate self, as Marlin is compelled by the plot to "behave in a way that is entirely unnatural both for him as an individual and for clownfish as a species . . . becom[ing] something other than what he is naturally meant to be."[41] Finally, though, "what the film really seems to say is simply that fatherhood is more basic than any of Marlin's other characteristics and that his innate love for his son is [the most] powerful natural impulse."[42]

Clearly, the celebrity identity—the flyboy—is coded as negative. The critique of consumerism implicit in the film's insistence that happiness is not located in one's material worth but one's loving relationships is fairly subtle (given the visual homage and joyous play in all Al's "Roundup" memorabilia), and the loving makeover montage wherein Woody is restored to mint probably does more harm than good to the film's narrative message against finding one's value in one's surface polish and market value), as we discuss in chapter 5, but even very small children can see that a museum in Japan is a lonely life, that what a celebrity will be denied is love and belonging. If Jessie wants to go to Japan because Emily doesn't love her, the film never suggests that anyone in Japan will either—as a museum piece, she might be admired, but not loved—so her loss is not likely to be compensated by her choice to run away. And if Woody goes to Japan, of course, he will never see Andy again, nor any of his friends, who are actively searching for him in the secondary action of the film. When Buzz teaches Woody his own lesson ("you are a toy, t-o-y"), and Jessie enthusiastically accompanies them both back to the playroom, it is clear that there is no place like home.

HOMESTEADER MASCULINITY AND CONFORMITY

The film's overt homesteader message is unambiguous, and by the end of each film, all the characters have embraced the truism that honor means putting your community before yourself. If *Toy Story* and *Toy Story 2* point to the midcentury moment at which the Crockett model effaced the Boone archetype, they tidily rewrite the moment's outcome, rewarding Boone in a nostalgic redefinition of masculine success. Furthermore, the fulfillment found in loving a child enough to put him first is incomparable, the act of parenting (even as a surrogate) providing the only path to happiness. The whole energy of the third film comes from the characters' struggle to find self-worth after Andy is grown, as we discuss more in chapter 6, and the plot finally gives them another child to love. By the trilogy's end, even the gruff Mr. Potato Head and the shallow Ken have become adoptive fathers.

Given the notorious conservatism of Disney's narratives, the celebration of an idealized historical masculine type, even if it does hearken all the way back to the "greatest generation," shouldn't surprise us. Further, given the role it chooses to endorse and the one it critiques, such nostalgia perhaps also might not concern us. After all, the films' messages are filled with many of the values we all try to instill in our children, values like love and civic responsibility. In our previous work, we have read these films as postfeminist texts that invite men into a newly forged gender landscape where definitions and roles have broadened and men may freely embrace those shared elements of humanity that the "male chauvinist pig" has been denied, including familial and communal bonds.[43] Reconsidering the historical point of origin for this masculine model doesn't need to undermine our general approbation for it: if Pixar's films promote loving fatherhood, they may be performing a social good, honoring a social necessity that is deeply rewarding for lots of men, promoting an ethic of responsibility that may literally "give [men's] lives meaning."[44]

Dismantling the flyboy male archetype might be fair and healthy for men, as well. Politically, we might see these plots as correcting an error, wish-fulfilling Pyle's dream of post-war manhood, putting Buzz Lightyear and other "big shots" down a peg and standing up for the common man otherwise lost in the wake of celebrity culture. In the absence of Andy and Molly's father, the male toys who assume responsibility to the community and to the child that needs them deserve credit for that noble work, and the self-aggrandizing delusions of one man have no real role in the social structure. Besides, the 1960s model of celebrity masculinity didn't work to "liberate," empower, or bring satisfaction to men either. The social construction of aggressive patriarchy, according to Kimmel and others, is chronically misunderstood as something that ever really brought power, contentment, and happiness to most individual men. What feminism did for men, says Kimmel, was not to *render* masculinity a flawed identity category but to *expose* it . . . to see the "impossible synthesis of sober responsible breadwinner, imperviously stoic master of his fate, and swashbuckling hero . . . finally . . . as a fraud."[45] Men striving for success under such a social template in the 1980s suffered even from health problems. That particular male ideal simply doesn't work for most men and clearly needs to be revised.

But Pixar piques our critical attention, rather than just our approval and fondness, partly because of the ubiquity of the homesteader ideal across its entire body of work. If Pixar's narratives stand in opposition to most boy culture narratives, they still stand as one across this powerhouse studio's entire oeuvre. Letting Woody and Buzz lead us toward this particular mid-century shift in idealized masculine roles and the celebration of the home-steader, we become aware that Lightning McQueen, Flik the Ant, Mr. Incredible, James P. Sullivan, and Carl Frederickson, not to mention tragic villains like Charles Muntz and Syndrome, all get similarly educated, not in a variety of progressive messages of feminism that might broaden their options, but in these narrow masculine values of yore. Mr. Incredible can't succeed until he learns to reengage with his family; Lightning won't be happy until he sacrifices his personal ambition to the values of his spiritual father, Doc Hudson; Sulley puts the care of Boo above his professional success and maybe even personal safety; even WALL-E is heteronormatively called to nurture the figuratively pregnant EVE and the life she's preserving in her abdomen. Paternal, homesteader masculinity becomes a compulsory performance for heterosexual masculinity: those who fail to nurture are punished, and those whom the films reward are rewarded only with the opportunity to nurture. Individual ambition is always subordinated to a parental role, which offers a masculine model very different from the persistent Crockett archetype, but in its way just as limiting.

For many men, fatherhood brings the realization of profound fulfillment. But perhaps the pendulum could swing too far. As motherhood has become for women, in a conversation that has unfolded over decades—even centuries—fatherhood ought to be a path to male success one can choose to embrace, without its being the only option available. *Toy Story* not only ridicules Buzz for thinking he's "the" instead of just "a" Buzz Lightyear but also teaches him that he's entirely meaningless—even fraudulent—until he embraces a servile relationship with another person. Besides, textual adulation of fatherhood, as Kimmel demonstrates, has sometimes emerged as a response to deeply broken cultural models of manhood, not just in spontaneous celebrations of "the intrinsic pleasures of domestic life."[46] In the 1950s, "domestic retreat and caring fatherhood were little compensation for the restless anxiety that has continued to haunt American men."[47]

Further, as is clearer (and/or more distressing) in some of the other films, the homesteader model of the past privileges self-effacement, obedience, and emotional stoicism, hardly healthy values for contemporary boys. The heroic role of the *Toy Story* male, like a good soldier, involves being available when you're needed for the good of the collective and quiet the rest of the time.[48] The role of the midcentury patriarch, Kimmel says, "may have required subordinating one's heroic vision to a dull routine, but it was exactly the sort of compromise that separated the mice from the men"; still, it could be "overconformist," rendering men "faceless, self-less nonentit[ies]."[49] Similarly, Card argues that the "unquestioning obedience" that comprises the moral of Disney's *Pinocchio* may have been an "important lesson in 1940 for children and adults alike,"[50] and indeed, maybe in times of war or frontier expansion it is appropriate to tell boys that the satisfaction of putting others first should always silence the clamor of ambition or individuality. But, obviously, it is not 1940s, or the 1950s, or even the 1990s anymore, and we must not uncritically echo this message.

Part of the genius of Pixar, admittedly, is that the films do work on so many levels at once—the rich appeal to parents and grandparents is part of what sets these films apart from their contemporaries and undoubtedly improves their bottom line—but their intended audience is not (just) nostalgic middle-aged parents and grandparents who find themselves and their own parents honored in the value structure of the films. The films aren't needed to provide social worth to returning WWII soldiers, underemployed and seeking to anchor their self-concepts in a world that simply doesn't need them in the ways they have come to expect. On the contrary, they speak pedagogically to children steeped in an energetic, celebrity-based media culture full of alpha messages of masculine value, children, furthermore, one in ten of whom is medicated into compliance with an institutional culture that prizes quiet, community-minded performance. To this audience, with none of the common experience necessary to even see the film's nostalgia as such, Pixar's lamentations of a nobler, "greatest generation" model of masculine heroism are not echoes of the past but lessons for the future. And the world in which they teach—this era, in which debates rage over whether, and to what extent, masculine identity in general and boy culture in particular is "in crisis"—makes all these messages ring differently than they might have done in another age.

Kimmel paints the 1940s grunt model/midcentury father as a kind of "frantic" social effort to revalue men in a world that was really hard on them, characterized by a profound "anxiety" and fear of "gender failure." Hanna Rosin's provocative analysis of the current moment, collected in *The End of Men (and the Rise of Women)*, suggests that masculine value is currently plummeting. Though "man has been the dominant sex since, well, the dawn of mankind," she says, "for the first time in human history, that is changing—and with shocking speed."[51] Citing education statistics, sociological field research, and employment statistics, Rosin, like Faludi and Kimmel, as well as Leonard Sax, Christina Hoff Sommers, and numerous other thinkers from across the broad rhetorical spectrum that comprises the current discourse about men and boys, describes the contemporary landscape as one largely hostile to the survival of the American male as we know him. Men, according to Rosin and other voices in the choir, are emotionally stunted, underachieving, and romantically challenged, increasingly seen as optional to rising women, and increasingly left behind.

Kimmel's history suggests that Rosin's claim to the novelty of manhood's decline is imprecise; certainly, reports of its demise may be somewhat exaggerated, in Rosin's title not least. And, frankly, to some feminists a "crisis" of traditional manhood may actually feel vindicating, as long as it coincides with a rise in women's professional achievement and other significant strides toward equality. But long before they are underemployed, underachieving, emotionally stunted, and depressed men, American males are little boys, and, according to the research, increasingly underachieving, emotionally stunted, overmedicated, bullying, and bullied little boys. Besides the plethora of unhealthy male role models in pop culture—from violent alphas to lovable losers as we discussed in the introduction to this book—boys in America populate a subculture characterized by its own set of problems, problems that, unlike the men's problems that Rosin enumerates, have nothing to do with the types of jobs available, the expectations of potential marriage partners, or various kinds of affirmative action. And little boys cannot be held responsible for the world that unfairly privileged their grandfathers over their grandmothers. At the heart of the *boy* crisis, it seems, is the hard truth that we don't like them very much anymore.

Rosin describes the turnabout in numbers of families deliberately attempting to have female children as one example of a cultural shift away from our historical privileging of boyhood. Though social progress usually seems slow, and the movement toward gender equality might feel like an "arduous form of catch-up," she says, by leaps and bounds for "American parents . . . as they imagine the pride of watching a child grow and develop and succeed as an adult, it is more often a girl that they see in their mind's eye."[52] If perhaps historically we have liked boys too much—enabling an unfair proportion of cultural privilege and a construct of entitlement that would compensate for the ways they misbehaved or lagged in school—they have, at very least, lost much of their advantage here in the early decades of the twenty-first century. Truly, research from a number of fields indicates that we have grown harshly critical of boys, particularly if they fail to behave in a certain way: physically calm and cooperative, at least, if not outright passive. Christopher Cornwell and his colleagues have identified a classroom "bonus" that frequently accompanies boys who comport themselves more like their female classmates.[53] William Pollack refers to a cultural belief in the "toxicity" of boyhood, the assumption that boys are "testosterone-driven monsters" whose poisonous behavior will spread if not aggressively treated.[54] Kindlon and Thompson claim that the growing tendency to medicate away certain undesirable behaviors (in several times as many boys as girls) suggests that we see them as broken, in need of "fixing."[55] And the staggering ADHD numbers—nearly one in ten children, and, depending on who you ask, two to three times as many boys as girls—will surely only rise with the new DSM revision, which broadens the target population. Jerome Groopman, Harvard Medical School professor, observes "a tremendous push where if the kid's behavior is thought to be quote-unquote abnormal—if they're not sitting quietly at their desk—that's pathological, instead of just childhood."[56] Particularly for the hyperactivity criteria, the DSM's passive-voice syntactical constructions (locating behaviors "in situations where remaining seated *is expected*") seem to further open the door to formally pathologizing what Pollack calls "MDD," or "male deficit disorder—with the deficiency lying not in our sons but within society's inability to correctly perceive [them]."[57] We certainly do not advocate an uncritical return to "boys will be boys" tolerances for cruelty and violence, nor can we accept a playing field that disadvantages girls, but it seems obvious that current conditions are also far from desirable.

As we explain in the introduction to this book, this has proven a difficult conversation to have. Attempts to address what Pollack calls the "inner needs" of boys often raise the specter of essentialism, sourcing them in chromosomes or testosterone, which may get even the most well-intentioned contributions thrown out with the bathwater, even though most of those writing on the subject clearly refrain from positing an answer to the question of how much of a role male physiology may play in boys' development. We would certainly not presume that all boys share a singular interior landscape, but that can't mean that we don't discuss the problem at all. The "inner needs" that Pollack laments we fail to nurture undoubtedly still include a kind of emotional wholeness that has historically been denied to boys socially, the "emotional literacy" that Kindlon and Thomspon see failing in epidemic numbers across boy culture. Furthermore, those needs might also include ambition, competition, gross-motor play, and self-expression; according to many of the psychologists, sociologists, and clinicians who have written on boys, they may be reflected in pushing boundaries and showing off, in physicality and competitiveness. Kindlon and Thompson say that boys often behave in what we might call mini-alpha ways: "celebrat[ing] themselves unabashedly, strutting, boasting, clamoring to be noticed," and identifying with the stereotypical boy-culture characters of "Spiderman, Batman [and other] heroic action figures . . . because they want so much to be seen in heroic proportions."[58] "Real boys," in Pollack's phrase, are often sensitive, even "feminine," and in need of a culture that lets them love and feel and relate without the tyranny of the homophobic boy police to inhibit them. But they are too Lightning McQueen, Mr. Incredible, and Buzz Lightyear, *before* those characters become family men, civic-minded, relationally valued, and generic.

GET BACK IN LINE, LIKE EVERYONE ELSE

This "strutting, clamoring," active, and ambitious boy type certainly appears in Pixar: in the catch phrases of the unreformed alpha characters (To Infinity and Beyond!" "Speed—I am Speed!"), in the early scenes of rising action (Nemo's attempt to touch the scuba-diving dentist's boat), in boy characters' rare moments of delightful unrestraint ("As fast as I can?" says Dash Parr, elated though facing mortal danger). Ironically, the merchandising campaigns often return to this earlier exuberance in their dolls, cars, books, plates, cups, bed sheets, bandages, and anything else that might be manufactured to repeat or display a slogan. But not one of these boys is left unscathed by his film's narrative trajectory—each gets reined in, reeducated, and/or reformed. If "real boys" enjoy performing exaggerated, self-aggrandizing versions of their own heroism, the most anti-boy gesture repeatedly performed by Pixar might be simply demanding that their protagonists come to see themselves as ordinary. As Mr. Incredible finds happiness within a newly cooperative family unit, he also has to accept that his particular talent is no longer widely valued or even socially appropriate. As Lightning learns to stop and smell the flowers, he also has to stifle his ambition and his emotions, willfully losing his Piston Cup race in the first film, and, in *Cars 2*, even having to apologize for feeling angry with Mater, who has thoughtlessly cost him his first race on the international stage. If Sulley learns to love Boo, he must also confront the shallowness of his previous values, the apparently silly desire to break a company record, to be recognized as the best.

This tendency of Pixar films, to discipline boyish self-celebration and ambition into conformity, stands out starkly in *A Bug's Life*. Flik, the protagonist, is the only free-thinker in a world of literal drones, anonymous and homogenous workers who work in a line and move in contagion, to the point of sheer panic if the slightest problem (a fallen leaf) should need a creative solution (like walking around it). An inventor and accidental adventurer, Flik also happens to be a nice guy, hard-working and community-oriented from the very the onset of the film, building his contraptions for the stated purpose of helping the colony collect grain faster and more efficiently than they do by traditional means, grain by grain. His community-mindedness, though, fuels his creativity and ambition rather than blind obedience and compliance with the status quo.

Despite the driving force of bully grasshoppers, who extort payment once a year to leave Ant Island intact, in the matriarchal society of the ant colony Flik's efforts are discouraged—even ridiculed—by his peers. "Get rid of that machine," Princess Atta tells him, "get back in line, and pick grain like everybody else." The only male ant willing to think outside the line(s), that is, is told in no uncertain terms that such free thinking and imagination will not be tolerated, that his inventions are foolish and doomed to failure, that appropriate behavior requires conformity and self-effacement. After a particularly ill-timed setback, when his contraption runs amok and knocks over the offering stone, dumping the collected bounty into the river just before the grasshoppers arrive to collect it, Flik is publicly humiliated, ostracized, and then expelled from the colony. In its simplest rendition, *A Bug's Life*—a male ant's life, at least—is characterized by either conformity or ridicule, with no other visible options.

Flik's history of clumsy failures ensures his exile—the offering stone debacle is treated more as a third-strike than a zero-tolerance offense—but his decision to adventure forth in search of a solution to the ants' annual problem, in his own interpretation at least, remains an ambitious pursuit. Holding on to his dreams of a superheroic solution to his plagued society's problem, Flik swallows his humiliation and ventures forth, but his language suggests that even he sees his failure as innate. Upon the discovery of his great mistake at the offering stone, Atta asks, "What did you *do*?" and Flik responds, "I'm sorry for the way I *am*." His behaviors are only tacitly gendered—in the wake of his technological failure, he seeks a militaristic solution, giving two responses stereotypically associated with masculinity—but even to Flik, his actions seem to stem from an essential self. The masculine gender of that self, invisible as it may be at first, may render the rejection he faces as not only deeply personal but also a subtle denigration of his manhood. As he departs, he's mocked by children in the words of their fathers, charting his failure on a specifically patriarchal taxonomy by telling him how their dads have wagered on his failure and death.

The film then even more conspicuously locates its ridicule of supposedly masculine tendencies in alternative male sexualities. The macho mercenaries Flik brings home are masculine failures in terms of both physical dominance and professional success, not only circus performers rather than the "magnificent seven" gunslingers Flik thinks he's found, but also unsuccessful circus performers to boot. Moreover, they occupy a surprising spectrum of gender performances or identities, as if the film needs to code male characters' failures as queer or effeminate, as if a man can't fail professionally, or in a fight, and still be fully a man. The figure of the effeminate or alternatively gendered male is used for comic relief: Heimlich, a caterpillar with an exaggeratedly effeminate intonation, can't stop talking about the beautiful butterfly wings for which he yearns (Heimlich, incidentally, is othered also by his German accent and, arguably, his fat body); and the androgynously named ladybug, Frances, identifies as male but gets read as a natural transvestite because of his physical markings and species signifier. Frances's confusing gender performance, conspicuously played for humor, takes the film to one fairly disturbing moment of sexual harassment: Frances is hassled by "flyboys" in a bar, to whom even his friends sardonically refer as "your boyfriends." Later in the film, Frances is made "den mother" to the ants' Blueberry troop and, becoming an excellent caretaker to the children, is complimented as a "natural mother."

In fact, nearly the whole circus troupe falls short of masculine stereotypes. The film's title, evocative of *Boys' Life,* the 1950s Boy Scout magazine often graced by Norman Rockwell covers, very subtly ties the film to an older rhetoric of masculine development, but unlike the strong and confident Rockwell boys on the cover of *Boys' Life,* the propaganda for *A Bug's Life* depicts Flik—peeking timidly through a hole in a leaf—and often surrounded by Heimlich, Frances, and the little girl Dot. The film does envision a type of embodied masculine power, in the bully villain, Hopper, large, loud, and equipped with a built-in motorcycle sound effect. Hopper's claim to power is rendered slightly problematic when he admits that his bluster and posturing arise from his fear of overthrow and, when angry with his brother, he regrets that his dead mother even now controls his violent behavior, but his physicality gives him a decided advantage over the ants he abuses and stands in as a marker of masculine force.

Embodied power, surprisingly enough, also emerges in the films' women. Even beyond the matriarchal ant colony, power in *A Bug's Life* is naturally feminine, inherent in the female body whether by its coloration, spinnerets, or maternal instinct. Rosie, the black widow spider whose job it is to rescue the pill bugs in the famous Flaming Death circus act, does so by spinning a web fast enough to keep them from hitting the flypaper. Gypsy Moth (who, stereotypically enough, is initially introduced as a wife and assistant) successfully protects the others by covering them with her beautiful camouflage. When Flik finally gets close to defeating Hopper with one of his inventions, a mechanical bird, he fails; boldly declaring that "ants are not meant to serve grasshoppers," Flik leads a sort of proletarian revolution, and though and his colony momentarily stands in solidarity behind him, this too fails to defeat their common enemy. Finally, it's a natural woman who saves the day, as the real mother bird shows up to protect her nest and ends up feeding Hopper to her babies. In short, Hopper's masculine power is revealed as the phobic bluster of the bully, Flik's has never materialized, and the circus troupe collects butterfly wings and den-mother status rather than masculine authority or success. Real power is feminine, and essentially so.

With Hopper's body in the bellies of the baby birds, Flik does get a little appreciation for all his efforts. For one small moment before the cheering colony, he is finally distinguished from the other ants in a positive rather than negative way, but his moment of glory is immediately usurped by the coronation of Atta, which occurs during the very same, unbroken round of applause. His true reward, it seems, is her affection, in a gender reversal of pretty much every fairy tale Disney ever told. Even though, in still illustrations over the closing credits, the film shows some of Flik's inventions being used, he is never lauded as a genius inventor—given, say, a lab and some tools and the support and gratitude of his community as he creates. He is not given any authority or power, say, a teaching position at a new ant-engineering academy. He is never thanked for being brave, for creative thinking, for bucking tradition and fighting the good fight against the oppressive system. He is welcomed back into the community, that is, but at the cost of his own ambition: his heteronormative pairing with the new queen puts him in a necessarily subordinate position, and, at least in the audience's view, his desire to achieve is never satisfied.

A THORN AMONG ROSES

Flik appears happy at the end of his film—as does Buzz, as does Woody, and as do the other reformed male characters—without a trace of resentment, frustration, or disappointment. Of course, we would expect nothing different from a feel-good children's film. One could read *A Bug's Life*, then, as the story of an ambitious and clever boy growing into a well-adjusted man who can privately strive for excellence while acknowledging his social responsibilities, relying on the efforts of others, and measuring his contributions by the health of the collective rather than individual status, finally, because he's found his primary source of happiness in the love of the woman who has chosen him. On the face of it, this reading is not especially troubling: in a sense, it contributes to the "New Man" model of postfeminist male satisfaction we've described before. Halberstam posits that "from the perspective of feminism, failure has always been better than success," as long as "success" is "measured by male standards."[59] Failure may offer unexpected freedoms and pleasures for Flik, to love and play and invent without the fear and pressure that come from continually jockeying for social status. But, for one thing, the film barely glimpses any of these freedoms and pleasures, emphasizing only the failure and offering only the qualified satisfaction of the final scene. And, again, the ubiquity of the pattern merits attention: Flik is not a singular instance but one of numerous Pixar boys encouraged to conform, taught to lose gracefully, and allowed to discover his supposedly "authentic" identity only in subordination to others. All that losing—that "get back in line . . . like everyone else"—becomes "we just all have to fit in" in *The Incredibles*, a film in which compulsory ordinariness is even more troubling because of the extraordinary nature of its characters.

Narratives that enable ordinary failures send a comforting message that it's okay to be ordinary. Narratives that compel such ordinariness, though, register their disapproval of the extraordinary. At a glance, children's media tends to champion the extraordinary, hiding it *in* the ordinary, or fantastically converting it *from* the ordinary. From the young Arthur to Shrek, boys in kids' films often begin their narrative arcs as apparently unremarkable people (or animals, or ogres, etc.), but they find inner strength or capability along the way, learning of the special traits they have within that call them to positions of power. Even in most typical superhero narrative structures, the ordinary figure is rendered heroic over the span of the story by an extraordinary discovery or circumstance. As Peter Parker's radioactive spider bite compels him to perform heroic actions with "great responsibility," Harry Potter leaves his cabinet under the stairs to find that he's the only one who can defeat Voldemort, and Percy Jackson gets kicked out of a school field trip only to learn he's a demigod. Even Rango finds the confidence, cleverness, and moral outrage necessary to save the town of Dirt. The "authentic" in these texts is understood to be the hidden specialness. The protagonists are compelled by their narratives to do anything *but* ignore their powers and conform to social norms. Secret identities give superheroes ways to hide from the things that will make their heroism impossible—the law, supervillains, overprotective aunts—but are seldom presented as simple concessions to social conformity. In *The Incredibles*, Pixar tells the story backward: foregrounding the special, the film's world insists that it must be stifled in the interest of "fitting in."

Of course, this is a counterintuitive look at a plot that, on a superficial level, does the exact opposite. The narrative position, the colorful and exciting opening scenes, and the ridiculousness of the litigiousness that has resulted in society's punitive anti-Super legislation all suggest that society is wrong to force the Supers underground. The *Watchmen*-esque plot backs up this critique, since the Superhero Relocation Act also exposes civilians to villains like Syndrome. And conformity is further denigrated by association with Syndrome himself, who explicitly articulates a villainous plot basically reducible to a vision of consumerist uniformity: when everyone is special because of the tools they can buy from him, he sneers, no one will be any more special than anyone else. As we discuss further in chapter 2, the visual evidence of Mr. Incredible's miserable attempts to conform to a society that both stifles him and lets muggers get away scot free further critiques this society's oppressiveness. Even very young child viewers can tell that something is very wrong indeed. But the other Super male in the film—Mr. Incredible's son, Dash—walks a different narrative path from his father, one that insists he sit down, shut up, keep his head down and his powers hidden. It is in this character that we see alarming echoes of the conformist journey undergone by Woody, Buzz, and Flik (as well as Lightning and other Pixar boys). Dash's entire childhood is to be a social performance, a deliberate suppression of who he is inside.

What Dash can do well, and what he loves to do, is run. Arguably, both his and his father's "powers" are stereotypically masculine physicalities, superior to certain "real boys" only in degree. His trouble at school—he uses his superspeed to put a tack on his teacher's chair undetected by even the security camera—may arise from his "higher activity level and lower level of impulse control that is normal for boys,"[60] further aligning his power with more ordinary boyness. When his antisocial prank both gives him joy and gets him suspended, he recalls one boy Kindlon and Thompson interviewed, a first-grader who complained about a new class that "you can't *do* anything." That child's trouble, they explain, "wasn't really that you couldn't do anything, of course, but that everything he loved to do—run, throw, wrestle, climb—was outlawed in the classroom. In this setting a boy's experience of school is as a thorn among roses; he is a different, lesser, and sometimes frowned-upon presence, and he knows it."[61] We hesitate to source this high-energy, physical behavior in some essential aspect of boys' bodies—psychiatrists and physicians who know more than we have also hesitated to posit definitive claims on the role of biology.[62] But Dash does seem emblematic of a common type of boy, one familiar to us, to our teacher friends, to the theorists and therapists we've encountered. Dash's gifts are "wrapped in high activity, impulsivity, and physicality," using the language of Kindlon and Thompson as they caution readers about how these very common boyhood traits may be interpreted as assets or liabilities, depending on boys' environments.[63]

Certainly, Dash ought not to trick his teacher with tacks; rules are crucial to classroom management, and besides, someone could get hurt. But Dash Parr's regular life never allows him to show off, to "strut," to "celebrate himself," or to "imagine himself in heroic proportions."[64] At home with the Parrs, Bob and Helen's parenting dilemma *du jour* centers around competitive sports. Dash's mother, denying him the opportunity to run competitively, insists that such performance would impair his ability to "fit in" and that fitting in is the very most important thing for him and the rest of the family to do. The conversation is narratively in the service of the film's larger plot, that detailing Mr. Incredible's midlife crisis and ultimate confrontation with Syndrome, but Dash nonetheless reacts to this prohibition on *his* opportunity with anger, sadness, and cynicism. Anticipating Syndrome's later line, Dash complains that the "everyone is special" parenting platitude just means that he's not.

Dash's dejection is poignantly contrasted with the one moment of sheer joy he experiences when, to escape enemy fire, his mother encourages him to run "as fast as [he] can." "As fast as I can?" he asks incredulously, his face lighting up in a tight close-up on his joy. In an exciting extended running scene—and giddy, even in the face of mortal danger—Dash experiences his talent fully. One would hope this singular experience is sufficient to last most of the rest of his life, since upon returning home, Dash has to put his light back under its bushel. Deliberately coming in second in his track meet, his parents frantically gesturing to indicate how much distance behind the first-place finisher seems necessary to maintaining his secret identity and allowing him to keep "fitting in," Dash delights in his father's attention and his silver trophy as the film winds to a close. Because Dash is happy with this result (despite his frustration earlier in the film about not getting to be special), this ending seems to offer a healthy counterpart to the "second place is the first loser" climate of boyhood elsewhere expressed in American culture.[65] But his second-place finish is part of a pattern in which Pixar boys *have* to lose, getting mocked or disciplined for trying to be extraordinary. As Flik's inventions fail, Buzz's flying is exposed as falling, Nemo faces death at the hands of a little girl, and Lightning walks away from the sponsorship he craves, Dash's contentment with a second-place finish might also be seen as a reward for conformity and his newfound ability to accept underachievement.

Of course, *The Incredibles*' fight against Syndrome ends with a brief public celebration of the Supers. Further, as they leave the track meet, the appearance of "the Underminer" causes the Parr family to put on their masks and strike their iconic action pose, teasing viewers with the idea of their future adventures. Even if a single still shot were enough to undo the message of the whole, though, the fact remains that the film leaves viewers with the sense that the Parrs have returned to a life of fitting in, living incognito, their opportunities to be Super occasional and secret surprises. From the opening montage, we learn that what Supers consider their "secret identity" is not their Super self but the false, social identity they assume to get by, to be able (in Elastigirl's example) to go to the supermarket. While the film dodges the question of justice for all the remaining Supers and the possibility of any legitimate future heroic action ("Let the politicians figure that one out," says Agent Dicker, the Parrs' Relocation handler), it offers just enough of a glimmer of "authenticity" to remind us that Dash's excellence—his true self—will always be hidden from view. As the Parrs' secret identities become their primary identities, to paraphrase the pro-Relocation speaker from the early television clip, Dash and his viewers learn unambiguously that only a boy's parents should ever know that he's extraordinary. To friends and classmates, he must always hide his talents.

Pixar does occasionally rejoice in the extremities of young boyhood. Boys too young to be taught how to nurture in the playroom, to get back in line, or to fit in, are delightful—but entirely uncivilized—creatures. The wonderful little Jack-Jack, the Incredibles' hyperactive baby with extreme presentations of intensity and expression, exercises no control whatsoever over his power(s). More obviously in the hilarious short than in the feature film, he's a literal spitfire who presents a nearly insurmountable challenge to his babysitter, Kari. She just chases him around with a fire extinguisher and tongs. These gifts, though they exhaust Kari, also save his life in the film, as a terrified Syndrome drops him instead of taking him with him to his jet-engine-assisted doom. The Clan DunBroch boys, in *Brave*, offer another playful moment of wild-boy childhood. Happily nude and apparently pre-verbal, the triplets occupy half the film in animal form, yet, like Jack-Jack, end up having some small ability to assist in the actions of the plot. Still, there's no narrative example of these children getting to retain their gifts *and* grow, even into elementary school. Jack-Jack will go to Dash's school and will either sit still and be quiet or get called in front of the principal; in *Brave*, since there are no other models at all, the triplets will presumably grow up to be adolescent dunces like those presented for Merida's hand. Maturing out of boyhood requires suppression and conformity.

There are risks in teaching that conformity is the most desirable response to one's innate differences, that one should stifle one's natural energy, talents, or ambitions in an attempt to fit in, to serve others, and to leave status quo unchallenged. For boys, one traditional risk is the construction of the emotional "fortress of solitude" in which far too many men live, without even "the words for their feelings."[66] Pollack claims that boys wear a "mask of masculinity," restricted by the "boy code" from "being their true selves."[67] Dash gets to pout a little when his mother tries to punish him for provoking his teacher, and he's obviously unhappy about not getting to play sports, but most of the masculine emotion in all these films is underplayed, even where complex feelings would be expected. Surely Flik feels ashamed, guilty, frustrated, curious, afraid, and excited, exiled for his failure and embarking on his new journey. Surely Mr. Incredible feels betrayed and angry and hopeless and defeated and proud. The apparently postfeminist plots that reform alpha men and boys into humble and nurturing roles don't do much to actually reeducate them in new ways of being.

Another risk seems especially ironic in *The Incredibles,* since superhero stories often wrestle with the question of moral responsibility. *The Incredibles* asks viewers to assume that Supers will behave morally, if in secret, simply because Mr. Incredible and Elastigirl do, and because Bob Parr is outraged over the unethical dealings of Insura-Care. But its overarching conformist plot might work counter to the development of moral agency in children, as Giroux and others have suggested, seeing conformity as more beneficial to a consumerist model of identity than to a particularly ethical one.[68] This is part of what Card says Disney's *Pinocchio* misses in its conversion from the Italian folk tale. Arguing that the source version requires Pinocchio to critique authority, to figure out a good lie from a bad one, and to learn empathy, Card claims that Disney just makes a rowdy boy obedient. His "bravery" isn't moral character but "macho heroism"[69]; his authentic personhood comes not from "reciprocity, trust, or caring," but from learning to obey those in power and "to avoid humiliation by pleasing one's father."[70] "Perhaps only in American popular culture," Card says, is this variety of heroism "an adequate substitute for having a sense of justice."[71] Dash's primary childhood lesson offers him nothing about knowing good from evil, nothing about using his powers for good, and nothing about accepting the great responsibility that comes with his extraordinary abilities: Dash simply learns how to stifle his real identity to go along with the crowd.

The argument that Pixar consistently makes its boys lose doesn't guarantee its corollary by which girls win. The Daniel Boone types do not relinquish their brand of male authority to a representative of female leadership in their embrace of conformist homesteader masculinity, and neither do Dash and Flik take second place to a visible manifestation of girl power. There are hardly enough girls in the films for head-to-head competitions, and the female successes in evidence tend to be displaced from masculine failure rather than consequent upon it. Only in *Brave* does Pixar make its boys actually lose to a girl, and even then, though Merida is a demonstrably better archer, the suitors' failures seem to have more to do with upholding their fathers' traditional expectations than any particular rivalry with the young princess. Flik's masculine failures are vaguely contrasted with Atta's accession to her mother's throne, and his invention fails to outperform the mother bird, but he does not lose in a direct contest with a female of his species, and Atta's own insecurities certainly help to negate any boys-versus-girls tension. The absence of outright competition with girls may make the trend of boys' failures less visible, however, since as a culture we've trained ourselves to see girl power more readily than boy trouble. If they're actually not being beaten by girls, we still assume that boys unproblematically occupy positions of patriarchal power. Still, if not to girls, Pixar's boys seem to be losing *something*. Perhaps it is just the right to be fully themselves—their hyperbolic, energetic, brilliant, kinetic, performative, Davy-Crockett selves. The films squander their potential to give their outgoing and inventive boys new ways of embracing, rather than silencing, their extraordinary and wonderful differences. In a boy culture "infected by this weird new virus of apathy," as Leonard Sax characterizes it, where the masculinity performed by "the boys at the back" is one typified by emotional "stoicism" and academic disengagement,[72] showing our boys new ways to stand out may be more important than insisting they just get back in line.

NOTES

1. Keith Booker, *Disney, Pixar, and the Hidden Messages of Children's Films* (Westport, CT: Greenwood, 2010), 6.

2. Henry A. Giroux, "Animating Youth: the Disnification of Children's Culture," *Socialist Review* 24, no. 3 (1995): 23–55; Henry Giroux, *The Mouse That Roared: Disney and the End of Innocence* (Plymouth, England: Rowman & Littlefield, 1999), 24, 84.

3. Booker, *Disney, Pixar,* 18.

4. Booker, *Disney, Pixar,* 78.

5. Giroux, *The Mouse that Roared,* 34.

6. David Price, *The Pixar Touch* (New York: Vintage Books, 2008).

7. Giroux, *The Mouse That Roared,* 8; Jack Zipes, "Breaking the Disney Spell," in *From Mouse to Mermaid: The Politics of Film, Gender, and Culture,* ed. Elizabeth Bell, Lynda Haas, and Laura Sells (Bloomington: Indiana University Press, 2008), 39.

8. Booker, *Disney, Pixar,* 6.

9. Booker, *Disney, Pixar,* 7.

10. Booker, *Disney, Pixar,* 3.

11. Booker, *Disney, Pixar,* 79.

12. Zipes, "Breaking the Disney Spell," 37.

13. Claudia Card, "Pinocchio," in *From Mouse to Mermaid: The Politics of Film, Gender, and Culture,* ed. Elizabeth Bell, Lynda Haas, and Laura Sells (Bloomington: Indiana University Press, 2008), 64.

14. Brian Attebery, "Beyond Captain Nemo: Disney's Science Fiction," in *From Mouse to Mermaid,* ed. Elizabeth Bell, Lynda Haas, and Laura Sells (Bloomington: Indiana University Press, 2008), 153; Susan Jeffords, "The Curse of Masculinity: Disney's *Beauty and the Beast,*" in *From Mouse to Mermaid: The Politics of Film, Gender, and Culture,* ed. Elizabeth Bell, Lynda Haas, and Laura Sells (Bloomington: Indiana University Press, 2008), 170.

15. Stephen Kline, *Out of the Garden: Toys and Children's Culture in the Age of TV Marketing* (New York: Verso, 1995), 199.

16. Michael Kimmel, *Manhood in America: A Cultural History,* 3rd ed. (New York: Oxford University Press, 2012), 145.

17. Kimmel, *Manhood in America,* 170–71.

18. Susan Faludi, *Stiffed: The Betrayal of the American Man* (New York: Harper Perennial, 2000), 12.

19. Davy Crockett quoted in Henry Allen, "An Inexplicable Gift for Fame," *Wall Street Journal*, 28 May 2011, http://online.wsj.com/news/articles/SB10001424052748703730804576319112014330104 (1 November 2013). Allen's article reviews Michael Wallis's biography, *David Crockett: The Lion of the West* (New York: Norton, 2011).

20. Allen, "An Inexplicable Gift," n.p.

21. Faludi, *Stiffed*, 10.

22. Faludi, *Stiffed*, 14.

23. Faludi, *Stiffed*, 10.

24. John M. Faragher, *Daniel Boone: The Life and Legend of an American Pioneer* (New York: Henry Holt), xvi.

25. Faludi, *Stiffed*, 11.

26. Kimmel, *Manhood in America*, 181.

27. Kimmel, *Manhood in America*, 182.

28. Faludi, *Stiffed*, 16.

29. Faludi, *Stiffed*, 17.

30. Faludi, *Stiffed*, 17.

31. Faludi, *Stiffed*, 19.

32. Faludi, *Stiffed*, 20.

33. Faludi, *Stiffed*, 17.

34. Faludi, *Stiffed*, 26, 29–32, 33.

35. Judith Halberstam, *The Queer Art of Failure* (Durham, NC: Duke University Press, 2011), 46.

36. Halberstam, *Queer Art of Failure*, 48.

37. Halberstam, *Queer Art of Failure*, 48.

38. Ken Gillam and Shannon R. Wooden, "Post Princess Models of Gender: The New Man in Disney/Pixar," *Journal of Popular Film and Television* 36, no. 1 (2008): 2–8

39. Dan Kindlon and Michael Thompson, *Raising Cain: Protecting the Emotional Life of Boys* (New York: Ballantine Books, 1999), 142.

40. Kindlon and Thompson, *Raising Cain*, 15.

41. Booker, *Disney, Pixar,* 90.

42. Booker, *Disney, Pixar,* 90.

43. Jeffords, "The Curse of Masculinity," 170.

44. Kimmel, *Manhood in America*, 296–97.

45. Kimmel, *Manhood in America*, 262.

46. Kimmel, *Manhood in America*, 180.

47. Kimmel, *Manhood in America*, 180.

48. Faludi, *Stiffed*, 17.

49. Kimmel, *Manhood in America*, 236.

50. Card, "Pinocchio," 9.

51. Hanna Rosin, "The End of Men." *Atlantic*, 8 June 2010, www.theatlantic.com/magazine/archive/2010/07/the-end-of-men/308135 (28 July 2013).

52. Rosin, "The End of Men," n.p.

53. Christopher Cornwell, David B. Mustard, and Jessica Van Parys, "Noncognitive Skills and the Gender Disparities in Test Scores and Teacher Assessments: Evidence from Primary School," *Journal of Human Resources* 48, no. 1 (Winter 2013): 236.

54. William Pollack, *Real Boys: Rescuing Our Sons from the Myths of Boyhood* (New York: Henry Holt, 1998), 243.

55. Kindlon and Thompson, *Raising Cain*, 44.

56. Groopman is quoted in Alan Schwarz and Sarah Cohen, "A.D.H.D. Seen in 11% of U.S. Children as Diagnoses Rise," *New York Times*, 1 April 2013, www.nytimes.com/services/xml/rss/yahoo/myyahoo/2013/04/01/health/more-diagnoses-of-hyperactivity-causing-concern.xml (26 September 2013).

57. Pollack, *Real Boys,* 257.

58. Kindlon and Thompson, *Raising Cain*, 30.

59. Halberstam, *Queer Art of Failure*, 4.

60. Kindlon and Thompson, *Raising Cain*, 23.

61. Kindlon and Thompson, *Raising Cain*, 23–24.

62. Kindlon and Thompson, *Raising Cain*, 4.

63. Kindlon and Thompson, *Raising Cain*, 30–31.

64. Kindlon and Thompson, *Raising Cain*, 30.

65. Lyn Brown, Sharon Lamb, and Mark Tappan, *Packaging Boyhood: Saving Our Sons from Superheroes, Slackers, and Other Media Stereotypes* (New York: St. Martin's Press, 2009), 4.

66. Kindlon and Thompson, *Raising Cain*, 142, 4.

67. Pollack, *Real Boys,* 9.

68. Giroux, *The Mouse That Roared,* 23–24.

69. Card, "Pinocchio," 66.

70. Card, "Pinocchio," 67.

71. Card, "Pinocchio," 69.

72. This closing statement weaves notions from several prominent voices in boy culture. Leonard Sax's quote about apathy comes from *Boys Adrift* (New York: Basic Books, 2007), 9. The "boys at the back" is Sommers's phrase ("The Boys at the Back," *New York Times*, 2 February 2013, SR1. http://opinionator.blogs.nytimes.com/2013/02/02/the-boys-at-the-back [30 October 2013]). Kindlon and Thompson's *Raising Cain* deals with "stoicism" as a typical response to boys' "emotional illiteracies" (15), and Kimmel theorizes that conceptualizations of masculinity itself may cause many boys to disengage academically ("Solving the 'Boy Crisis' in Schools," *Huffington Post*, 30 April 2013).

Chapter Two

Superior Bodies and Blue-Collar Brawn

"Real" and Rhetorical Manhoods

Through the lens of American manhood's history, focused on a mid-twentieth-century struggle between masculine ideals, the narrative trajectories of Buzz, Flik, and Dash may appear to nostalgically endorse the archetype that lost. The Pixar films' partiality to a particular combination of care, strength, humility, and social obedience, like that performed (and relearned) by Sheriff Woody, over the self-aggrandizing and ambitious posturing of the immature Buzz and others like him, disciplines into conformity even the more modest claims to individual excellence attempted by Flik or the familiar excesses of active boyhood depicted in Dash. To some degree, all these narratives echo the ways we try to parent our rowdy little boys into ethical citizens, the philosophies behind public education's classroom-management practices, and other dominant childrearing trends through which contemporary American society strives to help boys mature into healthy and well-adjusted men. Still, as we discussed in the previous chapter, we question whether such a blend of conformity and resignation is entirely wholesome. As Claudia Card notes about *Pinocchio,* and critics like Henry Giroux and Paolo Friere have theorized more extensively, social obedience doesn't necessarily ensure ethicality, so these narratives might actually work at cross-purposes to the goal of ethical citizenship.[1] Teaching boys that they should deny aspects of themselves in an effort to fit in to society—whether by "get[ting] back in line" or purposely coming in second or returning to the playroom to take care of the child—may ultimately serve Disney's corporate interests more than it provides the postfeminist role models we may take from the films at face

31

value. Further, in our current pharmacological climate, we may be repositioning the notion of normal so that "real boys" are seen—and see themselves—as "toxic," diseased, or broken if they fail to appropriately conform.[2] Finally, it is the unrelenting repetition of this template across the Pixar canon that we find the most disconcerting, particularly in a boy culture that itself largely privileges conformity and obedience over any other ways of being.

Into our own resistance to a ubiquitous culture of conformity, though, creeps an ironic social truism that elsewhere informs the Pixar films' representations of masculinity to boys, maybe even more insidiously. If these stories teach viewers that one should stifle aspects of one's true self in the interest of the social order—that one must live by a "secret" identity and render one's true identity secret, as do the Incredibles/Parrs after the Superhero Relocation Act—they simultaneously presume the existence of said "true" self. Despite promoting the learned behaviors that will allow one to "fit in," in other words, the Pixar films suggest that something essential underlies the social performance of identity: who you *are* is always present, lurking beneath whatever you choose to *do*. As such, they demonstrate a faith in a traditional notion of "authenticity" that, as Keith Booker explains, the Disney films have historically reiterated and that ultimately affirm the status quo, however imperfect. As Snow White must overcome the threat with which she is faced in order to reclaim "her natural place in life . . . [and] her authentic self," to borrow an example from Booker, the Disney canon typically presents a model of self "fixed and determined by birth,"[3] an identity structure that, while it seems to work well for a lost princess, also maintains the underprivileged position of many, many others. Though their narratives tend to move differently—traditional Disney fairy tales typically journeying toward a discovery of the true self while Pixar films seem to move from it into a more socially acceptable performance—both studios perpetuate the notion of authentic identity as fixed and inherent, even if obscured or obscurable.

Booker locates his argument in economics, noting the contradictions between such a feudal model of identity and the ideals of American capitalism,[4] but we would argue that the challenges of this identity model to boy culture are even more complex. To feminists, the idea of an "essential" or authentic self obviously risks the presumption of traditional gender norms and as such should be vigilantly critiqued. That Snow White's recovery of her supposedly true self should correspond to her mastery of domestic tasks and her heterosexual marriageability, for instance, at very least marks the film's old age (if it doesn't still alarm and aggravate feminist parents of girls, given the staying power of the Disney princess brand). When Merida's body, redrawn for the princess brand, was sexed-up and dressed in the outfit the film's protagonist *hates,* more than 200,000 petition-signers resisted, apparently interpreting the girl's identity first and foremost through her actions and preferences rather than locating her primarily in a traditionally gendered female body. Indeed, for women's studies scholars, the argument against essentialism is one of the most familiar and fundamental: "one is not born" a woman, as Simone de Beauvoir famously expressed it. Theorized and articulated by Judith Butler and others, the notion that gender identity is performed in a series of socially responsive and interpretable behaviors, rather than inhering in any essential bodily characteristics, means that we must not "assume that the meaning of women's social existence can be derived from some fact of their physiology."[5] Butler is emphatic: it is reductive, even harmful, to "reify and naturalize" the actual constructedness of gender, to presume that certain performances of femininity reflect some sort of "natural" or "authentic" womanhood. She makes it equally plain that essentializing masculinity is just as foolhardy. Still, though critics have neglected to cast it in gendered terms, an essentialist equation between masculine selves and male bodies is constant throughout the plots of the Pixar films. If Dash's super speed is the most obviously innate trait to complicate a character's social performance, Mr. Incredible, Lightning McQueen, James P. Sullivan, and other Pixar boys and men all must navigate what they *do* in terms of what they *are*.

Such a paradox as seems to logically arise between a culture of conformity and a belief in essential identity may seem to beg deconstruction, but for many American adolescents, its logic is unassailable, a basic underpinning of their dominant ideological structure, wherein the assumption of an inherent, bodily source beneath the performed self ultimately excludes some from the privileged strata despite their best efforts to conform. In *The Bully Society,* Jessie Klein describes the social caste systems that inform high schools across the United States, built on a set of shared subcultural values that transcend economic class distribution, ethnic diversity, and regional differences between schools. American adolescents' social identities and rank, she argues, and, often, their subsequent conclusions of personal identity and senses of individual value, are rooted in types of "capital." Among economic, social, and knowledge capital, Klein situates "body capital," the "certain kind of body" understood across the community as superior.[6]

Not surprisingly, such capital is rigidly gendered. Though in theory feminist arguments against essentialism are working to liberate women from social expectations previously thought to be "natural" to the female body, allowing new generations of girls to be both socially successful and, say, athletic and strong, the adolescent social idealization of masculinity seems to remain firmly tied to particular kinds of male bodies. For boys, says Klein, in an observation echoed in the work of Kimmel, Kindlon and Thompson, and many other scholars across the disciplines interested in boys, body capital is very narrowly inscribed, signified chiefly by physical ability and athleticism, a "hypermasculinity" marked by physical size, strength, and success in competitive sports.[7] Kindlon and Thompson insist that "physical size is an issue of emotional importance. . . . Boys are completely aware of their physical stature and how, in ranked order, they measure up."[8] Though the stereotype is so frequent in popular culture that it almost seems that it couldn't possibly be true in real life, Klein reports that there are few other options common across the universe of "the bully society" of American youth. Boys who face physical limitations, boys who are short or skinny or fat, and boys whose talents lie in artistic or intellectual pursuits are all set up to fail in the "social status wars," and in schools across the country, the "pressure to succeed physically" can override all other concerns.[9]

The athletic young Dash Parr, we assume, would thrive in this social world, at least if he could stay out of trouble in the early grades. That his hypermasculine athleticism is causing him problems might indicate the film's ironic inversion of the equation between physical excellence and social status. One might read the Parrs' difficulty passing for normal in light of their physical differences from the norm, especially alongside *Monsters Inc.* and *Monsters University*, as challenging the traditional social valuation of body capital by giving power to those typically understood as weaker (non-Supers in *The Incredibles,* and in Monstropolis, children). But even inverting the equation proves the fundamental rule of essential identity in the Pixar films. Indeed, the inversion itself—the humor generated from this play with audience expectations—depends on those expectations, assuming at least familiarity with an essentialist paradigm of masculine identity. Bodies are a priori to identity, in other words, regardless of whether we can momentarily mock the dominant hierarchies. If one is not naturally suited to the crowd to which one aspires—regardless of whether physical excellence or physical ordinariness sets the bar—one can only ever pretend to belong there, and it is amusing both to imagine these categories differently ranked and to watch a so-called fish out of water. Judith Halberstam posits that the nonhuman anatomies of the "Pixarvolt" films, including *Finding Nemo* and Dreamworks' *Over the Hedge* among others, afford a deconstruction of gender rather than an essentialist reiteration of traditional gender norms.[10] But in the animated male bodies of many Pixar protagonists, we see the very opposite thing happening, as exaggerations of idealized male body types visually represent masculine excellence, amazingly even in the "bodies" of cars, monsters, and toys, as well as men. Amidst ostensibly ironic inversions of power in the *Monsters* films and *The Incredibles*, male bodies are still ranked according to a tragically familiar social paradigm, whereby bigger, stronger, and more athletic men and boys are invariably understood as superior to smaller, more delicate, or intellectual ones.

Certainly Pixar didn't create these norms, but rather than realizing the potential of revising them, the films' very storytelling depends on their young audience's visual literacy in traditionally gendered images and an internalization of the taxonomy whereby those images are ranked. Even in a film that narratively disciplines a hypermasculine character's behavior—say, requiring him to stop posturing as a flyboy and to assume the duties of the homesteader—the idea of his essential male superiority remains unchallenged. Consider Buzz Lightyear in the opening moments of the original *Toy Story*. From the instant he arrives on the scene, Buzz is excellent. He's excellent despite being entirely misguided, arrogant, and foolish, excellent before anyone knows who or what he is. There is nothing about him to like, at first, but he nonetheless must be immediately understood as excellent, lest the story fail from the very beginning. Viewers must comprehend Woody's instant jealousy as quickly as he feels it.

Our quick grasp on the rivalry between the two is certainly nurtured by narrative elements: Andy's mom's surprise last-present maneuver raises the narrative tension, Andy's excitement to unwrap his Buzz cues viewers to the desirability of this particular gift, and Woody's physical displacement from the bed literally places one toy above the other. But his excellence is also visually marked by his body and its contrast to the lanky, old-fashioned Sheriff, clumsily crumpled in the spot where he was dropped. Buzz's body is newer, obviously, and equipped with gadgetry and weaponry (powers that allegedly give Woody "laser envy," subtly aligning Buzz's physical power with a notion of his superior virility), but moreover, with the shape of his suit inseparable from the human body presumed to inhabit it, Buzz is as bulky through the chest and arms as any hypermasculine action hero. With its impossible breadth across the chest and arms, its impossibly small waist and hips, his body presents a male equivalent to Barbie's ridiculous anatomy, beyond-steroidally amplified, as Brown et al. note about the modern G.I. Joe.[11] It is in terms of his body that the other playroom citizens respond to Buzz, modeling the desired audience responses. There aren't too many ways to read Bo Peep's purred approval, "I've got *my* moving buddy." With little other guidance as to what traits viewers are supposed to value, the success of the opening scenes in rendering Buzz a real threat to Woody's community standing indicates that even young children know how to read male bodies as signifiers of social status.

To complete the thought experiment, consider how *Toy Story's* opening would work differently if Buzz were not a hypermasculine action hero but a cool toy with a less legible body: a robot, a computer, a hand-held video game. Piggy banks and Speak & Spells are equally sentient in the world of Andy's playroom, but not even the mighty T-Rex threatens Woody's prominence until a supposedly more manly human arrives on the scene. Buzz's idealized male body, and the masculine value we all already know to ascribe to it, is necessary to the film's meaning from the beginning.

As we argued in the first chapter, an observation this relatively innocuous about one particular film may not warrant disapproving critique. The makers of *Toy Story* might reasonably enough have decided that a rivalry between two humanoid dolls would be easier for children to comprehend than an interspecies or otherwise existential struggle would have been (like that between Jessie and Emily's new nail polish in the heartrending growing-up montage of *Toy Story 2*). Artists, having to depict him one way or another, might as well have given Buzz the basic anatomical parameters of a G.I. Joe as anything else. But as with the homesteader pattern we describe, the ubiquity of masculine essentialism across the films is troublesome. Dash and his dad, Lightning, Sulley, the entire ROR fraternity at Monsters University— even the macho Doberman in *Up*, figuratively emasculated by the failure of his voice-enhancement device—exemplify and depend on a widespread cultural favoritism for a particular type of male body and the unspoken or proclaimed belief in that body's claim to a superior masculine identity.

As Booker says about *Finding Nemo*, it initially appears in some of these films that "nature" is the very thing being resisted in the films' narrative trajectories, allowing protagonists to escape predetermined identities and construct new ways of being: Flik rejects the ant colony mindset in order to invent and explore; Marlin quits his natural habitat in order to find his son; arguably, Lightning overcomes his built-in precision, speed, and aerodynamics in order to slow down, smell the roses, and eventually advocate for Radiator Springs. The list goes on. One can argue, though, as Booker does, that nature yet wins, as the even-stronger "natural" pull of heteronormative patriarchy always trumps the ostensible escape-from-nature plot. As Marlin's fatherhood is the urge that won't be stifled, Flik returns home to marry Atta in the aftermath of the battle against the grasshoppers; between the first and the second *Cars* films, Lightning similarly pairs with Sally and assumes a patriarchal role in his community as the heir apparent of the late Doc Hudson. In other cases, among secondary characters, the attempt to deny one's nature becomes ludicrous, the opportunity for excitement and comic relief. Of course Bruce the shark spectacularly fails to complete his twelve-step journey to vegetarianism; no matter how many times one rehearses the mantra "fish are friends, not food," the Great White remains carnivorous, triggered by the slightest odor of blood.

Ironically, girls get some power in the Pixar films from this very essentialist way of representing gender. Pixar has been criticized for having been a "boys club," at least until 2012's *Brave*, and it's true that the films want for leading roles by females. When female characters do appear, though, they are often strong, smart, and opinionated, and with surprising frequency, their power is depicted as inherent in their bodies. The mother bird who finally eats Hopper in *A Bug's Life* is only one of that film's naturally endowed female characters: Gypsy Moth and Rosie, the black widow spider, both succeed because of their innate abilities. Sally's beauty, in *Cars*, does not diminish her horsepower (she playfully asserts, as the film comes to a close, that she can hold her own against one of the best racecars in the world, and when the film ends, she is indeed in the lead), and Elastigirl uses her body throughout *The Incredibles* not only as a superheroine, stretching between sliding doors and knocking out three guards she can't even see, but also as a super-mom, performing such feats as becoming a human parachute to save her children and a human boat to transport them.

Such essential feminine talents may not be read as favorable in feminist discourse, though, particularly since these strong female bodies are yet socially gendered in somewhat unfortunate ways. Elastigirl's waist is as small as any Disney Princess's, if the width of her hips adds a visual maternality to her overall look, and her subtly sight-based secret name, Helen, pits her in a strange antagonism to Mirage, reinforced by the visual veneer of an extra-marital affair plot that pits one woman against another in a contest for Mr. Incredible's affection. In the *Toy Story* trilogy, Barbie and Bo Peep are overtly sexy—identified as objects of desire by the film and its male characters. Bo all but propositions Woody ("I'm just a couple of blocks over," she offers, so "why don't I get someone else to watch the sheep tonight?"), and Barbie's appeal inspires Hamm to ride shotgun on the sole rationale that he's single, while Mr. Potato Head frantically repeats to himself, "I'm a married spud. I'm a married spud." Even among Pixar's nonhuman characters, the favorably portrayed females—the women supposed to be likable and not laughable—inhabit skinny, sleek, (almost) sexy bodies. From Sally the Porsche to Cecilia the monster to EVE the robot, Pixar's good women manage to seem thin, youthful, and feminine. Larger sizes, rounder shapes, and older age signify a range from silly (Lizzie the Tin Lizzie), nagging (Mrs. Potato Head), and bossy (Edna Mode), to demanding (Roz), strict (Dean Hardscrabble), and terrifying (the MU librarian).

None of this is well-hidden. Bodies are at times explicitly traditionally gendered for comic effect: in *The Incredibles*, innate superpowers correspond directly to gender stereotypes, as Elastigirl's flexibility (which every mother, obviously, needs) helps her more efficiently vacuum and shy Violet's power includes the ability to hide her beauty until it's time to reveal it, like a teenage sexy librarian. Violet reads a magazine that touts itself as "the magazine for looking just like everyone else," in a split-second of a montage sequence, humorously mocking female adolescence and its suffocating peer pressure even as the film depicts a girl who will literally disappear to keep from standing out. Male bodies, in the same film, not only run and lift but also literally freeze out others: Frozone's contribution to the opening interview montage perfectly parallels his superpower, when he responds to a girlfriends' desire to share alter-egos ("to strengthen the relationship") with, "Girl, I don't even want to know."

The Incredibles and the *Monsters* films may be the clearest examples of an essentialized system of masculine value. You can take the Super out of lawful society and make him file insurance claims—you can domesticate some of his hypermasculine behaviors—but you can't excise the superiority from Bob Parr's innately Incredible body. Born to scare, Sulley's professional success at Monsters, Incorporated is virtually guaranteed by his body and his heritage. As with Snow White, the model works pretty well for these two protagonists, but the extent to which it fails the vast majority of boys necessitates our critique. As *Toy Story*'s nostalgic longings invite us to explore the histories of masculinity that source its idealized representations of manhood, so too do the variously temporal settings of *The Incredibles, Monsters, Inc.*, and *Monsters University* suggest a masculine model rooted in—or evolving over—American history. If, following Butler, we grant that gender identity ought not be presumed to be an authentic essence, discoverable through narrative journeying but always already in place, and yet we find the films' privileging individual characters' particular embodied traits as signifiers of masculinity, we must address a number of analytical questions: what bodily traits are privileged by and which excluded from social valuations of masculinity, which historical template(s) are naturalizing these views of masculine value, and what effects, if any, might these nostalgic gender scripts have on contemporary boy culture?

A SOCIAL HISTORY OF BRAWN

The Incredibles' nostalgic setting seems more historically identifiable than most of the Pixar films, citing actual dates and spans of time, albeit sparingly, and albeit from an alternate universe. The fashions of the prologue evoke the American 1950s. The styles of cars and hats, the price of newspaper "extras," and black-and-white television footage all suggest that Mr. Incredible and Elastigirl are young, childless adults sometime before, say, color television became widely available. Then, "15 years later," the film's scenes depict skinny ties, primitive computers, and teenagers wearing turtlenecks and miniskirts. At least until Bob's desire to get out of his rut drives him to buy a sports car, the Parrs drive a pink sedan with fins, another visual indication of the 1960s. Edna Mode reveals the latest date specifically mentioned in the film as 1958, the year of Thunderhead's death by cape. If this event occurred before the Supers were forced into hiding, the film may reach as late as 1973 or 1974 (suggesting only that the Parrs' car is not brand new).

The specter of McCarthyism, hanging over the Superhero Relocation Act, further roots this film in an imprecise but generally familiar past. Still, despite the political upheaval of actual America across the 1960s and 1970s, there aren't any obvious markers of race or gender politics in the film, no clear signs of political feminism—no expectation, for instance, that Helen Parr will do anything but stay home with Jack-Jack, while her husband "brings bacon." But in a way, this idealized 1960s–1970s era is anachronistically informed by modern feminism. Elastigirl's attitude is feminist even in the vintage 1950s prologue: "Girls, come on!" she says. "Leave the saving-the-world up to the men? I don't think so!" She and Mr. Incredible banter about who deserves the credit for catching a mugger (the mugger vouches for Elastigirl); shortly afterward, if in antagonism to the films' heroes, it is a woman behind the podium in the debate over whether the Supers should go into hiding. In the later action, the main setting of the film, the two professional women, Mirage and Edna, outnumber the stay-at-home Helen, with no sense that either's life is pioneering or even unusual.

And yet it seems that nothing less than Mr. Incredible's masculine identity is at stake as the main action of the film begins. Washed up, driven into hiding, and muddling through a life of quiet desperation in a suburb of Municiberg (Metroville), Bob Parr can only long for his glory days as a Super and, with his friend Frozone, occasionally hunch over the police scanner in an alley listening for the opportunity to perform some hero work on the sly. As Booker says, Disney films frequently draw an analogy between an individual's maturation and a society's progression, so we could try to enrich our reading of his individual narrative arc by inquiring into its social counterparts, and when we do we could perhaps imagine a way to connect the former hero's rather cliché male midlife crisis to the feminist movement. Indisputably, Mr. Incredible yearns for an era-gone-by, which on an individual level hearkens to his personal and professional life before the Superhero Relocation Act forced him into a dead-end job, and also, arguably, before marriage trapped him in a house in the suburbs with kids. After accidentally setting off the sprinkler system via illicit communique with Mirage, Bob apathetically blows books with a pink hairdryer, perhaps a sad visual metaphor for a kind of emasculation presumed to be inherent in domesticity. On a real historical timeline, of course, his glory days also ended just before the cultural influence of feminism created shifts in men's economic and domestic roles. Dealing with assertive professional women and, arguably, the feminization of his workplace, as well as a wife who insists that he "engage!" in parenting, Mr. Incredible might represent a so-called men's crisis in the wake of the feminist movement, despite the film evading the politics of the moment.

Such a reading, though, is a reach. If the film doesn't specifically honor feminism, neither does it clearly blame it for what has happened to Mr. Incredible in the fifteen years between the acts, the years that have contributed to his powerful midlife malaise. This historical explanation of what's eating Mr. Incredible—that his individual stagnation parallels the world of men in the face of the fight for women's rights—simply doesn't withstand scrutiny of the textual evidence. In the real history of the United States, of course, the more perfect past for which Bob Parr yearns does indeed predate modern feminism, but not only has the young Mr. Incredible formerly found

Elastigirl's ambition and ability more appealing than threatening (they banter, and then they marry), but also, after their marriage, she gives up her professional practice that once rivaled his. By happily enough embracing maternal domesticity, entirely supporting his traditional masculine performance of "provider," Helen Parr entirely relinquishes the specifically feminist claims to power that might challenge her husband's patriarchal sense of self. Indeed, what has changed in Mr. Incredible's life is that his wife has *stopped* working, that he has *become* the traditional patriarch. The emasculating Relocation process much more obviously evokes a Communist panic than any direct feminist influence.

Besides, as we discuss in the introduction to this book, this either/or argument—a crisis among men must be attributable to women—is one small example of a counterproductive rhetorical trend, in which many supposedly analytical examinations of gender that purport to be about men can't see masculinity except vis-à-vis femininity. Taking a longer and wider view of history, we can more interestingly situate the role of Mr. Incredible's body in the sometimes-contentious development of American manhood across the twentieth century.

The Incredibles may be, in one sense, about a man going through a midlife crisis, discovering that the things on which he relied for a manly identity in his youth have faded, that he's overweight and underemployed, that he's hit the halfway mark of his lifespan, and that he feels the urge to find a beautiful woman or a sports car or an exercise regimen to restore his feeling of vitality. At the same time, though, the out-of-shape Mr. Incredible is still pretty incredible, lifting cars to blow off steam, throwing pencil-neck administrators through not one but numerous cubicle walls, single-handedly battling giant robots. The film seems not entirely to agree with its own midlife-crisis premise of the body in decline, which, it seems, gets fatter but not much weaker, even in disuse. To understand his dissatisfaction, as feminists have argued for decades, Mr. Incredible's gendered body must be understood as socially construed. His midlife discovery stems not from his body's declining power but its declining value to those around him. Simply put, his brawn has always equaled his worth, but the rubric has changed, leaving him without a way to prove himself even to himself.

Certainly, this equation between physical brawn and socially valued "masculinity" did hold through much of American history, at least in many work environments. But social and economic changes long before feminism revised the equation, or threatened to, creating situations much more akin to that in which Mr. Incredible finds himself. Kimmel, in *Manhood in America,* describes a shift in attitudes toward American masculinity in the workplace at the turn of the twentieth century, as the "self-made, self-controlled" masculine model that had prevailed in the nineteenth century faced threats arising from changes in industrial production, the increasing urbanization of the

American landscape, and the rise of the "middle-class man." Though such a struggle transpired a generation or two before the earliest action in *The Incredibles*, it provides a useful template for exploring the film's juxtaposition of Mr. Incredible's brawny body, the middle-class mentality that devalues him, and even more tellingly, the techno-wunderkind who evolves from number-one fan to mortal foe.

Ruth Oldenziel, in *Making Technology Masculine*, argues that current ideas of middle-class masculinity were historically co-constructed with technological advances that informed various moments of struggle for male authority, an account supported by Kimmel's description of the decline of the "self-made man" archetype.[12] In short, the physicality of the laborer in the early nineteenth century coincided with the relative autonomy and authority of self-employment for many American men, creating a rhetorical construct of masculinity built on ambition, hard work, and individual freedom.[13] Though not without its negatives, argues Kimmel—downsides like anxiety and loneliness—"self-made" masculinity had, by the 1840s and 1850s become a "veritable cult," a pervasive definitional model of manhood in America.[14] Across the later nineteenth century, though, and in the first decades of the twentieth, as industrial production employed more and more men as subordinate laborers, and as engineering became an increasingly widespread, middle-class occupation situated between the work of laborers and the capital investments of owners, working-class masculinity underwent some profound conceptual changes, changes interpreted as "humiliating," even "emasculat[ing]."[15]

Surrounded by the physical brawn of the factory floor, engineers at the turn of the twentieth century staked a different but unequal claim to masculine authority, one based on education and intellect instead of physical strength. In the early emergence of this model of masculinity, engineers desperately needed to maintain authority over and command respect from the shop floor workers. The need for these aspiring middle-class men, whose skills were far more of the mind than the body, to "chart[ ] a revitalized male identity" was thus compelling.[16] Oldenziel recalls rhetorical efforts, both deliberate and indirect, to secure a middle-class manliness for engineers. In factories and more broadly across society, a new kind of respect for a new kind of masculinity had to emerge.

The shop floor itself provided a rhetorically necessary training ground for engineers at first, comprising a "moral gymnasium" and site of knowledge exchange that created the possibility of class divide that yet maintained mutual self-respect on both sides.[17] The skilled laborers—man's men who spent their work life in the fraternity of the shop floor—knew the job and taught it. Though seeking a status above the workers, aspiring engineers learned the trade from them, and by working shoulder-to-shoulder, they became "real men" in the eyes of the laborers as they did. In a short span of time, however, shop floor shoulder-rubbing became more symbolic, less necessary, as changes in industrial technology took decision-making out of the hands of the laborers, whose "skill" then became less and less necessary to their job performances.[18] The version of masculinity adopted by the engineer contrasted more and more to that which characterized the working man. School culture offered a further separation between the engineer and the men he led. Though the model of the academically educated engineer was even less popular with laborers,[19] engineering schools became just as powerful and ultimately more lasting a method of professional preparation than the shop floor fraternity. The academic engineer, physically separated from the shop floor but in a position of authority over it, slowly emerged as its own vision of masculinity.

Meanwhile, Kimmel says, the turn of the century saw workers "seem[ing] to lose control of their labor and the production process, which was transferred upwards to a new class of managers and supervisors."[20] Workers' bodies and their capacity for hard labor—basically, all that was left from the "self-made" social ideal of masculinity, with freedom and authority gone—were becoming economically appropriated: "docile," increasingly unskilled laborers, were seen as "human machines."[21]

As an academic, white-collar masculinity emerged for engineers, and the actual labor of the working man involved more and more surrender to it, the impact on blue-collar masculinity was profound. Nor were the gendered consequences of this shift lost on the laborers themselves. The gendered language from the discourse is not subtle, and rhetorical attempts to re-masculinize the laborer by feminizing the engineer abound: Kimmel includes dozens of quotes, like those from letters published in *Miner's Magazine* in 1904 and the *Boston Labor Leader* in 1887, which claim that workers must "stand erect in the full majesty of our manhood," against the "effeminate monopolistic system [and] effete methods of tyranny" that increasingly characterized capitalist labor practices.[22] An 1871 article in the *Journal of Social Science* bluntly states that moving a man to wage labor makes him "less of a man."[23] The genderedness of the changes to the production model was undoubtedly augmented by other factors—including the growing number of women in the workplace, particularly in the early decades of the twentieth century—but the link between a man's body, his physical labor, and his masculinity was being eroded in part by the changing nature of his work.

Of course brawn, as is obvious even in twenty-first-century popular culture, was never entirely divided from idealized masculine identity. As it declined in social and economic authority, Kimmel and Oldenziel argue, it became paradoxically manlier in art and sport, as laborers' bodies became visually and culturally celebrated. Oldenziel argues that "sport, fighting, [and] other contests of virile strength [were] associated with manual labor," and that pressures on engineers from "below," resolved in "a celebration of a shop-floor manliness when it was no longer viable."[24] The divide between types of masculinity thus rendered still conveys tremendous rhetorical power: in the 1950s, Charles Atlas and the ninety-eight-pound weakling, or, in today's parlance, the jock and the geek.

MR. INCREDIBLE'S MIDLIFE CRISIS

In light of this decline of "brawny" masculine authority in the workplace, Mr. Incredible's midlife crisis may be read as larger than idiosyncratic and indicative of a moment in gender history older than modern feminism. Mr. Incredible has been a "Super," one of a race of people endowed with extra-human traits and abilities, entrusted by society with a law-enforcement role. Though the Supers include both males and females, their work recalls the most satisfying aspects of the "self-made" model of manhood that Kimmel describes: while they work with the consent of actual law enforcement, there is no evidence that the Supers answer to the government, collect a paycheck, or heed a clock. Their professional decision-making is unfettered by bureaucracy or academic best practices, and their physicality uniquely suits them to their jobs. Their physical labor is portrayed as an honorable, fulfilling, and free pursuit. Indeed, the very freedom of their work initiates their downfall, as an outcry of politicians, lawyers, and litigious citizens force them into hiding.

In the main setting of the film, fifteen years after the heyday of the Supers, Mr. Incredible as Bob Parr is owned by a corporate bureaucracy. Squeezed into a cubicle, hectored by diminutive middle manager Mr. Huph, Bob is menaced by a row of clocks both literally (in the wall décor over his boss's desk) and figuratively (in Mr. Huph's tired metaphor for a high-functioning corporation).[25] In this dispiritingly measured existence Bob files—or, more precisely, denies—insurance claims. The film's depiction of Bob's giant body at work, dwarfing his small chair and his unfortunate client, conveys the oppressive nature of his new workplace and the inappropriateness of the job for the body doing it. An asset in the fight against villainy, his superfluous body for its cramped cubicle visually marks the unnaturalness of his doing such work.

His ill-fitting body is not all that hinders Mr. Parr's ability to do his new work well. His inner drive toward superheroic behavior resists the new corporate ethic to which he is asked to adhere. Entering the mainstream middle class means devaluing his body, once the source of his superior identity and close connection to the value of his labor, in other words, but it also means denying him the freedom and moral agency to which he is accustomed. Furthermore, this devaluation is systemic: from the time of the Relocation debate onward, Mr. Incredible has been directed by administrative authorities, from lawyers and politicians to his Insura-care boss. Though the Relocation agents seem relatively sensitive to the difficulty of such a decline, the further he gets from Super status the worse he's treated. Mr. Huph reprimands him like he's a naughty child, actually grabbing his face and saying, "Look at me when I'm talking to you!" If Mr. Incredible the Super exemplifies the "self-made" man, his degraded alter-ego Bob Parr represents the archetype in decline, his physical authority usurped by bureaucracy and the innate superiority of his body no longer adequate compensation for the loss.

Historically, this decline was frequently described in gendered language, and so too does it seem that Bob "Parr," though now on a "par" with other men, is unable to feel or convey any real sense of specifically masculine authenticity, that identity that he had previously connected to his hypermasculine body. As Kimmel says about office work, contrasted to shop floor labor in the early decades of the twentieth century, Bob's job seems "increasingly feminized" or emasculating, as it surrenders characteristics of the older masculine ideal.[26] It could be argued that the fault is in Mr. Incredible's old-fashioned—even sexist—notion of his own "masculinity," that a taxonomy of manhood that privileged the manually laboring, physically endowed body is unnecessarily limited, that Mr. Incredible need not succumb to such a traditionalist model when he could reinvent himself in new and interesting ways. But his old-fashioned notion of essential manhood is not the half of the equation that the film critiques: indeed, the self-made man is not only the role for which Mr. Incredible himself yearns but also the only ethical position represented in the film. Middle-class management is crookedly conformist, profit-seeking to the extreme, even cruel to those in need; engineering, as we'll discuss shortly, fares even worse. Mr. Incredible may be miserable with that giant body and its ill-fitting chair, but he's also honest and giving, wanting to the help both the policy-holder tricked by the business and the mugging victim he sees out the office window. His manly body may be in the wrong environment to support his sense of masculinity, but it seems to be because the environment—not the essentialist gender equation—is wrong.

As with Bruce the Great White, Bob's natural self cannot be suppressed for long, and the film doesn't let us forget that he's *not* really Mr. Parr; he's Mr. *Incredible*. When Bob's angst reaches crisis proportions, the film lets his brawny male body express itself through traditionally masculine outlets. First, the potential violence of his Super strength erupts in one dramatic act, as he throws Mr. Huph through layers and layers of cubicle walls, putting him in a body cast. Then, a sequence of scenes visually suggests an extramarital romantic dalliance: secret messages from a beautiful stranger lead to a sprinkler-enabled cold shower; phone calls are overheard piecemeal to the worst possible suspicions; a wife picks something—a hair? lipstick? no, just rubble—off of her husband's suit jacket to catch him in a lie; and a romantic dinner date with the mysterious stranger leads to an extremely odd conversation, in which the "other woman" starts talking about the fertility of the land to which she's invited him and asks him to "compare" what is before him, presumably with what his wife brings home from the supermarket. Finally, in a makeover montage—he starts working out (lifting train cars as free weights), flirting with his wife until she literally pulls him into the bedroom, and buying his-and-hers sports cars—the stereotypes of masculine midlife crisis seem particularly egregious. Bob gets his groove back, it seems, by shaking off the mantle of emasculating white-collar work, escaping corporate hierarchies, and rediscovering his innate, "authentic" masculinity, chiefly located in the physical power (and sexuality) of his body.

ENTER THE ENGINEER

Mr. Incredible's defeating Mr. Huph and faux-seducing Mirage, however, are not the main narrative points of *The Incredibles*, even if they do help him remember or discover his supposedly true self. The plot hinges on Syndrome. On the eve of his wedding, Mr. Incredible rebuffs the young Buddy Pine, his "number-one fan" and aspiring hero of his own. Buddy then spends the fifteen years between the film's two settings nursing his resentment and plotting his revenge. One legitimate and useful reading of the film, as we'll explore more in another chapter, is that Buddy is a hurt kid who grows up angry, a neglected boy turned bully (we resist "psychotic" and "sadistic" as the Disney Wikia and other fan sites have it).[27] But in the context of Mr. Incredible's masculine identity, its professional decline, and supposedly natural restoration, Buddy/Syndrome also represents a competing type of masculinity emerging in opposition to the "self-made" laborer of early American history. An inventor, engineer, and entrepreneur, he has spent his young life dramatically improving his rocket boot design, creating a whole arsenal of weapons, and getting rich selling his inventions abroad. By the time he encounters Mr. Incredible again, Syndrome has become the very picture of the emergent white-collar, socially climbing man, defining his new middle-class masculinity in opposition to the self-made labor model. Trained outside the shop floor fraternity, which Mr. Incredible denied him when he basically volunteered to apprentice, he further exemplifies the attempt to appropriate and control the brawny working-class male body as he simultaneously strives to outrank it on a broadening spectrum of masculinity.

If Syndrome had simply wanted to destroy Mr. Incredible, it seems that he would have had an easy enough time of it. Supers can die, and when Mirage locates "Bob" he is not only vulnerable but also entirely oblivious to any impending danger. If he only wanted him dead, theoretically, Syndrome could have just attacked him at home or work, poisoned him with all that incomparable food grown from fertile volcano soil. But Syndrome clearly has a more symbolically significant aim in mind: to guarantee his own masculine reputation, he needs to vanquish his rival in terms of not only who wins the fight but also who is more manly, or whose type of masculinity will prevail when that exemplified by engineering genius goes head to head with the more traditional model located in the brawny body.

Syndrome needs not only to defeat, in other words, but also to transcend his rival and the model of masculinity he has historically represented, an essentialist model that the small, brainy, non-Super Buddy simply does not embody. It stands to reason that the first thing he does to Mr. Incredible is hire him. Before he is confronted as a rival, Mr. Incredible is brought on as a hired subordinate, the work of his body appropriated and his labor controlled. It is undeniably work more suited to Mr. Incredible's sense of self than was his job at Insuracare, but it is not Super work in terms of agency or ethicality—only manual labor. And make no mistake: Mr. Incredible does indeed work for Syndrome. Admittedly, he enters into the job under fraudulent terms, as indicated by the list of "terminated" Supers who have previously battled versions of the Omnidroid, and Mr. Incredible is misled into believing he's helping the company by conquering the robot who's actually trying to kill him. Still, though Syndrome's plans for Mr. Incredible's death by Omnidroid may seem merely filtered through the discourse of the workplace, the employment arrangement surpasses its own rhetoric as Mr. Incredible's work actually does help Syndrome to improve his product. Mr. Incredible's physical might makes him employable, and valuably so, as a sort of brute product tester. In a small way, then, Syndrome exerts authority over Mr. Incredible's body even before directly challenging him as a rival.

Controlling him as a worker is not enough to satisfy Syndrome, who recalls early twentieth-century engineers, with their own masculinity to prove in the face of the manly brawn of manual labor. If living well is the best revenge, Syndrome has already won, having made a fortune off of the international distribution of his inventions, while Mr. Incredible wallows in the suburbs. Still, he seeks not only the destruction but also the total humiliation of his rival, and that means attacking him at his masculine identity. It is hard to read Mr. Incredible's capture—the literal and figurative low point in his narrative journey—as anything but figuratively emasculating. To get to Nomanisan, he descends to a kind of underworld, jetting under the ocean, through underwater caves and tunnels, to the inside of a volcano, but his katabasis culminates in a conspicuously gender-coded failure. When his wife uses a homing device to find him, she unwittingly exposes him to the security measures built into Syndrome's complex; he is then brought down by giant, swelling balls that cover his face and pull him to the ground. Finally, in case that's not enough, the last shot before the image goes completely dark frames Mirage's skirted lower half, splayed in a kind of mountain pose over him, the triangle of her crotch presumably the very last thing he sees before losing consciousness.

When Mr. Incredible wakes up, his humiliation continues with the apparent destruction of his family while he stands helplessly by. But the irony of the film is that while Syndrome seeks to conquer Mr. Incredible's sense of masculinity, he simultaneously emulates it, not successfully transcending or changing prevailing notions of "masculinity" to fit his strengths and talents but trying to travel by a different path to the very same end. Despite his success, having "learned to compensate" for being small and smart instead of hypermasculine and Super, Syndrome has bought into the manly model embodied by his rival and still needs him as a template to measure his own manliness.[28] On the surface of it, Syndrome's plan for global domination speaks indirectly to the potential foreseen by Halberstam or, more directly and cynically, to the influence of consumerism on conformity: once everyone can be "super," by their conscious and deliberate performances (purchases), no one will be Super, no one considered intrinsically better than anyone else. This overt attempt to rewrite the social codes that place the Supers at the top of the hierarchy (even, it would seem, when they have been forced into hiding) fails to imagine gender as an identity that could be differently performed, as if even Syndrome believes in the superiority of his enemy's body. His childhood worship of Mr. Incredible has led him to develop tools to make himself not only ostensibly (if fraudulently) more necessary to society as a protector but also more stereotypically manly in his very physical presence. With the refinements to his rocket boots (which Kindlon and Thompson might see as "compensatory mechanisms to make [him] feel bigger"),[29] the bantam supervillain even positions himself as taller than Mr. Incredible, hovering above him in their face-off in the jungle. Syndrome's desire to conquer Mr. Incredible cannot be separated from his desire to *be* Mr. Incredible—the Incredi-Boy of his youthful imagination. Particularly poignant is the fact that Syndrome's end game is not to conquer the world but to be popular in it; his Omnidroid, after all, is designed not to destroy but to be destroyed, in a choreographed performance of strength that he believes will at last make people respect him.

Ultimately, of course, Syndrome doesn't win: not the war he's waged on the Supers nor the campaign for the admiration of his fellow citizens. He earns the respect and compassion of neither the citizens of Municiberg nor the Incredible family nor the audience members. All that rhetorical and constructed masculinity is proven false as Syndrome publicly fails. His Omnidroid turns on him and he falls. With a terrified look on his face, he finds his arms too weak to push himself up again. Rather than becoming the city's rescuer, he once again gets saved. Finding no other masculine turf but paternity on which to challenge Mr. Incredible, he kidnaps the baby Jack-Jack, but when even the infant's superior body proves too much for him, he is conveniently sucked into a jet engine and killed.

The film, it seems, cannot place his version of masculinity—intellectual and rhetorical, but not essentially brawny—on the pedestal reserved for "real" men. Mr. Incredible, who never really changes but manages to change society's views back to the "old school" wherein he was happy, may get gently "disciplined" at the end of the film in a feminist sense, learning that he needs to team up with his wife and kids to truly succeed (and this is a reasonable argument, which we've made before). Even so, the film maintains the bodily authenticity of his masculine superiority and concludes with a kind of nostalgic hopefulness for its return. Despite the iconic family action shot that concludes the film as the Underminer burrows from the depths beneath the city, indicating the future (and opening the door for a sequel), the "no school like the old school" wistfulness of the Supers' fans—notably, older men in browline glasses—indicates that film simultaneously gestures backward, to a reality wherein progressive wrongs are made right and the Mr. Incredibles of the world—"real men"—have their day. The film nostalgically imagines that uncomplicated, essentialist masculinity, though temporarily driven underground by politics and economic change, may yet hold sway.

THE "TRUE MEASURE OF A MONSTER"

Like greater Municiberg, *Monsters, Inc.*'s Monstropolis evokes a nostalgic past that celebrates blue-collar masculinity and the shop floor fraternity in which it thrives. With details from the *Bewitched*-esque animated credits and the big-band soundtrack to Roz's cat-eye glasses and the round television screen on which the new Monsters Incorporated ad airs, *Monsters, Inc.* evokes the American midcentury despite its alternative-universe setting, populated by innumerable species and powered by energy distilled from human children's screams. The retro feel extends to the scare floor where Mike and Sulley work, a masculine idyll decorated with hardhats, lunch boxes, and locker rooms, where scarers express professional success in terms of competition, conquest, and humiliation. This fraternal space houses no women, save Cecilia, the receptionist, and, it initially appears, Roz the clerk. Though the prequel, *Monsters University,* shows female college students in attendance at Dean Hardscrabble's welcome lecture to the MU School of Scaring, their gender signified primarily by the curly eyelashes and hairstyles that elsewhere denote femininity in both films (and though in the *Monsters University* credits, some female scarers do have their own trading cards), no female monsters apparently secure work at Monsters, Incorporated after graduation alongside their onetime classmates, Mike, Sulley, and Randall. Without exception, the scarers and assistants on the scare floor are male (judging from available first names and voices, as well as the absence of the feminine gender cues elsewhere employed). The scarers enter the floor more like a sports team approaching a big game than shift workers reporting for duty, celebrated by slow motion, fanfare, and star-struck boys whose voices crack as they express their awe.

Monsters University rewrites the mythology of the first film somewhat, not only elevating professional scarers to a social pedestal that warrants things like trading cards and fan clubs but also establishing academic foundations in prestigious university programs of study. The pomp and circumstance of Monsters University's School of Scaring is one of two (the other, Fear Tech), whose alum are among Monsters, Incorporated's staff. Despite the revisionist inclusion of an academic tradition (nowhere anticipated by *Monsters, Inc.*), the actual work of the scream factory is decidedly blue-collar, physical labor, in which little academic learning or intellectual abstraction is visible. Though the film's faux-university website promotes the scholarship and teaching of its illustrious faculty, the pair of films arguably critiques higher education, as the trajectory of the legendary Sulley, who, by the second film, is the eleven-months-running employee of the month and All-time Scare Record hopeful, renders a formal education unnecessary at best. In his short stint at Monsters University, Sulley's chief application of books is to level the pong table, but never mind: expelled from the School of Scaring in the prequel, Mike and Sulley work their way up from the mail room through custodial and cafeteria work to rival—and consistently beat— the academically trained Randall, whose ambition has led him not to honorable success but to corruption. In the culture of Monstropolis, "book learning" at best gets a guy yelled at, as Randall's assistant Fungus regularly experiences, even when his skills might actually solve the problem at hand. At worst, being smart, educated, and strategic can turn a man into a real monster.

Given the physicality of the work, and the film's subtle denigration of intellectual approaches thereto, it is perhaps unsurprising that talent on the shop floor would inhere in the body. The scarier the body, it would seem, the more successful the scarer. In one way, the film is a democratic ideal for bodily diversity, as the idiosyncratic aspects of scarers' bodies make them uniquely suited to particular children, difference creating unique potential for success rather than obstacles to it. Indeed, the visual celebration of difference is one of the joys of the film, the sheer variety of monsters' bodies interrupted by few (or no) visible patterns of species or race, and traits presenting as either assets or liabilities depending on the environment. Still, though horror films have for decades maximized on the artistic potential of visualizing "scary"—as children, dolls, puppets, and clowns all agents of terror, sneaking, creeping, suprising, and menacing all approaches to generating terror—*Monsters, Inc.* simplifies the "scary" (and consequently successful) body of the blue-collar shop floor to traditionally "masculine" traits: the bulk and brawn of Buzz and Mr. Incredible. In every case, scarers are larger and burlier than their assistants; nearly all the assistants have skinny bodies, arms, and/or legs. Scarers' bodies are able and athletic—Sulley wakes to a morning workout montage, with Mike his coach—while assistants require the accommodations and protection of eyeglasses and hardhats. One even seems to wear a fur ruff on his otherwise smooth body. Scarers are animalistic—vaguely mammalian or reptilian, with visible hair or scales—while assistants embody smooth, colorful geometric shapes (Mike's round, green body, in a trailer for the film, doubling as a disco ball for a fraternity prank). Thus the shop floor takes its own privileging of hypermasculine body types as a given and, for all its alternate species, restricts alternate performances of masculinity.

In this space, Sulley is king, and *Monsters University* is even more explicit about his inextricably bound masculine and professional successes being attributable to his body and birthright. Though he may appear to Pixar's child viewers more like a big teddy bear than a terror (and thus a toy worth buying, no doubt), and to the plucky Boo like a giant blue "kitty," the film is unambiguous about Sulley's inherent scaring ability and the clear path to success it ensures. His young adult attitude assumes it: "You don't need to study scaring," he chides Mike. "You just do it!" His college peers recognize it, telling Mike that "real scarers look like us." His professors reinforce it: Professor Knight calls him "a monster who looks like a scarer." Even his friends at the Oozma Kappa fraternity believe in his essential superiority: "He's right," says Don. "We'll never look like them. We're built for other things." In class, while Mike is perfectly reciting his first right answer, Sulley just roars, satisfying Professor Knight, stealing Mike's thunder, and securing a place of social prominence. Even after his brief academic career, those around him read his body, hulking and powerful like Mr. Incredible's, as superior to many or most of the bodies around it. Unlike the loyal Mike, forever literally and figuratively obscured—by the corporate logo, the mailing label, and the reputation of his friend—Sulley is featured on television, encouraged on the street, complimented in the workplace, and granted access to elite social spots. Sulley is Mr. Incredible without the degradation of the Relocation Act, without the midlife crisis, and without the direct personal challenge of his rival.

Sulley has a rival, though, and Randall Boggs, like Syndrome, represents not only a competitor but also a competing masculine archetype. Randall, skinny and smart, is one of MU's freshman nerds before becoming a successful scarer; like Syndrome, his initial motivation is not merely professional but social. Like Syndrome, of course, Randall ultimately fails, humiliated in the first film by Sulley, insulted in the second by Waternoose, and always a few points short of the coveted Scare Record. By *Monsters, Inc.*, viewers learn, Randall's ambition has grown both grander and more insidious than the aboveboard quest for a record, and, like Syndrome's, his intellectual ability has led him to develop technology that he hopes will revolutionize the status quo and cement for him a position of status, regardless of how many people it hurts. Ultimately, as with *The Incredibles*, the pervasive system of essentialist masculine value that works well for the protagonist on a journey to self-discovery is the very system that seems to ensure the downfall of his nemesis. Though for Sulley scaring is literally a performance, a deliberately inauthentic gesture that belies the deeply kind personality beneath his surface, and though his narrative arc eventually brings him into the fold of Pixar's kind and gentle father figures, his is an essentially (hyper)masculine body—the traditionally honored body for the masculine self. In such a body from the beginning, Sulley (like Mr. Incredible, Buzz Lightyear, and Lightning McQueen) is afforded the luxury of performing a more domestic type of masculinity. Randall, like Syndrome, has no such luxury. Though he does have one powerful innate ability, his very talent is a cliché for inauthenticity: he is, after all, a monstrous version of chameleon. Furthermore, as someone whose most effective means of success is built, rather than embodied, and whose body is small, delicate, and insufficiently compensated by intelligence, Randall contrasts with—and finally loses to—Sulley's ostensibly more authentic masculine brawn.

Mike's masculine failure, just as inevitable, is far more poignant. Not a villain like Syndrome or Randall, Mike is nonetheless a child whose big dreams must be diverted—or crushed—by the world, and the body, in which he lives. Dean Hardscrabble says it plainly: "I know for a *fact* that one of you is not [scary]." Responding to Sulley's cavalier "just do it" slogan during the first days of college, the determined and disciplined young Mike naively insists: "Really? I think there's a little more to it than that," and then asks Sulley to leave so he can study. Having seen the first film, though, viewers already know that Mike's approach will not succeed and that Sulley's will: later in their lives, we know, Mike will be Sulley's cheerful assistant, his unequal partner who enables but does not perform scaring. Though the prequel allows his cleverness, intelligence, and hard academic labor to at least contribute to one team victory, earning him some status in a subculture of two as he strategizes his and Sulley's escape from the camp cabin, the films together guarantee that Mike's body will always prohibit him from reaching his lifelong goal. In the larger society—of the university, the scare floor, and the city it serves—he will only be a helper, a sidekick, or a comedian. Mike is funny, and the discovery tacked on to the end of *Monsters, Inc.*, that laughter conveys more energy than screams, redirects Sulley's spotlight for a moment to Mike's new nighttime stand-up routine. But as his jokes fail on the kids from whom he needs laughter and he resorts to self-abusive physical comedy, it is difficult to see such a future as an unproblematic resolution to the film's underlying ideologies.

Worse, the two *Monsters* films in tandem—along with *The Incredibles* and other Pixar films, notably *Cars 2*, as we discuss in the next chapter—structurally reinforce the foundations of what Klein calls "the jock cult."[30] Even when it looks like vengeful nerds may momentarily triumph, such small victories do not dismantle the system of their disenfranchisement as much as they ironically replicate it.[31] Nerds remain nerds, round people are funny, intellectual men will only ever be pencil-neck alternates to the truly successful hypermasculine jocks. Pixar's overt favoritism does not innocuously reiterates an essentialist model of masculinity, based in a traditional celebration of physical brawn, but tacitly endorses the social hierarchy that perpetuates our rampant bully culture.

NOTES

1. Claudia Card, "Pinocchio," in *From Mouse to Mermaid: The Politics of Film, Gender, and Culture*, ed. Elizabeth Bell, Lynda Haas, and Laura Sells (Bloomington: Indiana University Press, 2008), 66, 69. See also Friere and Giroux, who argue that the ideal function of public education is in "creating a public sphere of citizens who are able to exercise power over their own lives" but that it tends to "ignore its own complicity with those social relationsh that subjugate, infantilize, and corrupt" ("Pedagogy, Popular Culture, and Public Life: An Introduction," in *Popular Culture, Schooling and Everyday Life*, ed. Henry A. Giroux and Roger Simon [New York: Bergin & Garvey, 1989], viii).

2. William Pollack, *Real Boys: Rescuing Our Sons from the Myths of Boyhood* (New York: Henry Holt, 1998).

3. Keith Booker, *Disney, Pixar, and the Hidden Messages of Children's Films* (Westport, CT: Greenwood, 2010), 7.

4. Booker, *Disney, Pixar*, 7.

5. Judith Butler, "Performative Acts and Gender Constitution: an Essay in Phenomenology and Feminist Theory," *Theatre Journal* 40 no. 4 (December 1988), 520.

6. Jessie Klein, *The Bully Society: School Shootings and the Crisis of Bullying in America's Schools* (New York: New York University Press, 2012), 12.

7. Klein, *The Bully Society*, 26.

8. Dan Kindlon and Michael Thompson, *Raising Cain: Protecting the Emotional Life of Boys* (New York: Ballantine Books, 1999), 83.

9. Klein, *The Bully Society*, 29.

10. Judith Halberstam, *The Queer Art of Failure* (Durham, NC: Duke University Press, 2011), 46.

11. Lyn Brown, Sharon Lamb, and Mark Tappan. *Packaging Boyhood: Saving Our Sons from Superheroes, Slackers, and Other Media Stereotypes* (New York: St. Martin's Press, 2009), 208. See also Klein, *The Bully Society*, 28–29.

12. Ruth Oldenziel, *Making Technology Masculine: Men, Women, and Modern Machines in America, 1870–1945* (Amsterdam: Amsterdam University Press, 1999).

13. Michael Kimmel, *Manhood in America: A Cultural History*, 3rd ed. (New York: Oxford University Press, 2012), 17–20.

14. Kimmel, *Manhood in America*, 20.

15. Kimmel, *Manhood in America*, 62–63.

16. Oldenziel, *Making Technology Masculine*, 11.

17. Oldenziel, *Making Technology Masculine*, 59.

18. Oldenziel, *Making Technology Masculine*, 57–60.

19. Oldenziel, *Making Technology Masculine*, 65–66.

20. Kimmel, *Manhood in America*, 82.

21. Kimmel, *Manhood in America*, 83.

22. Kimmel, *Manhood in America*, 79.

23. Kimmel, *Manhood in America*, 63.

24. Oldenziel, *Making Technology Masculine*, 105, 109. See also Kimmel, *Manhood in America*, 88–89.

25. Citing the time-and-motion studies of Frederick Winslow Thomas at the turn of the twentieth century, Kimmel describes time clocks among the technologies that reduced workers to "human machines" (*Manhood in America,* 62).

26. Kimmel, *Manhood in America,* 77

27. These particular characterizations come from http://pixar.wikia.com/The_Incredibles, http://disney.wikia.com/wiki/Syndrome, and www.pixarplanet.com, but certainly the general spirit of them is the rule, not the exception.

28. Kindlon and Thompson, *Raising Cain*, 83.

29. Kindlon and Thompson, *Raising Cain*, 83.

30. Klein, *The Bully Society*, 25.

31. Klein, *The Bully Society*, 41–42.

Chapter Three

"I am speed"

Athleticism, Competition, and the Bully Society

The bully/jock is so commonplace in children's media that Roar Omega Roar fraternity president Johnny Worthington really needs no introduction and, in truth, the character uses relatively few lines to exert his formidable presence in the school culture of Monsters University. The social overthrow plot of such classics as *Revenge of the Nerds* and *Animal House,* paid homage if not retold outright by *Monsters University,* employs such familiar social stereo-types that it requires merely a symbol of "popular" to direct the revenge endlessly sought by its "unpopular" protagonists. Worthington's status as hegemonic man on campus is as legible today in its essentialist masculine body type as it might have been decades ago, his tall, broad-chested, narrow-hipped body almost superfluously adorned with the faux-Greek characters that further signify prestige and belonging. As viewers' instantaneous recog-nition of Worthington's type and its inherent social power indicates, the nerds-rule plot structure remains notoriously unsuccessful as a deconstruc-tive tool, the ever-resilient stock types resonating long after any momentary inversion of the status quo. Even more ironically, the inversions themselves may more successfully reify than dismantle the hierarchy of valuation upon which they are based. Unfortunately—and at times, horrifically—this seem-ingly impervious hierarchy, which gives shape to so many film narratives, complete with jocks, "nerds," and other misfits, mirrors the very real ideo-logical foundation of American adolescence, and even the most dramatic real-life overthrow plots succeed only in effecting tragedy, not change. As Jessie Klein observes in *The Bully Society: School Shootings and the Crisis of Bullying in American Schools*, the extreme revenge fantasies of school shooters over the past thirty years much more often reiterate than reinvent the systemic inequalities and prejudices that have bred their pain and resentment. Even those who rebel against the hierarchy, it seems, can only imagine themselves momentarily perched at the top of it, not an altogether new, and more just, way of being a kid in America.

In the context of the ubiquitous and "singularly cruel peer culture" that Dan Kindlon and Michael Thompson lament and that Klein documents, those perpetual "social status wars" in which "children found lacking are pushed to the bottom of their school's social hierarchy, where life can be unbearable,"[1] we find it at least mildly disappointing that a powerhouse like Pixar uses, but doesn't alter, the tired structural device of "popular kids" versus "losers." As Henry Giroux and others have noted about Disney, and Pixar's distribution numbers indicate is equally true for its output, the pedagogical reach of these mainstream films and their marketing machines can be vast and powerful, a "public school system" unto itself, in terms of teaching the ideological under-pinnings of society.[2] What's far more disappointing than Pixar's abdication of their unique position to effect positive change, given this cultural author-ity, is its willingness to go one step further in the wrong direction. Pixar's vengeful nerds and lovable misfits generally don't manage to don the mantle of privilege even temporarily. Instead, across its various social worlds and alternate realities, from Monstropolis to Metroville to Radiator Springs, Pixar plays favorites in dishearteningly traditional ways, actually shoring up the taxonomy that places hypermasculine success stories—and these boys alone—atop the social hierarchies of American childhood and adolescence. The two *Monsters* films, *The Incredibles, Cars,* and *Cars 2* all structurally reinforce the foundations of what Klein calls "the jock cult," that insidious system that elevates particularly athletic, aggressive, and competitive boys while devaluing the rest.[3] Moreover, the films overtly sanction—sometimes even participate in—surprisingly violent methods of policing and maintain-ing those foundations.

Klein argues that the "bully society" of American adolescence is so insid-ious that adults sometimes don't see it even when it's right in front of us. Teachers, parents, administrators, and the purveyors of cultural texts often if unwittingly adhere to normalized but arbitrary standards of gendered behav-ior and reinforce as natural a resultant structure of valuation that can be seriously damaging to many children on their way to adulthood. In eruptions of resistance like the school shootings that comprise much of Klein's re-search, the foundations of the bully society become visible, and still we frequently ignore them, instead attributing shooters' behaviors to external and idiosyncratic factors—the music one listened to, another's parents, yet another's possible mental illnesses. In this chapter, our counter-readings may be less counter to the films' messages themselves than to the blinders of the audiences who consume them. In the films overtly about adolescent or young adult men competing with one another—*Monsters University* and *Cars 2*—

the link between athleticism, competition, and idealized, hegemonic masculinity is plain. The films delineate the victors and the vanquished unambiguously and predictably according to the familiar social hierarchy based on that link: winners win and losers lose. Still, as Klein describes, the structure and its inherent biases can be hard to see, hidden in plain sight amid structural truisms to which we all may gravitate. Even in their moments of nonviolent competition, the films maintain the ground on which actual violence is enacted every day.

THE BULLY SOCIETY OF MONSTERS UNIVERSITY

Though Mike Wazowski would rather study than party, willing to postpone the trappings of success until he's a superstar scarer, *Monsters University* bluntly teaches the lesson that fitting in is both highly desirable and synonymous with membership in the most selective organizations. If Mike doesn't care about popularity, the film seems to say, that preference alone isolates him from his peers. Early in the fall semester, Randall Boggs, then "Randy," affirms these truisms, somewhat desperately, insisting that rush parties present the freshmen's "only chance to get in with the cool kids." Though his "lame" cupcakes cast doubt on his prospects from the beginning, his very exclusion seems to uphold his assessment of the situation. The already-lauded "Jimmy" Sullivan endorses Randy's perspective, reminding viewers as he informs Mike that Roar Omega Roar is the best because it only accepts "the highly elite." The fun-loving pig chase culminating in Mike's humiliation further reinforces the lesson. Sulley holds the small monster up to the crowd as if to place him on equal terms with Archie the Fear Tech mascot, even though Mike's the one who has caught the pig, and the RΩRs deny Mike entry to their party anyway. The bookish work-study student might have a superior strategy for achieving academic success, but the film makes it pretty clear that he's not "cool."

What Mike lacks, in Dean Hardscrabble's words, "cannot be taught." It is what Klein calls "body capital," arguing (alongside Kimmel and many others) that for boys, size and athleticism definitely matter.[4] Indeed, the approbation of the fraternity on whose approval all of one's aspirations depend—the very definition of success—is rooted in the exaggeratedly male body Pixar elsewhere celebrates. The brawny Worthington is explicit, claiming that "real scarers look like us," as he refuses Mike (who, of course, doesn't). Mike is the one who catches Archie the pig, but his actions can earn him no credit without a body that signifies masculine authority. The idealized masculine body literally becomes a necessary condition for any and all success Mike might achieve at MU: "fitting in" to a fraternity or sorority, however humiliating and arbitrary attaining such membership may be, is a prerequisite to participation in the Scare Games; the Scare Games represent Mike's only hope for "proving [he's] the best" and thus getting back into the School of Scaring; and the School of Scaring holds the key to his lifelong ambition of being a scarer. One can't win if he doesn't play, the film pronounces, but he can't play if he doesn't belong, and he can't belong unless he's born (looking like) a winner. Mike begins college believing his "chances are just as good as" anybody's, but his peers quickly correct him: "You're not even in the same league as me," Sulley sneers.

In this vicious circle of popularity, where success both depends on and paradoxically requires belonging, success is also necessarily competitive, based on actual winning rather than merely achieving. Mike initially (and reasonably enough) expects that school success will mean mastering material, but he finds himself involved instead in direct competition with his peers, even before the Greek organizations face off in the annual Scare Games. From the moment of his rejection at the fraternity party—to which he was never interested in going anyway—Mike slightly revises his notion of success to include proving himself by out-achieving those who denigrate him, but he remains committed to his plan of academic achievement: his goal is to do his best. Sulley, on the other hand, socially out-ranking Mike from the beginning and, presumably, with little to prove by besting him, begins to define his success as specifically contingent on his rival's failure. Taking Sullivan's RΩRs jacket, as a "precaution" in case he doesn't pass his Scare exam, Worthington dramatically states the connection between success and belonging. Moreover, though there's nothing to suggest that Mike and Sulley could not both pass the exam and thus both succeed in the scare school, he articulates the exam as a head-to-head contest. RΩRs, after all, "can't have a member getting shown up by a beach ball."

Boy culture relentlessly polices this peer culture of competitiveness, which measures success not by one's ability but by his conquest over others; the "boy police," as Klein argues, ensures that even the socially successful boys maintain aggressive and competitive postures toward one another. The pressures of competition are never alleviated by winning, in other words, but get redirected onto personal interactions with other boys. Klein says, "The [small minority of] boys most successful at staying on top . . . can never relax their vigilance. . . . Even the most seemingly masculine athletes bear the social burden of constantly proving their manhood through aggression."[5] When the RΩR brothers enter the back of the lecture hall to witness Sulley's performance, the rising anxiety in Sulley's face is unmistakable. A probational RΩR facing an exam for which he is not academically prepared, and on which both his professional and social aspirations hinge, Sulley may reasonably enough feel nervous, but he acts out *against Mike*, pushing his books onto the floor, not only in misdirected fear but also in a social performance of manhood for the audience of his contingent brothers.

Thus begins the immediate conflict that, upsetting Dean Hardscrabble's scream canister, initiates the whole Scare Games plot in the first place. But the film does not critique the social hierarchy it presumes. Clearly, Sulley's aggression toward Mike was unprovoked by anything but the RΩRs' warped sense of their own masculine power, and clearly, Mike's own competitive desire, fueled by his lifelong professional ambition, was seeking an appropriate academic outlet (and, to his further credit, he is at least initially willing to walk away from Sulley's provocation), but no one ever calls Sulley out for his behavior toward the smaller monster. Instead, Mike and Sulley bear equal responsibility for the skirmish, at the will of Dean Hardscrabble and the film itself. Since punishment dealt in equal measure is presented as an unproblematic conclusion to the boys' altercation—their yoked destinies become the very essence of the film and the beginning of the friendship viewers know will eventually blossom—the film tacitly acknowledges that Sulley's treatment of Mike is to be expected, seeing Mike as either equally blameworthy for others' mistreatment of him or unprotectable from the supposedly natural hierarchy that generates such treatment toward him.

What is shocking, really, in a funny, happy-go-lucky film like *Monsters University,* is that such mistreatment has been a constant in Mike's life. Since spilling Mike's books is a relatively slight (and not directly violent) act, since Mike talks back to Sulley with more outrage than fear, and since the film indicates Sulley's relative discomfort with the situation, viewers might not see Sulley's gesture as evidence of a pervasive bully society or Mike's being a victim of chronic bullying. But Mike's entire history as we know it is marked by such mistreatment. It is naïve to see Mike as an ambitious, self-disciplined, but otherwise happy and well-adjusted college kid drawn into a rivalry by mere circumstance, as if any of a number of other social groups—MU has a debate team, an art club—might have led him to a satisfying social life and the eventual fulfillment of his dreams. Even as a very young child, Mike occupies the lowest rung on the social ladder. On his elementary school field trip he is told in no uncertain terms that he doesn't "belong." Not a friend, not a classmate, not even his cousin will buddy up with him. No one speaks to him except to taunt. Furthermore, and perhaps even more disconcertingly, there is no protective institutional structure; no adults notice or care. His teacher seems only weary of having to hang around with him, and neither she nor anyone else acts on Mike's perfectly reasonable, problem-solving suggestion that would give all the children equal access to the presentation he can't see ("How about we do tallest in the back?" he inquires). His optimism, enthusiasm, and extraversion all imperfectly mask the brutal truth of his young life: he has no one to enjoy, care for, or protect him. Mike endures his low status position with a smile, but the film never lets up. Even getting off the bus at MU, when he cheerfully takes leave of several riders by name, not one of them even responds, not to return the gesture, not to wish him well.

Given the insidious nature of the bully society, Klein might argue, why would we expect Ms. Graves or anyone else to speak for (or to) Mike? The set of definitions whereby a small, smart, friendly kid like the young Wazowski gets socially devalued and consequently treated as lesser—the hegemonic masculinity built largely of aggression, athleticism, competitive success, and emotional isolation—is widely normalized, seeming "inevitable" and "immutable" to adults and kids alike, across American schools. [6] Kids at the top of the bully society see their behavior—exiling, ridiculing, even physically abusing the children they've deemed "outcasts"—as natural. "Even after the [Columbine] shooting," Klein explains, "many students seemed to see nothing wrong with bullying students like Eric and Dylan." [7] Despite the shooters' resentment and anger explicitly directed against the social hierarchies of the school, many still considered mistreating them "a reasonable thing to do," calling them names and defending themselves for having taunted the pair. [8] "They're freaks," a student athlete allegedly told a reporter after the attack, among several who seemed to feel justified picking on the boys. [9] Perhaps, then, it is not strange enough that in Sulley's response to Mike's assertion of his right to equal opportunities—"you're not even in my league"—we don't hear an echo of Columbine alum Brooks Brown's description of his high school's mentality: "pathetic geeks like you are not on my level." [10]

Furthermore, bullies act with broad consent and/or the protection of a blindness wrought by the continual perpetuation of the power structure. Though Klebold and Harris had been actively bullied by only a few students, Klein notes, the rest of the school "seemed to have watched their humiliation with either indifference or some degree of pleasure." [11] The highest social groups in any school comprise only a small minority of kids, but those in the larger middle social tiers can "identify[ ] with the powerful group" by consenting to the subordination of others. [12] Their complicity earns them small but sufficient rewards, like safety from their own persecution. A bully society works because the power to maintain it is broadly distributed and silently accepted beyond the apparent locus of domination. Not incidentally, this is how gender theorists like R. W. Connell describe the maintenance of gender hegemonies as well: adopting "complicit" masculine identity pays small "dividends," Connell explains, at least in the right to separate oneself from subordinate or marginalized masculine groups. Even those outcast groups may internalize or "buy in" to the ideological foundations. [13] Teachers and administrators may further "perpetuate and model [these] dynamics" by deliberately "look[ing] the other way," even in the face of atrocious behavior, including physical and emotional mistreatment. [14] More insidious is their tacit consent, when so normalized is the hierarchy that "the dynamics don't register as abusive." [15]

Monsters University's account of the bully society's taxonomy of mascu-linities is utterly predictable and sadly accurate. Long before Johnny Worth-ington and Professor Knight tell him he doesn't "look like" a scarer, Mike's body type indicates his placement on the spectrum of alternative masculin-ities rather than on the upper ranks of hegemonic masculinity, From the opening scene, when viewers can see but have not yet met him, the simple fact that he's small silently justifies the cruel neglect of his peers. Indeed, at that point in the film, his size is the only information available to shape viewers' response to his elementary school experience, but apparently it is enough to generate fond amusement rather than outrage in the vast majority of audience members. Later, of course, his intelligence and hard work—he is an "outstanding" student, as Professor Knight praises—will likewise obstruct any claim to social status, but the unambiguous display of this discrimination may inspire just as little indignation from viewers. Klein remarks on the typical hierarchical placement of academic "nerds": at best, she says, kids who deliberately strive for intellectual and academic success may end up "outside the popular crowd, while at worst it can make them downright outcasts"; Columbine shooter Dylan Klebold, she observes, had been booed at a high school assembly for being a state debate champion.[16] Particularly endemic among boys, this vilification of academic intelligence is also so common as to be nearly invisible. Garnering no surprise or anger from audi-ences, *Monsters University* presents Mike's inability to leverage smarts into success as appropriate, indeed, a crucial part of the lesson he must learn.

As Lyn Mikel Brown et al. complain, "It strikes us that we're laughing a lot at the stupidity and anti-intellectualism of boys."[17] Of course, other traits than book-smarts can exempt boys from the in-crowd. If the narrow stratum of hegemonic masculinity in adolescence allows boys only hypermasculinity as a defining trait, the broad spectrum of alternative masculinities (supposed-ly populated by losers, nerds, and misfits) houses everything else: academic intelligence, interpersonal dependence, respect for women, financial priva-tion or anxiety, emotional literacy, generosity, manners, and enthusiasm for the performing arts. The Oozma Kappa membership roster reads as a laundry list of the commonly damning, supposedly non-masculine traits that fre-quently land boys at the bottom of the social heap. The soft, pink Squishy lives with his mother; Don, a pudgy nontraditional student, has recently lost his job; the contemplative Art keeps a rainbow/unicorn dream journal and enthusiastically shares his emotions with his friends. None of the OK broth-ers but Sulley has shoulders to speak of, broad or otherwise. The quasi-hermaphroditic Terri/Terry—both of whose heads speak with male voices, though one identifies by the traditionally feminine spelling of their name—is a virtual metaphor for restrictive gender codes, the "feminine" half of the boy wanting to dance and the "masculine" half embarrassed by, even hostile to, that public performance. The emotional traits and interpersonal friendships of the "losers" may be particularly notable in a world where, as Kindlon and Thompson explain, boys' emotional illiteracy is often destructive both to the self and to others. Klein claims that in the bully society being "too nice," especially to girls, exposes boys to ridicule: "The demonization of whatever is considered 'feminine' forces these boys to sacrifice depth and intimacy."[18] Though the film is structured so that the underdogs are lovable, and though, in the closing moments of the film, viewers are told that some do go on to successful careers, the social position of the OK brothers is not only maintained by but also necessary to the film's basic narrative tension, and their traits are far more obviously cast as humorous social liabilities than characteristics to adopt.

Monsters University does incorporate one clearly articulated, almost-inspiring message against the foundations of the bully society. Having snuck in to the Monsters, Incorporated factory, the Oozma Kappas observe and openly admire the sheer diversity of the scarers. The prequel thus recalls the potential for celebrating diversity built into the mythology of the first film (but not capitalized on, as we discuss in the previous chapter). The administration of the scare industry carefully matches scarers' unique abilities and traits with particular children, who are of course scared by different things. "What do all these scarers have in common?" Mike asks his new brothers, and when they fumble for answers he reveals the point of his trick question. Regardless of how many professors claim that they can identify potential scarers on sight, as Professor Knight has done to Sulley, Mike insists that "the best scarers use their differences to their advantage." For a moment, the film could be speaking directly from disability studies theory, advocating for a paradigm by which bodily differences are understood to be fundamental to the human condition and should not just be accommodated by but incorporated into a more highly functioning and more socially just society. Of course, the gag that frames the film from the first day of fall semester to the very end of the credits is a snail-type monster with such limited mobility that he can't even make it to a single class—more consistent with Klein's observation about the bully society's generally unsupportive treatment of children with disabilities than with the mission statement of the Society for Disability Studies[19]—but the language of difference is, at least for a moment, beautifully present.

For a time, too, the characteristics and talents of the Oozma Kappas do pay off, even when they vary from the hypermasculine norms embodied by the JθX and the RΩRs and widely celebrated across American society. In the first challenge, Mike and Sulley's hypermasculine face-off fails spectacularly, as they don't listen to the rule about team cohesion and are beaten by not only the two dominant fraternity teams but also all three sororities. Fortunately, when the JθX are discovered cheating, their disqualification puts the OK brothers back in the running, but they realize that they must develop a different strategy. Terri/Terry, though his stage magic needs work, encourage their team's use of "misdirection" to win the second Scare Games challenge, distracting the gigantic but nearsighted librarian. Academic and strategic intelligence, as well as patience, help the OKs avoid elimination in the third and fourth challenges. Still, as Sulley reminds them, "that's not *real* scaring," for which their aptitude, assumed to be inadequate, has yet to be tested.

Their qualified success at "not real scaring" also doesn't earn them "real" status. Attending their first fraternity party, the OK brothers feel successful, accepted, invited to "party like scarers." Perhaps only adult viewers of a certain age anticipate what happens next, as the film mocks up the prom scene from *Carrie*, which Michael Bronski calls out as the epitome of the bully backlash film. Dousing its characters in brightly colored paint rather than pig's blood, the film spares its viewers the grotesqueness of the original, but following up with glitter and stuffed animals almost makes the OKs' torment worse—or slyly but complexly adapts the menstrual-blood trope of the original—by not only humiliating its victims but also humiliating them in a pointedly gendered way, figuratively emasculating them. This strategy is absolutely consistent with the ideologies and behaviors of the real-world bully society. Even beyond the "gay-bashing" suffered by boys who actually are gay, the act of publicly stripping boys of any and all claims to hegemonic masculinity is a fairly a common method of further lowering their social status, "preserv[ing] and promot[ing] the exaggerated gender roles that prevail."[20] Klebold and Harris were the targets of gay rumors, and they are not alone, even among the bullied shooters Klein details. The figurative emasculation of the OK brothers rendered by cross-dressing them in colorful sparkles, then publicized by plastering photographs across the quad, perhaps resonates even more eerily in our age of cyberbullying, where bullies may spread their attacks on students' gender identities instantaneously and infinitely across social media and the internet.

Adults who have internalized the "mean-spirited hierarchy" of the bully society may "take it for granted that the less popular students would be treated badly" and, as a result, may not hesitate to bully themselves.[21] Dean Hardscrabble's pedagogy is outdated at best; indeed, her philosophy seems to belie much faith in teaching altogether, since she believes "mediocre" freshmen can never become anything more than slightly "less mediocre." By her own admission, she sees her program as gatekeeping, weeding out the second-rate and teaching only the already talented. More egregiously, her behavior toward Mike is rooted in a prejudicial reading of his physical appearance, as well as her anger over the scream can fiasco. In her pique and prejudice, she won't even let Mike attempt the exam, instead publicly insulting him and then exiling him to the department of Scream Can Design. Klein describes similar "teacher bullies" who assert their authority by threatening, insulting, and provoking students to commit punishable offenses or, "taught by the same harsh rules during their own school years," have internalized the hierarchy that enables bullying behavior.[22] Though Dean Hardscrabble's past as a legendary scarer includes no indication of her having been bullied, one could easily speculate that her membership in a seriously underrepresented group (women in professional scaring) has rendered her path a bit more "hardscrabble" than it might otherwise have been. One might recall Colette, in *Ratatouille*, fully aware of the "antiquated hierarchy build upon rules written by stupid old men," which has made her success as a chef so hard-earned. At any rate, the film makes clear Hardscrabble's acceptance of an essentialist hierarchy and her belief in the rightness of ruthlessly policing it.[23]

Klein also critiques adults who, from their own partiality to athletics, perpetuate a systematic favoritism of jocks, institutions "notorious for looking past the negatives" of the bully society's worship of hypermasculinity and "willing to look the other way if the local 'jocks' behave badly."[24] Monsters University in general—if not the School of Scaring's dean herself—emblematizes this "jock cult," if tacitly, by disqualifying but not expelling the JθX who cheat in the first Scare Games challenge. The discovery of Sulley's comparable crime, which he confesses in a moment of conscience later in the film, is met with Dean Hardscrabble's unmitigated contempt: she orders him to leave campus the next day and calls him "a disgrace" not just to MU but to his family. When the JθX are caught with performance-enhancing substances, by contrast, Hardscrabble's harsh words are directed *at Mike*: "Your luck will run out," she tells him, "eventually."

Finally, of course, it does. Until the final challenge, Sulley is right: the OK brothers' success—qualified as it is, since they've never actually won a challenge, merely avoiding elimination—has not come from "real scaring," and their early performances do not promise a positive outcome in the ultimate test of the Scare Simulator. When push comes to shove, the film suggests, the alternate masculinities of Oozma Kappa fall. Sulley is still able to scare, decisively beating Randy (whose humiliation is enhanced by emasculation; when the chameleon falls on the simulated child's rug, his own innate talent of camouflage works against his masculine performance by cross-dressing his body in a pink heart pattern, in front of everyone, subtly paralleling the paint-and-glitter prank at the RΩR house). The results of the rest of the team, though, are mixed at best. Don's intelligence racks up more points than Bruiser's clumsiness, and Squishy's creepy face puts up a respectable score, but Art's gymnastics can't compete with his counterpart, and Terri/Terry similarly lose in their round. Then it's Mike's turn. His careful performance—lent tension and poignancy by the deep insecurities he forces himself to overcome—is spectacular, decisively wrapping up his team's victory. But his triumph is short-lived and, we soon learn, illegitimate. When he discovers that Sulley has cheated on his behalf, Mike is devastated, not only by a sense of betrayal from his friend's belief in his innate inadequacy, but also by those wracking self-doubts about his ability and potential. Viewers' own growing suspicion that Mike just doesn't "have it" is nurtured when Sulley repeats it yet again in defense of his decision to cheat, and the film thus initiates the final conversion of any remaining faith viewers have in Mike—or in the underdog plot we might have believed we were watching—to pity.

And yet the film could still redeem itself. Dean Hardscrabble, Professor Knight, Johnny Worthington, and Sulley could all still be wrong about Mike Wazowski. There was no way to accurately measure that last scream, after all. Or, as the very end of the original film hints, by swapping scream energy with laugh energy, there might be a way to revise the very paradigm. Mike could still figure out a way to be terrifying, revolutionizing the industry with strategic new approaches. Certainly, as Halberstam indicates, the possibilities of animated storytelling are virtually limitless. But finally, *Monsters University* proves its bullies *right* about Mike's inevitable, embodied failure, sending a clear message about the appropriateness of the bully society's hierarchical truisms. [25]

To complete its ridicule of alternative masculinities—the mama's boys, the sensitive musicians, the theatrical, the smart, the small, and the physically disabled—the film tests Mike against a camp cabin full of little girls. He roars, but they are not afraid. They roar back. Though Sulley arrives on the scene to give a speech on how difficult it is for him to be in the upper echelons of social rank, Mike's fate is sealed. He draws on his academic knowledge to formulate a clever, multiphase plan to generate scream energy and reopen the portal back to their world, and he rigs the room to set the plan in motion, but at the end of the day it is the same old Sullivan roar that saves them. Dean Hardscrabble's biggest error has been not in underestimating Mike but in claiming that "one frightening face does not a scarer make," suggesting that Sulley's academic underachievement might not be adequately compensated by his exceptional body. It turns out that one hypermasculine body is exactly all you need, and, indeed, the only thing that will get you by. Klein says such a paradigm is so pervasive across American high schools that many students simply "get used to it"[26]; in Messner's terms, the "buy-in" of the disenfranchised is essential to the maintenance of the hegemony. [27] By the end of the film, Mike has indeed bought in: "It's time I leave the greatness to the other monsters," he says. "I'm OK just being OK." Out of context, such a statement is a pithy play on his fraternity initials and a pleasant enough affirmation of contentment as a life goal, but given the mind, drive, and work ethic of this unusual kid, and the experiences of his short college career, settling for "okay" at eighteen years old is more than a shame.

What kind of message is this, really, to the little boys watching the film? If you're not born to fit some essentialist idea of hypermasculine success, you'd better just get used to a life of underachievement, prejudice, and mistreatment? You must strive for membership in the hypermasculine tier or suffer at the hands of your peers, adults, and institutions? Leaving the theater, our boys and their friends—even the five-year-olds—had all already decided that they would want to be in the RΩR fraternity, later bickering over who got to be a RΩR or a JθX in the online game. Boys like Mike—he's funny—but they know that Worthington and Sulley are the guys they're supposed to emulate. Indeed, the very structure of the film would fail if the majority of audience members did not read these characters in this way: without assuming the desirability of being a RΩR, Sulley's attack on Mike is either absurd or an ugly sort of gang initiation behavior; without assuming the essential inferiority of Mike's body, the injustice and neglect he suffers is not funny but outrageous. Even Randy's "lame" cupcake pratfall would be far more sad than humorous.

This silent, perpetual reiteration of the bully society informs contemporary boy culture, and this should matter, a lot, to parents of boys. If children are constantly taught that the definitions of excellence are immutable and the mean, even brutal maintenance of a stratified social world based thereon are natural, then the hierarchy remains unassailable, yet dangerously volatile. The Pixar films, like much of contemporary culture, utilize the foundations of the bully society in their storytelling without attempting the necessary deconstruction that contemporary boy culture desperately needs. Perhaps we can't control the mainstream narratives that teach our boys how to be men, but as feminists have done for girls, we can (and must) notice and critique them.

"PRECISION INSTRUMENTS"

It may seem that a film in which all the characters are machines would have a hard time essentializing masculinity and condemning alternate performances of manliness. Ironically, though, even in the Pixar films most celebratory of technology—*Cars* and *Cars 2*—which idolize in art and story those "precision instruments of speed and aerodynamics" that populate the world of auto racing, a sense of embodied masculinity reigns supreme, reifying the traits that yet characterize hegemonic American manhood, and contrasting dramatically with alternative masculinities. The original film's plot may domestically redirect Lightning's acclaimed horsepower—showing him how to fix roads, to rescue old friends, and to attract a new girlfriend rather than just vanquish other young men in sport—but its essential masculine superiority remains unquestioned. Doc, one of the most decorated Piston Cup racers of all time, narratively represents a spiritual father figure, handing down knowledge and wisdom from his experience with racing and its business culture, but he also marks a lineage of body type, having won three of the coveted trophies himself before injuries forced him into retirement. If any doubt remains as to the bodily superiority of the racecar over less powerful automobiles, the film directly praises Lightning's body numerous times, from his own brags to Sally's observation about his horsepower to Lizzie's crowding around to admire the "sexy hotrod." If, younger and less mature than established alpha males like Doc and the King, Lightning needs to develop self-control and a social conscience, his is held up as an exemplary male body all the same: Mater's, Guido's, Fillmore's, and even Sarge's bodies are not in the same league. (The large, quiet, but emotionally volatile Red, it seems, dutifully watering his flowers, belongs in another category altogether.)

By the time the sequel begins, Lightning, at least four years older and wiser, has assumed his rightful place as Doc's heir, not only as a pillar of Radiator Springs but also apparently as the winner of several Piston Cups himself. Nevertheless, the narrative catalyst of *Cars 2* calls Lightning's essentially superior manhood into question. In light of the gauntlet publicly thrown down by Miles Axelrod and Francesco Bernoulli, through their invitation to compete in the World Grand Prix, Lightning's winning one more race unexpectedly becomes necessary for him to maintain his hypermasculine position. Lightning's American frame is far from a shoo-in for victory when pitted against Formula 1 and Indy cars on the global stage. But the plot ends up measuring his masculinity against rubrics other than rival race cars, contrasting his supposedly excellent embodiment of manhood with a variety of alternative masculine types. Lightning not only faces the delicate-framed European favored (by some) to win the race, after all, but also, like Mr. Incredible, encounters an angry engineer capitalist and, like Sulley, crosses paths with a group of unfashionable, physically inferior "losers." Once again, size and ability triumph over all other qualities in what becomes an international celebration of the American jock and his blue-collar brawn. Worse, in this film, the bully society turns violent, literally. As the bullied group of "lemons" rises up against the structure of their persecution, causing destruction and mayhem in their rage, the protagonists aggressively set the paradigm to rights, forcibly putting the "losers" back in their place. Klein insists that "there are inextricable connections between school shooting outbursts, the 'everyday' violence of bullying, and the destructive gender pressures and social demands created by . . . culture and . . . schools."[28] *Cars 2* plays out this tragically familiar eruption in the woefully damaged status quo.

Hegemonic masculinity's being essentialized does not exempt it from the obligatory performance of a specific set of behaviors. Masculinity is as performative as femininity, as Kimmel and others have explained, and, in *Cars 2*, it is meticulously performed. Even the guy in the demonstrably superior body cannot appear weak, frightened, or vulnerable: "no sissy stuff," as Kimmel says.[29] Lightning's acceptance of the World Grand Prix challenge is entirely rhetorical: his participation is not actually necessary to his safety, his family, his finances, not even his professional reputation. But in full view of his girlfriend and his group of male friends, he cannot back away from a challenge. Mater forces the question in defense of his friend's honor against the provocative English billionaire and the taunting Italian, recognizing their rhetoric as targeted at the heart of Lightning's masculine identity and not just, say, his professional choices. Ironically, he first defends his friend by attempting to validate Lightning's choice to opt out of hypermasculine performance temporarily, to rest and enjoy his surrogate family after a long and exhausting season. In so doing, he unwittingly makes Lightning sound weak ("slow") and thus forces him to again prove himself as powerful, hardworking, and competitive.

In a small way, then, from the outset, the exemplar of masculinity is denied access to such emotionally necessary things as rest, relaxation, and the safety of family ties. Throughout the film, his access to his emotions is ever more rigidly demarcated. Beginning with data that indicate the equal emotional capacities of very young boys and girls, Kindlon and Thompson well articulate the need to cultivate emotional wholeness and empathy, lamenting the "emotional *mis*education of boys . . . [the] training away from healthful attachment and emotional understanding."[30] For boys, such "training begins early," echo Klein and Kimmel, their childhoods "discourag[ing] . . . weakness, sadness, or any form of dependence," and teaching them instead to "refrain from crying, to suppress their emotions, never to display vulnerability."[31] As very young children, boys' interior landscapes are as rich as girls', but through their childhood they are coerced into trading in their emotional complexity for what Pollack calls the "mask of masculinity."[32] "As a result," Kimmel explains, "boys feel effeminate not only if they express their emotions but even if they feel them."[33] *Cars 2* as rigorously maintains these emotional borders of masculinity as it does those of bravery and strength. Lightning can only stew silently when he's worried about his missing best friend, for instance, sorry and ashamed for hurting Mater's feelings. Even so, perceiving his sadness, Francesco taunts him for his vulnerability, applying it directly to the actual contest before them: "I will beat his cry baby bottom today!" he crows.

All things considered, Lightning wears his "mask of masculinity" pretty convincingly. He is not actually crying, after all, when Francesco starts taunting him, and he has expressed his sadness at the memory of Doc Hudson appropriately enough, earlier in the film, through a quiet sigh and a symbolic competitive win rather than tears or any other display of vulnerability. His emotional reserve is nonetheless policed, and not only by his peers but also by the entire meaning-making structure of the narrative. The very behavior for which he feels regret—the behavior for which the film demands epiphany and apology—has arisen from reasonable enough feelings of frustration, anger, embarrassment, and disappointment over losing a big, widely hyped race because of a silly mistake directly traceable to his best friend's sheer and utter thoughtlessness. Unless we grant that Mater has some sort of special needs that should excuse his refusal to attend to his friend's particular circumstances (and, elsewhere, to learn and respect the conventions of another culture), Lightning's emotional responses seem justifiable, if not ideal. From another angle, Mater's behavior might be what warrants the big apology. Having traveled halfway across the world at the invitation of his friend, expressly to support him in a huge professional endeavor, Mater is immediately distracted by a pretty girl, and distracted enough to compromise—and abandon—his friend without a second thought. But a real man, it seems, knows—or learns—how to stifle his emotions, however legitimate, so as to more effectively serve as patriarch and protector. Luigi's Uncle Topolino corrects Lightning more gently than Francesco does but he unambiguously holds him responsible for suppressing his feelings: "You gotta make up fast . . . no fight more important than friendship," he says. Instead of allowing a man to acknowledge and sort through the complex emotions wrought by an emotionally complicated situation, in other words, hegemonic masculinity dictates his shame if he accidentally lets any of his difficulty show. The film's very structure—the young man's hotheaded comment, the wise instruction of an old man, and the ensuing apology/resolution—reinforces this "boys don't cry" truism.

Francesco's taunting illustrates the boy police at work, exposing what Lightning risks any time he lets down his mask, but his function in the film is more complex. Through Sally's giddy attraction, the film initially presents Francesco as a romantic rival to Lightning, not just a fellow competitor. Indeed, the idea of his girlfriend's approval provides the narrative catalyst, as Lightning first pouts over her complimentary notice of his "open-wheel design" ("I thought you liked my fenders," he complains) and then accepts the challenge to compete. The two racecars spar over whose win will be dedicated to Sally. Kimmel finds such behavior typical among men, arguing that "women themselves often serve as a kind of currency," their approval a benchmark for a man's social success.[34] Trilling her *r*'s and lingering over the syllables in "Francesco Bernoulli," Sally's gushing over Francesco echoes Bo Peep's response to seeing Buzz Lightyear "fall with style" in the first *Toy Story*: "I've found *my* moving buddy," she murmurs, stoking the resentment and jealousy so central to that film's plot.

Even more than establishing a rivalry, though, Sally's attraction sets the stage for a test of American hegemonic masculinity. It may be that without Sally's guidance, Francesco's body would be hard for audiences to read in comparison to Lightning's, since, though similarly strong and powerful, it looks quite different from the essentialist hypermasculine model so dominant in the other Pixar films and beyond. If Lightning's youthful curves and bright smile were more appealing than Chick's sharp edges and heavy moustache in the first film, the two were nonetheless visually comparable as fierce competitors. Francesco, on the other hand, is sleek, delicate, even "fragile," as he tacitly admits, more a model of the European "metrosexual" than the squarer, larger, and stockier Lightning McQueen. Built to go faster and corner more precisely, Indy and Formula cars are certainly no less mighty than NASCAR cars, if NASCAR racing features more aggressive head-to-head contests and frequent lead changes. Francesco's real-world counterparts would probably decisively beat Lightning's in a race like the World Grand Prix, with its curvy and irregular courses. But baited by Sally's apparent comparison and with the benefit of the visual contrast alone, Francesco might seem the weaker man. Just in case viewers can't come to this conclusion by the visuals alone, he is also associated with stereotypically feminine traits or queer clichés like emotional literacy, dependence on his mother, and fashion-consciousness. It is, after all, his "design" over which Sally and Flo swoon.

One might argue that being "othered" from hegemonic gender roles affords Francesco some freedom the American racecar doesn't have, an "art of failure" like those Halberstam explores in other "Pixarvolt" films. He can taunt Lightning for wanting his mommy even as he enjoys his own mother's support, for one thing. But in a flag-waving film franchise like *Cars*, Francesco's European, metrosexual manhood can hardly provide a viable alternative to a masculinity like the one McQueen's team has built out of American steel. Francesco never poses a real threat, romantically or professionally—Sally doesn't even meet him until the end, and he only wins a single race because of the confusion Mater causes in the pit—and finally, he is shunted into an insignificant side plot as the main action of the film unfolds. The film uses the contrast between Lightning and Francesco, then, less to build and sustain narrative tension than to define and reinforce a distinctly American model of hegemonic masculinity.

This quintessentially American model of masculinity holds generally true across the history of the American nation, as Kimmel recounts it, from the frontiersman forward. Whatever complications of circumstance over time have variously thrown it into "crisis," the ideal American man is, or aspires to be, aggressive, strong, individualistic, emotionless, and competitive: a "self-made" winner. As we discuss in the previous chapter, twentieth-century culture often waxes nostalgic for a particularly blue-collar "shop floor" version of this self-made man, privileging (or fetishizing) the physical brawn suited to manual labor over more intellectual talents. Though the *Cars* franchise is ambivalent on questions of actual money—Lightning is, after all, a rich celebrity who in the first film materially helps his friends (themselves in relatively low-status jobs like auto repair, fast food, pawn, and motel management) by buying and promoting their products—the hotshot racecar retains his blue-collar credentials by association with Mater, with Radiator Springs, and (arguably) with NASCAR itself. His work, however well it pays, he does with his body, with nary an acknowledgment of his own technological inner working. As Mater's movie, the sequel even more clearly celebrates a blue-collar, "old-school" version of masculinity in the body of the old tow truck, whose simple but reliable machinery ends up not only infallible but also the very key to the mystery.

Going global with the idyllic American heartland theme of the first *Cars*, *Cars 2* conflates its depiction of American hegemonic masculinity with its very representation of America. Susan Jeffords demonstrates how, in various films of the 1980s and 1990s, "hard-body" masculinity rhetorically presented American power abroad in the Reagan era; Messner further notes that this model "thrives symbiotically with pervasive fears of threats by outsiders."[35] Lightning is logically enough presented in head-to-head competition with foreign others, but the immediate threat matters less than the innate sense of competitiveness and domination. Like Jeffords, Messner sees the rise of the bulked-up, hypermasculine action hero in the 1980s as emblematic of America's public face reiterated anew under the presidency of Ronald Reagan. Militaristically strong, emotionally restrained, fiercely individualistic, and "self-made" by each successful citizen's bootstraps, a manly America resists the feminizing influences of "bleeding-heart" domestic policy and pacifistic, diplomatic, or otherwise weak (in Schwarzenegger's words, "girlie") behavior abroad.[36] Obviously, the metrosexual European cannot win the World Grand Prix or the true affection of Sally—nor can he be seen as offering a viable alternative masculinity to that of American superman Lightning McQueen—lest America itself be critiqued alongside its manly metonym's narrative trajectory. The national character honored by his inevitable defeat is one of aggressive competitiveness, emotional impoverishment, and, as becomes clearer later in the film, faith in a very stereotypically gendered taxonomy of power.

THE BULLY SOCIETY

Cars 2's values emerge in even sharper relief when we contrast the lovable Radiator Springs gang to characters more dramatically different than Francesco. Like *The Incredibles,* the film is hard on performances of masculinity not presumed to inhere in an excellent male body but enabled by technology and rhetoric. Engineered enhancements to a supposedly inferior male body—like Syndrome's use of rocket boots and weaponry to compensate for his short stature and relative physical weakness—are not only critiqued as inauthentic but also associated with unethicality, even evil. In *Cars 2*, even before specific men can be stripped of their built identities and outed as masculine frauds, technology itself is suspect. Perhaps no character exemplifies authenticity better than Mater, dents and all; his true self, the film exhorts, ought never to be compromised even by cultural competencies or basic manners. The bumpkin-abroad scenes at the World Grand Prix's opening-night party, humorous as they are, result in Lightning's—not Mater's—being repri-manded. Though Mater's behavior is embarrassing to Lightning and impolite to his hosts, when he loudly interrupts a presentation to announce that the party is serving spoiled pistachio ice cream, for instance, rather than learning what wasabi is, it is Lightning to whom Uncle Topolino sagely poses the question: "Why would you ask him to be someone else?" When Mater is confronted with the idea of technological body enhancement, his steadfast opposition contributes to the film's exalted notion of his authenticity and the incompatibility of the "real" male body with technology. Mater has fun for a minute or two with British Intelligence's voice-activated disguise machine (though it may be that he is enjoying voice-commanding a machine more than actually playing dress up), but when disguise means actually manipulat-ing his body, he is deeply, even personally, offended. Unconcerned that he might actually die if the disguise doesn't work, which he knows by this point in the film, Mater still won't let Holly so much as buff out a dent to improve its adherence. His physical body is presented as perfectly equivalent to his true self and his cherished relationships with others.

Going a step further than *The Incredibles*, which separates technology from an idealized, essential masculinity by making Syndrome artificial, un-ethical, and finally unsuccessful, *Cars 2* adds to its masculine critique of technology by literally connecting it to the feminine. This connection, slight as it may seem, may be very influential on boy viewers, even if it is nearly invisible. As Kimmel, Klein, and others note, the relentlessly homophobic "boy police" may exact severe penalties on boys who become associated with anything even in proximity to the idea of femininity or anything arbi-trarily but consistently interpreted as feminine.[37] Despite its relative dearth of strong female characters, in keeping with the rest of the Pixar "boys club," *Cars 2* invites girls to enjoy "all the good hardware." It's Holly Shiftwell,[38] not Finn McMissile, who possesses the most advanced spy gear, including things like wings, which she coyly dismisses as now "standard issue," that add visual interest and excitement to the film. Holly herself associates tech-nological savvy with weakness, protesting a field assignment by insisting that she is only "technical," and thus presumably not qualified for the arena of physical work. To boys already steeped in the homophobic cult of hyper-masculinity, technological knowledge may thus begin to seem girly, or, in the catch-all expression of the bully society, "gay."[39] In American schools, boy culture's fierce aversion to the feminine, coupled with an unfairly broad-ened definition of "femininity," unfortunately tends to render many impor-tant things off limits for boys, things like academic achievement, emotional intimacies, and the arts. Including "technology" on this list of things deemed feminine may defy conventional wisdom on gender norms, but as Oldenziel says, technology has not always been associated with men, the brawny working laborer once a compelling antecedent for the emerging engineer. Further, because of its inherent artificiality, and its source in the intellectual rather than the manual, technology symbolically works to prove the rule of supposedly "authentic" manhood.

Holly, at least, is one of the allies. In the film's most slapstick depiction of feminized technology, new advancements present imminent danger to old-fashioned American men, who seem suddenly vulnerable to surprise attacks in the strangest places. Mater begins his foray into the Japanese bathroom with literal gender confusion, unable to read the iconography on the doors. Quickly correcting his initial error, he is locked in a stall, held down by the tires, and virtually assaulted by the wide-eyed giggling pink car on the control screen, horrified and helpless as pink soap is shot into his undercarriage. For visual contrast, the fight going on outside the stall is so unproblematically "manly" that Holly hesitates to enter it, saying, "I can't go in the men's loo!" despite the fact that the business of the loo has become spy business, not men's business.

Finally, of course, the emblem of American hegemonic masculinity, Lightning McQueen, is literally under attack by the supposed technological breakthrough of the film's criminal mastermind, Miles Axelrod. Though Axelrod's purpose is convoluted—his true advocacy is for big oil, not the new biofuel he outwardly promotes—the film visually and narratively marks Allinol as fatal, a method of torture that leads to death and the immediate cause of race-day explosions that destroy (and kill) the competitors. Allinol, finally, comprises a central concern for Lightning's safety, until the magnetic pulse meant to ignite it fails and the characters scramble to locate the bomb. Though his minions actually perform the dirty work, Axelrod, as the face of Allinol, is also the film's face of evil. Moreover, he embodies all the film's denigrated alternative masculinities simultaneously. Unlike Lightning, his body is a lemon; unlike Mater, he's willing to mask his authentic self with technology and disguise. Like Francesco, his masculinity is European and white-collar. And if the voice of "executive transvestite" comedian Eddie Izzard goes unnoticed by most children, Axelrod wears branches from a banana tree in his hair like a makeshift Carmen Miranda hat, as if to undercut with femininity the otherwise macho image of hiking out of the jungle alone. His plotting is villainous enough, ostensibly born of greed and vengeance, but the multiple failures of his masculinity even more compellingly signify inferiority, unethicality, and even evil.

In the final analysis, the superiority of Mater's simple but reliable body (which doesn't leak oil after all) holds the key to the mystery, and the Radiator Springs gang's prejudicial distrust of Axelrod and his new technology is the whole reason Lightning is alive, Sarge's having replaced his Allinol—the fuel all racers were supposed to use—for a "big oil"–based product. The real man—he who refuses to alter or augment his authentic and superior body and who distrusts technology for the inauthenticity and danger it poses in the future—is decidedly "old school." Thus arguably the least visually nostalgic of the Pixar films taps into the same nostalgic homage to traditional, blue-collar American manhood.

Cars 2's global assertion of American hegemonic masculinity, rather than a flag-waving transcontinental romp that might inspire American children's curiosity in the world outside our borders, is an untimely celebration of emotional ignorance, xenophobia, and gas-guzzling entitlement. The loyalty of Lightning's "tree hugger" friend, Fillmore, might have supplied a truly successful and homegrown biofuel to counter what they all believed to be the dangerous Allinol, setting an example that would put to shame Axelrod's rhetorical maneuvering and desire to unscrupulously profit from nonsustainable resources. Instead, the success of the veteran soldier's allegiance to "big oil" not only fuses fossil fuels with masculinity, and both with American national identity, but also makes them a symbol of wisdom and friendship between men. Green energy, the film all but says, is unpatriotic, disloyal, and effeminate. Ironically, Axelrod's plan is to make alternative fuel look so bad that everyone will cling to gasoline; though he personally fails, the film executes his plan to perfection.

LONG LIVE LEMONS!

Even at home, American culture as a whole is inextricable from our cultural ideologies of masculinity. As Jeffords and Messner each argue, the conflation of hypermasculinity with American national identity often shapes political rhetoric domestically and abroad. Klein, furthermore, sees a vicious circle between our hypermasculine national character and the harshly policed gender hierarchies in the "microcosms of American society" that are our schools. "The values . . . at the core of bullying behavior," she says, "are also the foundation upon which much of the economic, political, and social life of our nation is built."[40] Our "bully economy" of "hard-core competition" and "harsh inequalities," in other words, is based on—and recursively informs—the ideological underpinnings of "bully society" so ubiquitous in American youth culture.[41] In this respect, *Cars 2*'s values may be even more immediately dire to contemporary boy culture. The film's patriotic American masculinity, like *Monsters University*'s glorification of university frat houses, reiterates the hierarchy that enables the bullying rampant across American childhood. Even worse than the perpetual victory of the hegemonic male, in *Cars 2*, is the relentless punishment of its various losers.

Of course the slight, elegant metrosexual Italian loses. Granted one preliminary win, when Mater's inattention causes Lightning to err, Francesco's luck goes downhill ever after. Despite a course that would presumably favor Indy and Formula 1 cars in the real world, he still finishes second in the second race. By the third race, he's barely present in the film, ignorant of all the major plot events, and even so he is figuratively beaten by Mater *towing* Lightning, and Holly also flies by him in her rush to stop the bomb. In the closing scene, a visitor to Radiator Springs, Francesco gets bested once again by Mater (albeit Mater playing with the spies' rocket-propulsion device, a detail that is apparently lost on Francesco), making his last line the frustrated and incredulous *"Impossibile!"* Francesco, competitive to the last but always unsuccessful, is systematically devalued until his repeated failure becomes a humorous visual conceit.

The second loser of *Cars 2*, as with *The Incredibles* and *Monsters, Inc.*, is the inventor/engineer who attempts to use his technological knowledge to compensate for the essential masculine superiority he simply doesn't have. Axelrod joins the rogues' gallery of Pixar villains like Syndrome, Randall, even Waternoose who try to earn social and economic capital from their inventions because they lack a bodily claim to such capital. Up against the blue-collar, experiential intelligence of Mater or the bodily authority of Mr. Incredible and Sulley, the techno-genius always fails. *Cars 2* is remarkable, though, for how it depicts this failure and the subsequent restoration of order. Syndrome and Randall both meet violent ends—Syndrome gets sucked into a jet engine and Randall beaten with a board in a backwoods trailer—but Axelrod's comeuppance comes closer to public humiliation than cosmic justice, however brutal. Axelrod loses not to the authorities who foil his diabolical scheme and take him into custody but to Mater in a final, public game of chicken. As he details the scheme and compellingly implicates Axelrod, Mater also basically tells a crowd that the inventor wets his pants, forces him to say uncle (literally, "deactivate"), and finally, throwing open his hood to expose his leaky engine, figuratively denudes him. This behavior, rather than coming across as bullying, warrants praise, seemingly entirely justifiable by Axelrod's villainy. However humiliating or violent their just deserts, the film implies, the bad guys deserve what they get. That's a bit troubling on the face of it, eschewing as it does civilized notions of legal ethics for a playground-jungle model of justice. Worse, though, is that Axelrod is not just a techno-genius; he's a lemon, and his villainy arises from the very social hierarchy that eventually punishes it.

Axelrod's treatment is not idiosyncratic, either; he is not a lone gun. He represents a group of men, joined together by a common social position presumably based on common traits. When their anger reaches the point at which they will no longer comply with the hardships of their position, their actions invite further, punitive bullying that sets the hierarchy to rights. Entrenched in the value system of the bully society, the film authorizes fear and cruelty as appropriate responses to the outrage of the abused classes, entirely begging the question of their class placement and the endemic brutality of the hierarchy against which such outrage is directed. With Mater's pithy description of the "tow truck's bread and butter . . . cars that don't never work right," the film defines *lemon* according to a medical model of disability that locates it in the body rather than in the relationship between the body and the inaccessible society in which it cannot thrive. Then, as Klein reports is common in the bully society for kids with physical challenges, it systematically withholds "compassion and support," instead "shun[ning], degrad[ing]," and otherwise bullying the physically less fit. [42]

The Pixar universe is a strange place for questions of disability. Though *Finding Nemo* has been praised as a film that celebrates physical difference, it largely avoids the difficult questions of disability that persist in American society. An "epic" example of tolerance and diversity, as Ann Millett claims, [43] the universal design of the film's ocean environment basically renders "disability" a moot point. In its celebration of diverse and differently abled bodies, in other words, no one is actually disabled. Even with a "lucky fin," Nemo swims just fine; the child who's "H2O intolerant" apparently inhabits his aquatic home in perfect health and safety; the boy who claims "obnoxious" as his particular condition clearly just wants to have something to say. Even Dory's short-term memory loss causes no greater hardship than Marlin's occasional impatience. Refusing to incorporate any environmental obstacles by which physical differences would be "disabling," *Finding Nemo* may stand as an object lesson in the social model of disability, but it neither demonstrates how certain individuals might need accommodation nor critiques a society that fails to accommodate them.

A social model of disability might mean, paraphrasing Dash Parr and his evil doppelganger, that once everyone's accommodated, no one is any more "special" than anyone else. Of course, *The Incredibles* indicates that such universal access would be *bad,* that the availability of tools that would help all achieve equally would unfairly—unnaturally, even—negate the inborn superiority of some. In *Cars 2,* similarly, the physical incapacity of the Lemons is depicted as inborn, natural, and inevitable. In the world of *Cars,* however, other cars can be repaired. Through the two films' depiction of race culture and its advertising, it is clear that car parts are available in this universe and that broken cars—like Doc Hudson and the King—can be rebuilt. Lemons only exist as such because they live in an environment that loudly proclaims its celebrity-worship of perfect, powerful bodies and refuses to extend accommodation to those whose needs seem innate rather than circumstantial. Complacent enough with the lack of such accommodation for those presumed to be essentially inferior, the film forces them into back alleys filled with "treacherous lowlife" parts dealers to surreptitiously acquire what their repairs call for. From the beginning, the film ensures, their only options are incapacity or criminality.

That Pixar would mock and exile some for their particular bodily needs is perhaps less strange if we accept a social stratification that allows the (doubtfully) "average intelligence" Mater to insult "dumber" trucks for the sake of humor and depicts knocking other vehicles over as a fun, exciting, and ethically unproblematic activity. Across many of the Pixar films, physical challenges are likewise treated as whimsical and amusing rather than actually disabling and worth others' consideration and care. One finds in the original *Cars* little or no sensitivity to differences not freely chosen, even beyond the questionable practice of tractor tipping. The veteran Sarge can be stricter than Fillmore the aging hippie, for instance, but neither requires accommodation for equal access to anything. Even Lizzie, the oldest resident of Radiator Springs, enjoys perfect mobility and independence, her harmless dotage providing only another occasion for audiences to laugh. *Up*'s climactic battle likewise plays age-related physical limitations for humor in what is at least a fair fight between Carl Fredrickson and Charles Muntz, as both men's stiff backs temporarily interrupt their duel. Carl's cane, so necessary to his mobility early in the film, finally serves not as an accommodation but as a symbol for the emotional distance he's traveled; suddenly agile enough not only to walk unassisted but also to dodge and parry, he brandishes it over his head as a weapon. (His other accommodation, dentures, are also conscripted as humorous weaponry.)

When physical differences in Pixar are not funny, they are feared. *Toy Story 2* initially, if fatalistically, assumes that when one's body breaks down one gets discarded, though Woody resists the body's being destiny. Not only does he risk his personal safety to rescue Wheezy, redistributing value from the body to the affectionate bonds of community, but he also sees his own arm sloppily but lovingly mended at the end of the film. The original *Toy Story* may even more effectively revise a reductive and restrictive view of physical disability. Though Buzz and Woody both initially respond to Sid's mutant toys with horror—agreeing that "kill" is an appropriate laser setting for the situation—they eventually see past the damaged toys' differences and employ their variety of unique abilities to stage a rebellion against the environmental source of their challenges. Rather than correct the society that disables its lemons, on the contrary, *Cars 2* gives an instructive example of how lemons should behave. Helped out by his "friend" Mater (though in full view of their customer/provider relationship), the docile Otis displays gratitude and self-deprecation in the opening Radiator Springs scene: "Ah, who am I kidding? I'll always be a lemon," he says to Mater, who is cheerfully providing his tenth tow of the month. Otis acknowledges the social hardship of disability, even if audiences never see it, telling Mater, "You're the only one that's nice to lemons like me." Just as Mike Wazowski acquiesces to the ideology that prohibits his success—"I'm OK just being OK"—this good lemon buys in, accepting his categorical role in the ideology of domination and grateful for any exception, however temporary, to the regular mistreatment of lemons.

Among Axelrod's gang though, the category of "lemon" is more problematic than Mater's definition allows. Though they do commiserate over frequent breakdowns, employ a fleet of tow trucks, and frequently need replacement parts, not all the Lemons appear physically challenged. Most of them, in fact, get around just fine, to sneak, spy, chase, and fight. Among their real-world counterparts, only the Yugo ("Hugo," in the film) was a notorious mechanical failure. The Pacer ("Acer") and the Gremlin ("Grem") were mainly denigrated for looking weird. But *Cars 2* indiscriminately lumps together all low-status cars, regardless of mechanical soundness, suggesting that the social categorization itself matters more than the ostensible (physical) cause. Small, smart, odd, unfashionable, and sometimes physically disabled, the Lemons are not even thinly veiled stand-ins for the kids on the lowest rungs of the bully society's social ladder. Even Otis suffers socially as much or more than he does physically. Whether he will ever get across the county line matters less than the fact that the "only one that's nice," even in a community as apparently close-knit as Radiator Springs, is the guy he pays to tow him.

Narratively, Otis's breakdown presents only the opportunity for him to model appropriately complaisant lemon behavior. But the rest of *Cars 2*'s Lemons are not willing to bow and scrape and accept the habitual disrespect of their society. They're angry. Grouped into what Klein calls "oppositional masculinity," they do not exemplify hegemonic masculine behaviors or hypermasculine bodies, and, actively resisting the hierarchy that devalues them, they seek alternative access to the social authority they have been denied. Axelrod's motivational speech unambiguously outlines their social-justice motive and the fact that it is the only motive: "The world turned their back on cars like us," he says. "They've called us terrible names [and] laughed at us. But now it's our turn to laugh back. . . . [We] will become the most powerful cars in the world! . . . They will come to us and they will have no choice, because they will need us. . . . And they will finally respect us. So hold your hoods high. After today you will never again be ashamed of who you are!"

The echoes of real-world school shooters are deafening. In 1997, before shooting nine people in his Pearl, Mississippi, school, Luke Woodham wrote, "I killed because people like me are mistreated everyday. I did this to show society, push us and we will push back. . . . All throughout my life, I was ridiculed, always beaten, always hated. Can you, society, truly blame me for what I do? It was not a cry for attention, it was not a cry for help. It was a scream in sheer agony."[44] Columbine's Eric Harris addressed teachers and parents the day before his 1999 attack, writing, "Your children who have ridiculed me, who have chosen not to accept me, who have treated me like I am not worth their time are dead. . . . You have taught these kids to not accept what is different. YOU ARE IN THE WRONG. I have taken their lives and my own—but it was your doing."[45] After killing three and injuring eight more in West Paducah, Kentucky, in 1997, Michael Carneal reported feeling "proud, strong, good and more respected. I accomplished something."[46] That Axelrod could tap into such adolescent anguish—and from that anguish be seen as unproblematically villainous—is remarkable. That legions of parents and critics seem not to have noticed (or cared about) the connection is alarming.

Katherine Newman, author of *Rampage: The Social Roots of School Shootings*, explains that school shooters are usually motivated by failures to find social acceptance. Contrary to conventional wisdom, she notes, "The shooter is rarely a loner. He is, rather, a 'failed joiner,' someone who has tried, time and again, to find a niche, a clique, a social group that will accept him, but his daily experience is one of rejection, friction and marginality."[47] The first irony, in *Cars 2* and in its tragic real-world analogies, may be that these rebellions restore, rather than dismantle, the system. Klein says that the school shooters she has studied "didn't seek to change the values in their schools; instead, they meant to win at the same game."[48] Moreover, obviously, they can't. Mater insists that not even money and power will help the Lemons earn respect—nothing, it seems, is "gonna make [them] feel better." Yet further, it seems that change is hardly conceivable. Newman posits, hopefully, that "we could promote a more diverse set of male images," but we don't, not even within the free imaginative spaces afforded by animation.[49]

Finally, the punishments *Cars 2* metes out further affirm the hierarchical system and the cruel behaviors it justifies. The bullied lemons-turned-villains don't get heard, they don't get rehabilitated, and they don't even get punished within a legal apparatus: *they get bullied again.* Defeated in their quest for acceptance, for "respect," for an erasure of the shame that has shaped their lives, they are also, at last, ganged up on by the cool kids. Even as Mater claims to understand what they feel like, saying "everyone has been laughing at me my whole life, too," their refusal to submit to their rightful place ensures swift and brutal punishment. The entire Radiator Springs race team, inexplicably having arrived on the scene in London, circles two on the street, menacing, until they escape in terror. Another two accidentally wind up in a pub, where the locals (who can't possibly know they've done anything wrong) also circle, menace, and then apparently beat them until their tires fall off. Not only do the protagonists save the day, in other words, but they also enforce a particular type of masculine behavior that includes literal violence against those who fall short of the hegemonic ideal. In short, the film once again honors the popular jock, recreates jock culture, and naturalizes the social pecking order that produces such terror and dysfunction in our schools.

As we cheer for our protagonists, we give our consent to the collective abuse of their strength and power, as if to say with Columbine's unrepentant, "They're freaks; why wouldn't we make fun of them?"

The Pixar films, for all their wholesome surface messages, do nothing to rewrite the bully script by which many American kids suffer. If they punish tyrants like Lotso Huggin' Bear, as we discuss later in this book, they nonetheless tolerate cliquishness and cruelty in keeping with the pervasive social hierarchy of contemporary youth culture. They utterly fail to imagine a new and broader construct of masculine value that might enable more children to thrive in safe and nurturing schools. Of course, this passive acquiescence is tragically common; we assume that Pixar's storytellers and viewers—including ourselves upon our earliest viewings of the films—have so internalized the values of the bully society that we do not see right in front of us. Still, for our boys and their friends, and for all the rest of them too, we wish that the films could reimagine, rather than simply reiterate, the dangerous ideology of "jocks" and "losers."

NOTES

1. Dan Kindlon and Michael Thompson, *Raising Cain: Protecting the Emotional Life of Boys* (New York: Ballantine Books, 1999), 5; Jessie Klein, *The Bully Society: School Shootings and the Crisis of Bullying in America's Schools* (New York: New York University Press, 2012), 11.

2. Stanley Aronowitz, *The Politics of Identity* (New York: Routledge, 1992), quoted in Elizabeth Bell, Lynda Haas, and Laura Sells, eds., *From Mouse to Mermaid: The Politics of Film, Gender, and Culture* (Bloomington: Indiana University Press, 2008), 7.

3. "The jock cult," quoted elsewhere, is Klein's phrase (*The Bully Society*, 25). Giroux, discussing Disney, describes how many of the Disney films use the animal kingdom to similar ends, "the mechanism for presenting and legitimating caste . . . and structural inequality as part of the national order. . . . Strict discipline is imposed through social hierarchies . . . suggest[ing] a yearning for a return to a more rigidly stratified society" (*The Mouse That Roared: Disney and the End of Innocence* [Plymouth, England: Rowman & Littlefield, 1999], 107).

4. Klein, *The Bully Society*, 26–29; Kindlon and Thompson, *Raising Cain*, 83.

5. Klein, *The Bully Society*, 26.

6. R. W. Connell and James Messerschmidt, "Hegemonic Masculinity: Rethinking the Concept," *Gender & Society* 19, no. 6 (December 2005): 840. See also Michael Bronski, "High School Hell," *Z Net - The Spirit Of Resistance Lives*, 1999, www.zcommunications.org/high-school-hell-by-michael-bronski (30 October 2013).

7. Klein, *The Bully Society*, 15.

8. Eliot Aronson, *Nobody Left to Hate: Teaching Compassion after Columbine* (New York: Henry Holt, 2001), quoted in Klein, *The Bully Society*, 15.

9. Dave Cullen, "The Rumor That Won't Go Away," *Salon*, 24 April 1999, www.salon.com/1999/04/24/rumors (1 November 2013); Jodi Wilgoren, "Terror in Littleton: The Group," *New York Times*, 25 April 1999, www.nytimes.com/1999/04/25/us/terror-in-littleton-the-group-society-of-outcasts-began-with-a-99-black-coat.html (30 October 2013).

10. Brooks Brown and Rob Merritt, *No Easy Answers: The Truth Behind Death at Columbine* (New York: Lantern Books, 2002), 47. Brown is quoted in Klein, *The Bully Society*, 26. Obviously, a great deal has been written about Columbine itself, including efforts to debunk the very theories we're relying on here. Without claiming expertise on Harris and Klebold, we lean on Klein's comparative work between numerous shootings more than on the site-specific

research like that of *Slate* writer Dave Cullen, whose 2010 book *Columbine* purports to correct many of the misconceptions about Columbine myths, beginning with the outcast narrative; citing psychologist Robert Hare, Cullen argues that Harris was a psychopath, not a bully victim. The memoir of the shooters' friend Brooks Brown, though, and numerous anecdotal accounts that have been widely reported, supports the idea that, with or without diagnosable mental illness, they were angry about not fitting in and that they were in fact subjected to physical and emotional abuse.

11. Klein, *The Bully Society*, 15.

12. Susan Gilbert, "A Conversation with Elliot Aronson; No One Left to Hate: Averting Columbines," *New York Times*, 27 March 2001, www.nytimes.com/2001/03/27/health/a-conversation-with-elliot-aronson-no-one-left-to-hate-averting-columbines.html (1 November 2013).

13. Michael A. Messner, "The Masculinity of the Governator: Muscle and Compassion in American Politics," *Gender & Society* 21 (2007): 463. Messner says that hegemonic masculinity depends on "less powerful men's (and many women's consent and complicity with the institutions, social practices, and symbols that ensure some men's privileges . . . a 'buy-in' by subordinated and marginalized men."

14. Klein, *The Bully Society*, 26.

15. Klein, *The Bully Society*, 154.

16. Klein, *The Bully Society*, 30-32.

17. Lyn Brown, Sharon Lamb, and Mark Tappan, *Packaging Boyhood: Saving Our Sons from Superheroes, Slackers, and Other Media Stereotypes* (New York: St. Martin's Press, 2009), 55.

18. Klein, *The Bully Society*, 28, 45.

19. Klein, *The Bully Society*, 29. The Society for Disability Studies, a group dedicated to academic and pragmatic interrogations of ability, "recognizes that disability is a key aspect of human experience, and that the study of disability has important political, social, and economic implications for society as a whole, including both disabled and nondisabled people." www.disstudies.org/about/mission-and-history (1 November 2013).

20. Klein, *The Bully Society*, 86. See also Bronski, "High School Hell," n.p.

21. Klein, *The Bully Society*, 128.

22. Klein, *The Bully Society*, 144.

23. Early versions of the film apparently drew the dean as male, an alligator-type monster somewhat evocative of John Houseman's Professor Kingsfield in *The Paper Chase*. See Adam B. Vary's "The *Monsters University* Character Who Changed Gender at the Last Minute" for an illustration of the original design concept (www.buzzfeed.com/adambvary/monsters-university-dean-hardscrabble-change-gender). Deciding a woman might be more intimidating—and our sons enthusiastically agree with their decision—the artists struggled with the female Hardscrabble's body type before setting on the Amazonian giant centipede. No one seems to have noticed the humor of the powerful woman being Amazonian.

24. Klein, *The Bully Society*, 26.

25. The notion of Mike's failure is built even into his intimate relationships. As Brown et al. note about many animated representations of male friendship, including *Monsters, Inc.* and *Cars* among non-Pixar films like *Ice Age* and *Shrek*, they claim, "The buddy relationships in these films are less about mutual friendships than an opportunity for a dominant male character to work out his issues. Like the quarterback on a high school football team, the star of these movies can afford to learn a lesson or two because he's already proven his masculinity in a whole variety of ways." The masculinity of the buddy constructed by contrast, he represents "what the main character isn't: smaller, weaker, needier, more emotional, not as smart" (84). We'd counter the last item on the list of liabilities, particularly in Mike's case, since one can apparently be too smart for the "boy code." But the rest of the observation definitely holds.

26. Klein, *The Bully Society*, 35.

27. Messner, "The Masculinity of the Governator," 463.

28. Klein, *The Bully Society*, 3.

29. Michael Kimmel, *Guyland: The Perilous World Where Boys Become Men* (New York: HarperCollins, 2008), 45.

30. Kindlon and Thompson, *Raising Cain*, 10–11, 4.

31. Klein, *The Bully Society*, 45; Kimmel, *Guyland*, 53.

32. Kindlon and Thompson, *Raising Cain*, 10–11; William Pollack, *Real Boys: Rescuing Our Sons from the Myths of Boyhood* (New York: Henry Holt, 1998), 3.

33. Kimmel, *Guyland*, 53.

34. Michael Kimmel, *Manhood in America: A Cultural History*, 3rd ed. (New York: Oxford University Press, 2012), 7.

35. Susan Jeffords, *Hard Bodies: Hollywood Masculinity in the Reagan Era* (New Brunswick, NJ: Rutgers University Press, 1993), 191; Messner, "The Masculinity of the Governor," 468.

36. Messner, "The Masculinity of the Governor," 469.

37. Kimmel, *Guyland,* 7; Klein, *The Bully Society,* 5.

38. It is interesting that among *Cars 2*'s secret agents, strong bodies still seem essentially gendered, as with Elastigirl in previous chapter, whose talent for "stretching" makes her a demonstrably more efficient and successful mother. In *Cars 2*, the mighty males are named for speed and weaponry: "Turbo" and "McMissile" are new counterparts to the powerful "Lightning," while Holly's surname, "Shiftwell," seems to privilege a more domestic comfort and functionality. In the context of gender and naming, Lightning's rival from the first film, "Chick," seems subtly feminized, as we said in our previous article on Pixar masculinities (though his character's behavior is not obviously effeminate). "Francesco," though a very common name for Italian men, is akin to the androgynous "Frances" in English (which is also, incidentally, the name of the ladybug in *A Bug's Life*).

39. Klein, *The Bully Society*, 84.

40. Klein, *The Bully Society*, 155.

41. Klein, *The Bully Society*, 155–56.

42. Klein, *The Bully Society*, 29.

43. Ann Millett, "'Other' Fish in the Sea: *Finding Nemo* as an Epic Representation of Disability," *Disability Studies Quarterly* 24, no. 1 (Winter 2004): n.p. http://dsq-sds.org/article/view/873/1048 (1 November 2013).

44. Woodham's "manifesto" from June 1997 is quoted in Klein, *The Bully Society*, 177. An image of his notebook page is also available in Phil Chalmers, *Inside the Mind of a Teen Killer* (Nashville, TN: Thomas Nelson, 2009).

45. Klein, *The Bully Society*, 127.

46. Klein, *The Bully Society*, 44.

47. Katherine S. Newman, "School Shootings: Why They Do It," *Baltimore Sun,* 28 August 2012, http://articles.baltimoresun.com/2012-08-28/news/bs-ed-school-shootings-20120828_1_random-shootings-rampage-social-media (1 November 2013).

48. Klein, *The Bully Society*, 40.

49. Katherine S. Newman, "Roots of a Rampage," *The Nation*, 19 December 2012. www.thenation.com/article/171866/roots-rampage (1 November 2013).

Chapter Four

"Hey, double prizes!"

Pixar's Boy Villains' Gifts and Intensities

Historically, Disney's greatest villains have personified emotions beyond the experience, or even the imagination, of most child viewers. Though all unambiguously signified as bad with visual and narrative details, the villains act from distinctly adult motivations: Cruella's rapacity (*101 Dalmatians*), Ursula's resentment (*The Little Mermaid*), Jafar's ambition (*Aladdin*), the Evil Queen's jealousy (*Snow White and the Seven Dwarves*), Stromboli's greed (*Pinocchio*), and Judge Frollo's racism and lust (*Hunchback of Notre Dame*), all render their characters entirely unsympathetic to child viewers —even incomprehensible, beyond a simplistic notion of evil. Pixar's films, however, often unfold without a clear villain at all. Nemo and Lightning basically just get lost; Merida's and Remy's chief antagonists are cultural expectations. Though secondary characters may be visually marked as bad and momentarily presented as antagonistic, these frightening or otherwise unlikeable characters present merely situational threats. Chick Hicks in *Cars*, *Finding Nemo*'s dentist's niece, and *Brave*'s Mor'du are less villains than they are distractions, ultimately uninvolved with, or completely ignorant of, their respective films' main narrative journeys toward the protagonists' wisdom and/ or idealized "home." Chick's win of the Piston Cup bears not at all on Lightning's personal growth; the rookie's decision to lose completes the narrative arc that has taken him through Radiator Springs, where Chick was never even present. Mor'du threatens Merida and her mother's safety in the woods, but the journey through witchcraft and misunderstanding that puts them there has little to do with the cursed bear/prince besides analogy.

Those films that do present a villain likewise depart from the classic Disney template by including a relatable childhood back story that complicates the villain's supposedly evil, adult values. Buddy/Syndrome's vengeance and Miles Axlerod's bitterness come from being spurned and mistreated; Lotso Huggin' Bear's tyrannical turn is a direct response to the trauma of abandonment; even Hopper's extortion of Ant Island is finally chalked up to fear. Attention to these back stories might render a lot of the Pixar villains more sympathetic than they first appear, and the films seem to invite us, generously, to see a person's outward villainy as masking a vulnerability or pain inside. Particularly when the young pre-antagonist is a bullied nerd, such a back story may reveal a glimmer of potential for confronting the cyclic nature of bully violence. But Pixar seldom extends the notion of the hurt and (rightly) angry youth into the main narrative moment in a meaningful way. Instead, the films assume—correctly, it seems—that if their viewers are mildly interested in a villain's back story, they will nonetheless remain unforgiving of his present actions.

Indeed, the films by their very structure encourage this impassive reading of a villain's past. *Cars 2*, for instance, as we discuss in the previous chapter, almost entirely marginalizes the Lemons' brutal youth as dramatic irony, since Mater is the only "good" character who hears Axlerod's personal justification for his criminal plan. He tells others only of Axlerod's profit motive. Viewers, who identify with the protagonists for numerous reasons, from franchise familiarity to form, are similarly discouraged from weaving the film's two narratives—that of the Lemons as victims and that of Axlerod as criminal mastermind—to any complex or potentially ethical end. Since the main characters don't seem to need the back story of the abused nerd to decide on their course of action, since that course of action plays out as the right one for all involved, and since no revelation of that back story causes reflection on the ethicality of the action that transpired in ignorance thereof, the film does not present the villains' back story as one worth considering—not as sympathetic, not as even marginally relevant to the matters at hand. Instead, the "good" characters simply and successfully police the status quo, putting the *violent* bullied nerd back in his place as a *contained* bullied nerd.

Pixar's apparent disapproval of the non-jock guy extends to young boys, even those the films draw with such remarkable creative and intellectual ability that individualized education programs or academic curricula designed specifically for gifted children would seem more appropriate than the scorn with which they are treated. Even before protagonists intervene, Pixar's narratives do their own dirty work, imposing punishment on those who don't measure up; the narrative structures of *The Incredibles* and *Toy Story* themselves vilify a gifted child even before he does anything morally wrong. James T. Webb et al. argue that American media, including films like Pixar's, "commonly portray highly intelligent children as oddities, geeks, or nerds . . . often transpos[ing] the children's abilities, interests, and emotions from assets into liabilities."[1] The consequences can be serious, as media representations authorize real-world mistreatment—taunts, bullying, and rejection from childhood and adolescent social circles. Klein cites a study in which two out of three gifted kids reported being bullied by the time they were eighth-graders, many specifically for their academic abilities.[2] Admittedly, it can be hard to identify a child as gifted, particularly with our media constantly training us to see things like emotional intensity, fierce creativity, and independence from social codes as bad things, especially in boys. Far too often, these hallmark characteristics of giftedness traits get misread, wrongly diagnosed, and otherwise unnurtured. Furthermore, like many boys with "alternative" masculine interests and talents, boys with intense emotions, artistic inclinations, and driving intellectual curiosity find themselves in perpetual violation of the "boy code," and end up either "resent[ing] the idea that their intensity cannot be directed toward intellectual or creative behavior" or "hold[ing] themselves to impossible hypermasculine standards."[3] Like far too many of their real-world counterparts, Pixar's gifted boys act up or drop out.

GO HOME, BUDDY!

Before he becomes an angry engineering genius acting out against the man who hurt him and endangering society in order to earn their respect, *The Incredibles'* Syndrome is Buddy Pine, a boy who reveres superheroes and invents rocket boots that actually fly. Showing off his accomplishment for the approval of his idol, Mr. Incredible, Buddy interrupts a crime being foiled, falling out a window and, thus needing rescue, accidentally facilitating the criminal's escape. Earning no admiration or encouragement for his remarkable invention, Buddy instead is punished for being in the way. As Mr. Incredible closes the door of the police car appointed to taking the child home, he instructs the officers to make sure "his mother" is involved in his punishment. Moreover, visually muddling the success of Buddy's boots with the detonation of Bomb Voyage's explosive device—it is the bomb, not the rocket boots, that causes the explosion—the film itself reinforces the notion that Buddy has done wrong, that his inventions cause problems, that police (and maternal) custody is necessary and appropriate to contain the delinquent child. Even if he wasn't yet strong or strategic enough to use them, and even if his ill-timed attempt to do so distracted Mr. Incredible from his important law-enforcement work, the rocket boots themselves surely indicate the work of a profoundly gifted child, one who is inventive, creative, and capable, but the film withholds any and all praise. Coming from the same intellectual and creative gifts, his later successes are no more surprising and yet merit no more acclaim. Of course he is capable of inventing and nearly perfecting learning robots that quickly adapt to the fighting styles of their opponents, but of course such a project must be viewed in an exclusively negative light.

The film does not fail to notice *one* boy's gifts, if they too need focus and discipline. In a fifteen-years-later scene that visually mirrors the young Buddy's brush with the law, it is Dash Parr in the backseat of a car facing the disciplinary gaze of his mother. Unlike Buddy, though, Dash is told that his gifts make him better than the rest of society. Of course, his gifts are athletic, endowing him with the "capital" most valuable for boys at the top of the bully society. If still socially problematic, still needing to be kept under control, as we discuss in chapter 1, Dash's talents are nonetheless praised. Though told to hide his gifts, he is not shunned for them but told unequivocally that they make him "special." The film thus instructs its viewers clearly in the taxonomy of masculine talents: Dash's super body might make him naughty, but not bad, while Buddy's superior mind indicates a budding delinquent, someone to be feared and shunned. His mother's support is all it takes to secure Dash's general well-being, though he feels momentarily underappreciated by society.

Webb et al. argue, with numerous other advocates for gifted education, that for gifted kids with similar nurture, even less socially acclaimed talents can be turned back into assets, at least at home or within focused educational settings. For other gifted kids, though, the sense of alienation that comes from a world devaluing the very things that set one apart may contribute to profound unhappiness, loneliness, and other emotional problems. Being an outsider is standard fare for many kids, and of course in American schools, being an outsider can have even worse consequences than alienation. Some of the most notorious school shooters in Klein's research had IQ scores well above the mean and, by their own admission, were tired of being mistreated by a peer group that didn't understand them. Even if they never act out against others, Webb et al. suggest that gifted children whose particular needs go unmet may be at greater risk for serious depression, possibly suicide.[4] While Dash's mother tries to teach him to fit in despite his own unquestioned superiority, Buddy sets out all alone on a path far too familiar to many highly gifted kids.

Because their abilities go unrecognized, their behaviors get misinterpreted, or their talents are socially devalued, gifted kids may struggle to find the mentors and friends whom they desperately need to provide some understanding and direction.[5] With no sympathetic parent or teacher in the film, and any such potentially nurturing social contact replaced by an unyielding police presence and underscored by Mr. Incredible's outright refusal to accept the child's remarkable offering, it should come as no surprise that Buddy fails to find a way to use his gifts to better society instead of to disrupt (or, later, to necessitate) adults' crime-fighting work. Even without peer bullies to shun and ridicule the nerd in an obvious representation of the bully society, the film itself does the job, its narrative structures enforcing the discipline needed to maintain a familiar social hierarchy. Punishing him for his failure to appropriately channel his energies and talents—in effect, holding him accountable for his own lack of guidance and support—the film exiles him to Nomanisan, where his anger festers, it seems, for years.

For any boy, this "fortress of solitude" would be a dangerous place to spend adolescence. As Dan Kindlon and Michael Thompson note, "cut off from meaningful connections . . . ill-equipped to find their own way out of hiding, many boys become stranded, digging deeper and deeper into emotional isolation, building stronger and higher walls around their emotions [and becoming] more likely to look for a scapegoat, blaming other people or circumstances for [their] problems."[6] Holed up on Nomanisan, Buddy's developing anger leads to elaborate, violent plotting, laser-focused on revenge and respect. Like Axlerod's, Buddy's scheming may be comparable to the elaborate planning of school shooters like Klebold and Harris. "Monologuing" to the incapacitated Mr. Incredible, he identifies "respect" as his chief motivation: all he wants is to make everyone see him as heroic, not dissimilar from how Michael Carneal, in prison after shooting eight of his high school classmates at age fourteen, reported that "people respect [him] now."[7] Buddy's motives, immature and anti-social as they may be, are hardly mysterious. What's far stranger is that the entire rest of the film explores just how bad it feels for one's gifts to be socially devalued, criticized, and forced into hiding. The very process that has resulted in Mr. Incredible's identity crisis—and the entire film's plot—is somehow entirely appropriate when done to the intellectually and creatively gifted child. In full view of the possible psychological and emotional difficulties of the unappreciated, the film's treatment of Buddy/Syndrome can only be justified by privileging the hypermasculine gifts of athleticism and strength far beneath intellectual ones.

The adult Syndrome's personality, villainous as it seems, suggests giftedness beyond mere intellect and creativity. Many theorists of gifted education argue that the struggles of gifted kids may be exacerbated by other emotional hallmarks, including perfectionism and emotional intensity, characteristics often missing from simplistic depictions of gifted children wherein exaggerated academic talents, particularly in science and math, stand in for "the full range of personhood."[8] Perfectionism, leading some children to set impossible standards for themselves and to feel like failures when they achieve "anything less than perfect," may lead to "intense stress and suffering . . . continual dissatisf[action]" throughout their lives, even anxiety and depression.[9] The sheer number of Omnidroids he goes through before confronting his nemesis suggests Syndrome's propensity to perfectionism, as well as the fact that even his international entrepreneurial success isn't enough to satisfy him. He has to be a "real" superhero or nothing. Furthermore, though it might seem counterintuitive to identify someone all too ready to wreak havoc on a populated city as emotionally intense, a characteristic that often presents as empathy, on second glance it becomes apparent that Syndrome's entire orientation to the world is highly emotionally charged. From intensely seeking Mr. Incredible's approval to deliberately redirecting his profound love into unmitigated anger, he displays an exaggerated sense of self-righteousness when finally confronting Mr. Incredible, like the many children who experience emotional intensity as an acute sense of justice. Syndrome is exemplary of emotionally intense gifted children who are "very sensitive . . . to injustice, and also to criticism and their own pain."[10] His "fortress of solitude" does not dampen his feelings but bottles them up. His unhappy adult life, still marked by childhood pain after the numerous technological and commercial achievements he has realized, may come after a long struggle with perfectionism, emotional intensity, and a profound sense of alienation. With no one to help negotiate his potentially destructive intensities and emotions, it is the child who suffers, long before the plot comes to its climax.

The film ensures that the audience remains ignorant of the child's suffering, conflating it with the aggressively adult traits signified by classic Disney villains. Instead of recognizing his perfectionism as the sharply self-critical delusion of a powerful but immature intellect and imagination, and his anger as acute moral outrage undiluted by healthy and mature perspective, we instead interpret Syndrome's actions as simple expressions of monomaniacal vengeance. Despite the back story, and despite Mr. Incredible's superficial acknowledgment of his own mistreatment of the child, viewers are never invited to read Syndrome's adult actions sympathetically as the culmination of childhood pain, intensity, and misdirected gifts. Though Mr. Incredible apologizes at least for hurting the young Buddy's feelings, the film doesn't pause to let Mr. Incredible's apology sink in; on the contrary, offered under duress in the middle of a fight, the apology itself may seem disingenuous, the kind a child will offer in an attempt to avoid punishment rather than from true remorse. When Syndrome demands to know, "Am I good enough now?" the desperation of his question is not even dignified with a response, interrupted rather by Mr. Incredible's sudden attempt to escape. From this point forward, the film does not again wed Syndrome's past with his present (at least until he has kidnapped the baby Jack-Jack, and then only elliptically, and in his own angry words), instead casting his motives as the typical "evil" adult ones that elsewhere fuel Disney's narratives: Ursula's resentment, maybe, plus Jafar's hunger for power. The jock versus geek plot settles onto the familiar good versus evil, and the typical misrepresentation of the gifted in mainstream media that Webb et al. describe—our cultural shorthand that denies emotional complexity to anomalous, unacceptable, "odd" kids—goes unchallenged.

We may speculate that our cultural training as readers of Disney films itself blocks the child's back story from view, foregrounding the adult villainy we have come to expect. More incontrovertibly, the film's plot—showing Syndrome no mercy as it punishes him for threatening the recognizable true heroes, even, unforgivably, the children and baby—distracts the audience's gaze from the boy's tale and virtually eliminates the possibility for sympathy. Ironically, it may be the frame itself that lets us see the young Buddy as gifted, as his adult accomplishments and intensity are more legible than the inventor-child's disappointment alone would be. With images from both the past and the present, we can imagine a more holistic picture of an emotionally and psychologically difficult life. It is not always so easy to diagnose giftedness in kids, however, when gifts may present not as academic ability but as behavioral problems, as other diagnosable phenomena, even as learning difficulties. Who knows what we might have seen in Buddy's workshop had we been there through his adolescence, which of his failed projects might have looked like sheer destructiveness, what vitriolic journals might have signified mental disturbance. Indeed, we might have seen someone like *Toy Story*'s Sid Phillips.

OH, NO! NOT SID!

Sid's villainy is perceived just as unequivocally as Syndrome's. Commanding a slot on nearly every fan list of Disney-Pixar villains, and even frequently canonized alongside the famed villains of classic Disney, Sid has been called sociopathic, evil, and demented; even critics have deemed him "psychotic," "sadistic," and "pathologically violent."[11] Disney itself calls his an "unwell mind."[12] Like Syndrome, though, such a characterization simplifies what the film actually does with, and to, the character. The plot of the original *Toy Story* more closely resembles *Finding Nemo* or *Cars* than it does *The Incredibles*: like Nemo and Lightning, Buzz and Woody get lost at the outset and spend the rest of the film trying to forge a way home. The chief narrative conflict occurs between Buzz and Woody, not between either and a ruthless enemy, driven by anger and seeking to exact vengeance or wreak havoc on an unsuspecting metropolitan community; indeed, Sid doesn't have anything against Buzz and Woody, or anyone else, really. The film's heartwarming narrative resolution finally has more to do with finding one's purpose in life than vanquishing one's foes. Yet the overwhelming consensus of critics, reviewers, and fans is that Sid is a bad guy, even vicious, even mentally disturbed.

Sid is displaced from the immediate narrative tension of the plot, which charts the journey of one toy overcoming his jealousy and prejudice against a new rival and resolves when the two become friends and allies. How, then, is he so easily interpreted as a tween-boy version of Cruella de Vil or the Evil Queen? In the descriptive language of the folktale's structural patterns, Sid can easily enough be seen as a structural antagonist, representing an obstacle to the forward narrative progress of the protagonist. Historically, as Vladimir Propp explained, villains were thinly developed disruptors of the hero's peace, serving the narrative function of struggling against the hero's journey, personifying fairly simple "evil" in juxtaposition to the hero's "good."[13] Evil or no, it is undeniable that Sid stands between Andy's toys and their play-room, and it is equally clear that he does not intend to let them go home. Judging from fan chatter on the internet, though, as well as numerous li-censed *Toy Story* products from board books to coloring pages, calling him "The Mean Kid" at best, the villainy that emanates from Sid is interpreted as far more sinister than circumstantial. The evidence of the film—broken toy bodies, the lamentations of the playroom gang—clearly raises the specter of physical harm and intimates violent intentions, so that the absence of person-al motive might make his villainy seem even worse than the incomprehen-sible criminal pursuits of the classic fairy tale villains: not jealous or greedy or mad, Sid must be psychopathic.

Visually, the film allows very little ambiguity in its characterization of Sid as the villain. The very composition of frames might make viewers feel small, like at-risk toys ourselves, our gaze angling upward to a tight shot on Sid's menacing smile, enlarged further by his magnifying glass. The wood paneling of his room creates a close, dark space similar to Ursula's cave, the skull on his shirt serving as a *memento mori* like the one voodoo priest Dr. Facilier wears on his hat in *The Princess and the Frog*. The posters on Sid's walls—concert posters for bands like "Megadork" and "Wraith Rock Mon-ster"—might position him as an outsider to mainstream popular culture (most obviously evoking heavy metal band Megadeth), but even more surely they indicate his age as at least older than the target audience of *Toy Story*, his adolescence itself perhaps intimidating to small children. His giant head, close-cropped, not quite shaved and strangely congruent to the skull on his shirt, might evoke militaristic authority but at very least accentuates his sharp, menacing eyebrows, and his terrifying braces, actually magnified in his glass, manage to look both predatory and not quite human. In case these details aren't enough on their own, nearly every one has a contrasting counterpart in Andy's house: the good child's bright playroom with its sky-painted walls, his clean white shirt, his bright red cowboy hat. Even more bluntly, the trusted denizens of the playroom educate viewers in how to interpret Sid. Not just home from camp, he was "kicked out early this year," suggesting habitual misbehavior and frequent institutional discipline; not the "happy child" who Buzz thinks he sees playing in his yard with his dog and his toys, he "tortures toys!" as Rex corrects the playroom gang's newest member.

His behavior does indeed seem to reinforce what we're told about him: he does blow up a Combat Carl, after all, further proving to Buzz, and to us, that his laughter signifies not happiness but homicidal tendencies. But his villainy is hopelessly complicated by the ontological construction of the film. Many of Pixar's films—*Cars, A Bug's Life, The Incredibles, Brave*—occupy fairly simplistic fantastic realms, where extraordinary things seem ordinary.[14] Cars can talk, ants get married, some people have superpowers, and daughters can cast spells on mothers to turn them into bears, and those who live in those worlds take their fantastic elements as given. Even in *Ratatouille*, where the chefs and rats never learn to *talk* to one another, no true ontological breach divides the "real world" of humans and a fantastic world invisible to them: Colette and Linguini eventually accept that Remy can cook, even if the society outside of their kitchen is not yet so tolerant. The *Toy Story* and *Monsters* films, though, self-consciously blend a "real world" of humans, presumably one very much like that inhabited by their viewers, with a fantasy world to which the viewers have no real access. Each film narratively depends on two spheres of being, only one of which is conscious of the other. Beyond humor, beyond tongue-in-cheek reversals like children's fear *of* monsters becoming their toxicity *to* monsters, *Toy Story*'s very narrative structure—the great moment of mutant toy rebellion—depends on this ontological dualism.

In a purely fantastic world, Sid's treatment of his toys might look like Ursula's stealing of souls in *The Little Mermaid*, maniacally wielding his power over the helpless. Worse (arguably), if he knew what the toys know and still chose to mutilate them, Sid would become a monstrous Dr. Moreau, a sadistic psychopath. A realistic set up, however, would wholly fail to draw Sid's behavior as seriously deviant. In the human world, Sid is a ten-year-old boy who spends a lot of time alone in his room, who acts rambunctious in pizza arcades and excitedly, even impatiently, anticipates an extra prize from the claw game. Sid teases his sister by altering her toys; he rides a skateboard and throws chew toys to his dog. He locks his family out of his room with numerous deadbolts. He orders age-inappropriate playthings through the mail. But he does no one physical harm and never expresses genuine, non-performative aggression or hostility—that is, nothing outside of the imagined performances of his play—toward a human or an animal. The film requires viewers to believe two things at once: first, from the fantastic realm, that toys can suffer pain, fear, and even death; second, from the human world, that *Sid does not know this truth.* If he so much as suspected, the very device the film uses to bring about his come-uppance would fail utterly. He must be surprised—horrified to match the horrors he has created—in order to be appropriately punished for his crimes, which in turn, by his very surprise, must be understood as unintentional.

Sid's other apparent crimes—we've heard him accused of bullying his sister and stealing Andy's property, in addition to kidnapping and "torturing" toys—all have other, equally compelling explanations. In terms of actual screen time, Sid's sister taunts as much as she is taunted, certainly suggesting sibling rivalry (if not a more troubled sibling relationship), but belying his unidirectional reign of terror. Andy's toys, having jumped or fallen out the playroom window, make their own way to Pizza Planet, where it is the aliens who ensure that Woody can't stop Sid's collecting them. Nothing implies that the exploded Combat Carl was ever in Andy's possession. If he doesn't bully and he doesn't steal, and by the very nature of the film, he cannot be an intentional abuser of sentient creatures, Sid's punishment seems deserved only by the nature of his play. Sid is a bad kid, the film seems to say, because he plays wrong.

Nor is it the violence—the meanness—of his play that the film disciplines. Interestingly, it is not Sid but the film's other characters, including Andy, who imitate or intimate violence and anti-social behavior: in Andy's games, toys steal from one another and threaten each other with violence; when he's not looking, the toys themselves—sarcastically or fearfully—wish others harm. Buzz does not hesitate to turn his laser "from stun to kill," for instance, when first encountering Sid's mutants, and Woody admits he'd like to see Buzz where Combat Carl had been: "like a crater." In Sid's imagination, on the other hand, he performs pioneering experimental surgery, sends astronauts into space, interrogates prisoners, and serves in the trenches with soldiers at war. His play is intentionally and concretely harmful to the toys— toy brain surgery actually means cutting off a doll's head, and his war games and aeronautics do involve explosives—but it is not intentional *as violence* (at least, not outside of a military context). It is not configured as one entity deliberately trying to harm another for pleasure or power in the other's pain: he saws off Janie's head primarily to perform a transplant; he threatens Buzz only to launch him into space. Yet Sid is perceived as deliberately, even gleefully violent: a delinquent, a budding sociopath, a danger to the calmer norms emblematized by Andy's house.

In juxtaposition to Syndrome, and in view of the literature on gifted education, perhaps it is not surprising that Sid's actions are so woefully misunderstood by—and misrepresented to—the audience. Perhaps it's no coincidence that he role-plays as both a brain surgeon and a rocket scientist. Like the young Buddy Pine's rocket boots, Sid's mutant menagerie demonstrates some remarkable achievements in invention and building. It is not every child who can build such an army of original but functional toys out of mismatched parts: a doll head on robotic spider legs, a fishing pole where a Barbie's torso and head once appeared, a duck that hops around on a spring. From a vantage point other than Buzz and Woody's prejudice and fear, such a workshop (and the young inventor's isolation therein) might suggest the intellectual aptitude and emotional struggle of the gifted child who has no informed support network. Gifted boys often play with toys "in ways that were not intended," explain Barbara Kerr and Sanford Cohn, demonstrating their creativity, curiosity, and intensity as well as just ability. Sid's play—characterized by breaking, rebuilding, and performing—resembles that of many a creatively gifted child, while his inclination toward behaviors that appear delinquent (and his three-film trajectory to garbage man) may indicate what can happen when creative and intellectual gifts are thwarted.

Andy's play is also imaginative, in its way. Many viewers enjoy the film and its spectacular display of vintage toys particularly for its celebration of his old-fashioned child's play. The stories he acts out with his toys are given a prominent place of honor at the opening of each film, in the second actually set in the imaginative spaces of his mind by the animation itself. But the two boys' expressions of creativity are very different from one another. Andy's creative play depends on his general acceptance of the prescribed identity of each toy, for instance, seldom repurposing brand-identifiable toys for dramatically original purposes. His toys' adventures reveal his familiarity with cliché narrative tropes (the bank robber faces off with the sheriff while the damsel is tied to the railroad tracks) more than his radically creative originality. There is nothing unusual or deficient in Andy's play; Gail Lewis might see it as indicative of a conformist society, where creativity presents in "more imitative and reproductive" than "artistic" ways. [15] But Sid's play is markedly different from Andy's: he imitates scenes, but he casts himself in them; he begins with the brand product, and then destroys it.

As we've argued elsewhere, the film visually condemns Sid's play by linking it to the visual "horror" of categorical violations. Noel Carroll explains how cinematic horror is built on such cognitive disruption: zombies who are both alive and dead, werewolves who are both human and animal, toys that are both babydoll heads and robotic spider legs. [16] In this sense, the construction and engineering are the terrifying elements of the mutant menagerie, the gifted inventor—like Syndrome, or Victor Frankenstein—mounting Promethean efforts to play god, to create the unthinkable. But destruction is the other half of the problem the film has with Sid. All that breakage—the decapitation and other dismemberment, the wounded soldier, the bleary remains of a baby doll's abused face—signifies as well. For all the uncanny constructions, it is the damage that the toys resist: "We don't like being smashed, Sid, or blown up, or ripped apart," Woody lectures. For creatively gifted kids, creative and destructive behaviors may be "closely related," like two halves of a wave. [17] As the film disapproves, so too does a frequently uncomprehending society. Lewis notes that the creatively gifted child's processes of creating and destroying often invite "sanctions" and other pressures to suppress. "Creativity," she argues, "is not an easy gift." [18]

The relationship between creative gifts and delinquency is not simply conceptual but can actually be causal. If stifled, creative gifts are "less likely to be extinguished than to take an anti-social turn," Lewis notes, and "unguided creativity may turn to destructive behavior." [19] Reviewing the re-

search on creative personalities, Lewis supports the conventional wisdom
that throughout history, many creatively gifted people have suffered emotional difficulties and feelings of alienation and hostility. As early as elementary school, she explains, the sense that one's creativity is becoming increasingly less tolerated can lead to certain unacceptable behaviors like fighting
and vandalism. Without direction, that creative energy "which depart[s] too
radically from society's value," particularly antithetical to the conformist
values of school, can find delinquent, even dangerous, outlets. [20] Indeed, the
first phase of her own study revealed surprisingly similar aggression scores
between the creatively gifted and delinquent populations she interviewed, all
teenagers, the first group including actors with experience beyond school
plays, the second repeat criminal offenders with at least one offence against
persons or property. [21] The biggest discrepancy in their scores, Lewis reports,
was in "creative productivity," suggesting that the delinquents' creative potential "had rarely been put to use." [22]

What makes the difference between a successful creatively gifted person
and a delinquent? Why are some creative energies focused into healthy outlets while others turn anti-social and destructive? Research indicates that
support of those who recognize and value the creative child's potential can
make a tremendous difference. [23] Lewis sees the creative gifted personality
on a continuum between constructive and destructive poles: "the task of
society," she says, "is to see that the balance is more heavily weighted
toward constructive behavior." [24] If Sid's creative gifts are already skewing
toward destruction, a look at his personal "society" may be illuminating.
Regardless of whether the playroom gang has accurately represented his
experience at camp, his parents are both absent presences. The man we might
presume to be his dad snores in an armchair in front of television cartoons in
the middle of the day, a pile of crumpled cans beside him; his mom (whom
he does not hesitate to ask for matches, apparently fearing no interference or
discipline) only appears as the voice yelling up to offer him a toaster pastry.
Someone has delivered a package of explosives, clearly marked "keep out of
the hands of children," directly to his bedroom. And his feelings toward them
seem clearly signified by the numerous deadbolts on his bedroom door. Even
at the pizza parlor, Sid has no friends, no family, and no institutional support.

Furthermore, the society educated by the cultural pedagogy of the film
itself—the society we all occupy—learns from *Toy Story* how to further deny
creatively gifted people the support and imaginative opportunities they need.
Before the plot has even gotten underway, Pixar takes a bright, talented,
exuberant, imaginative kid and ostracizes him, shutting him up in a room
alone without kindness or encouragement from anyone, and unambiguously
alerts viewers that he's to be feared and shunned at all costs. Expelled,
exiled, and isolated, he still manages to find creative outlets and joy, if
perverted into more destructive than constructive behaviors. So in its final

punishment, the film takes the one thing he needs most. The delinquents in Lewis's study, those whose creative energies had not found productive outlets, shut down particularly in terms of their ability to fantasize, revealing a "fear" of daydreaming beyond concrete, problem-solving imaginings. "Thus the chief functions of fantasy," Lewis argues, particularly the "discharge of painful, unpleasant, or unacceptable material and diversion—are denied them."[25] Pixar's toy rebellion not only teaches Sid to stop breaking stuff but also utterly undermines his fantasy world. Punished in classic bully fashion by the threat of constant surveillance, and doomed to a life of garbage collection by the time of his cameo in the third film, Sid may also lose something even more vital to his emotional health and achievement. "We must not destroy the child's ability to fantasize. . . . The suppression of creativity, of the ability to fantasize, is a dangerous move."[26]

Beyond the anecdotal research that boys like to play kinetically, often by breaking stuff and fictionalizing aggressive relationships between toys or peers, and beyond the commonplace that their behavior is frequently viewed negatively by teachers and others,[27] the pressures on gifted boys may be uniquely intense. Highly gifted boys and girls alike may have trouble fitting in; as Webb et al. describe, as long as girls are supposed to be pretty and boys are supposed to be athletic, the kid whose intellect is his or her defining mark will have to find his or her own way. But their issues are different. Kerr and Cohn, Jesse Klein, Michael Kimmel, and numerous others note that boys have very few socially sanctioned outlets for some of the most common features of giftedness. If emotionally sensitive or intense, boys are at risk of being marked "crybabies"; if intellectually driven and smart, "nerds"; if highly creative and performative, "gay" (whether they identify as homosexual or not)."[28] And, as many of those decrying the "boy crisis" have documented, bright boys seem to be increasingly unmotivated, disengaging, and underachieving.[29]

Certainly, *Toy Story*'s treatment of Sid normalizes an unfortunate but common set of preferences. Lewis is blunt: "It is easier to love a child who behaves . . . than to love a child accused of vandalism or worse,"[30] and the most brutally honest of the researchers on gifted children acknowledge that parents and teachers alike sometimes wish extraordinary children were a little more ordinary.[31] But from its incomparable position of cultural pedagogical power, Pixar could authorize a less typical and more productive set of audience reactions to those who depart from the norms. Why must we see Andy's quieter, more sociable childhood as superior to Sid's? Why must the film draw Sid as vicious in his constructive and destructive play rather than just circumstantially dangerous to the toys who cross his path? And, as we've argued throughout this book, why across a thirteen-film catalog are there no exceptions to this rule? Pixar's gifted and talented are frequently present, but always ludicrous, creepy, or downright dangerous. Even as children, they are punished when they might have been positively redirected. Though distracted by his headphones in *Toy Story 3*, hiding behind his sunglasses, and happily enough collecting the trash in front of Andy's house, the adult Sid Philips ends up like too many gifted boys, underachieving in a world that either can't see his gifts or simply won't give him space to nurture them.

NOTES

1. James T. Webb, Janet L. Gore, Edward R. Amend, and Arlene R. DeVries, *A Parent's Guide to Gifted Children* (Scottsdale, AZ: Great Potential Press, 2007), 120.

2. D. A. Kinney, "From Nerds to Normals: The Recovery of Identity Among Adolescents from Middle School to High School," *Sociology of Education* 66, no. 1 (1993), quoted in Jessie Klein, *The Bully Society: School Shootings and the Crisis of Bullying in America's Schools* (New York: New York University Press, 2012), 30.

3. Barbara A. Kerr and Sanford J. Cohn, *Smart Boys: Talent, Manhood, and the Search for Meaning* (Scottsdale, AZ: Great Potential Press, 2001), 84, 134.

4. Webb et al., *A Parent's Guide*, 150–52. Webb et al. are thoughtful in their analysis of the data on depression and suicide in gifted children. Though some professionals claim that gifted children are in fact at higher risk, and argue plausibly enough from the union of alienation and other emotional hallmarks of giftedness like perfectionism, intensity, and extreme introversion, research studies show comparable rates of suicide between gifted children and other kids. Webb et al., though, also note the conditions under which such studies take place and posit that if children have been identified as "gifted" for the purposes of the study, it is likely that they are in gifted education programs, in which case at least some of their needs are being met. It is impossible, of course, to measure the rates of depression in profoundly gifted children who are still being misunderstood or misdiagnosed, still in educational situations not suited to their particular needs.

5. Webb et al., *A Parent's Guide*, 174, 277.

6. Dan Kindlon and Michael Thompson, *Raising Cain: Protecting the Emotional Life of Boys* (New York: Ballantine Books, 1999), 143

7. Carneal is quoted in Michael Kimmel, *Guyland: The Perilous World Where Boys Become Men* (New York: HarperCollins, 2008), 88.

8. Webb et al., *A Parent's Guide*, 120.

9. Webb et al., *A Parent's Guide*, 125, 123–24, 159.

10. Susan Daniels and Michael M. Piechowski, eds., *Living with Intensity: Understanding the Sensitivity, Excitability, and the Emotional Development of Gifted Children, Adolescents, and Adults* (Scottsdale, AZ: Great Potential Press, 2008), 14.

11. Eleanor Byrne and Martin McQuillan, *Deconstructing Disney* (Sterling, VA: Pluto Press, 2000); Alan Ackerman, "The Spirit of Toys: Resurrection and Redemption in *Toy Story* and *Toy Story 2*," *University of Toronto Quarterly* 74, no. 4 (2005): 896–97. Ackerman calls Sid a "toy-sadist" and "a figure for terror and destruction."

12. "Mutant Toys," *Disney.com*, n.d., www.disney.go.com/disneyvideos/animatedfilms/toystory/characters/mutant.htm (1 November 2013).

13. Vladmir Propp, *Morphology of the Folktale* (Austin: University of Texas Press, 1968).

14. Noel Carroll, *The Philosophy of Horror: Or, Paradoxes of the Heart* (New York: Routledge, 1990), 16.

15. Gail Lewis, "The Need to Create: Constructive and Destructive Behavior in Creatively Gifted Children," *Gifted Education International* 7, no. 2 (January 1991): 3.

16. Carroll, *The Philosophy of Horror*, 16.

17. Lewis, "The Need to Create," 62.

18. Lewis, "The Need to Create," 62.

19. Lewis, "The Need to Create," 67.

20. Lewis, "The Need to Create," 63.

21. Lewis, "The Need to Create," 65.

22. Lewis, "The Need to Create," 66.

23. Lewis, "The Need to Create," 63, 67.

24. Lewis, "The Need to Create," 62.

25. Lewis, "The Need to Create," 66.

26. Lewis, "The Need to Create," 67.

27. Kindlon and Thompson, *Raising Cain,* 29–30.

28. Kids who *do* openly identify as gay generally fare much worse. See Klein, *The Bully Society,* chapter four, "Gay Bashing," and Ken Corbett, *Boyhoods: Rethinking Masculinities* (New Haven, CT: Yale University Press, 2009).

29. Leonard Sax, *Boys Adrift: The Five Factors Driving the Growing Epidemic of Unmotivated Boys and Underachieving Young Men* (New York: Basic Books, 2007).

30. Lewis, "The Need to Create," 67.

31. Webb et al., *A Parent's Guide,* xiii.

Chapter Five

Consumerist Conformity and the Ornamental Masculine Self

Even when the bully society is not clearly in evidence, when plots do not pit the "cool" kids against the "nerds" in conspicuously competitive arenas, the character traits Pixar consistently chooses to vilify may indicate the value structure on which the films are built and that they reinforce with their tremendous, if oblique, pedagogical power. Though at a glance Pixar's bad guys may seem to vary widely—from a wannabe superhero to a mint-condition toy, from an ambitious lizard to a disgraced adventurer, from a mean tween to a grasshopper to a computer with a mind of its own—the villains of Pixar actually have a great deal in common. Pixar is consistently hard on intellectuals and other "alternative" masculinities, but the films further situate their villainous nerds amid a decidedly consumer culture, which they unfailingly endorse and perpetuate. As a result, the Pixar universe not only nostalgically reiterates a traditional, supposedly essential, hegemonic masculinity from the American past—a model that persists, fueling the contemporary adolescent "bully society"—but also endorses the economic premises of that dominant hierarchical structure as well. In its celebration of the postmodern, consumerist man, and its subsequent rejection of those who circumvent or rebel against commodity culture, Pixar extends its call for masculine conformity past the individual and institutional compliance we posit in the previous chapters and into consumer behavior, a shift utterly in keeping with the present reality of children's film as a merchandise-based, rather than strictly narrative-based, enterprise.

TRY BLUE! IT'S THE NEW RED!

In the rivalries that characterize many of Pixar's plots, as we have argued throughout this book, a hypermasculine, athletic male strives against an intellectually and creatively gifted boy or man to the inevitable defeat or displacement of the latter. The former's victory often coincides with a sort of domestic redemption. Big, athletic, popular guys like Mr. Incredible, Lightning McQueen, Buzz Lightyear, and James P. Sullivan develop ethically over the course of their narrative journeys, especially when called upon to care for a child, family, or community, but even while learning to channel their masculine excellences in more social and emotional directions than they have historically pursued, they retain their supposedly essential masculine privilege, often conspicuously through the celebration of their bodies. Skinny, short, smart guys, on the other hand, are laughable and lovable at best, like Flik the ant and Mike Wazowski; at worst, they're bullied and punished, like Miles Axlerod and Buddy/Syndrome. As we have argued further, invited by the overt nostalgia of the films' plots, settings, and visual detail, to historicize this stereotypical "jock versus geek" contest, we may profitably situate it amid a long twentieth-century struggle over the ideal of American masculinity in a changing workplace. The oppositions of Syndrome against Mr. Incredible, Randall against Sulley, and Axlerod against the entire McQueen race team draw the "geek" as an ambitious intellectual, attempting to rise to a comparable status with his "jock" opponent, a hero of the "self-made man" type idealized across early American history. [1] Pixar's hypermasculine, "self-made" heroes, if not literally self-employed, are yet concretely associated with their labor and afforded some degree of freedom and autonomy in how they perform it: Mr. Incredible, Lightning—even Sulley, in the employ of the "incorporated" scream factory—use their bodies to work in self-directed and authoritative ways, finding success and satisfaction in the physical performance of their labor.

Without exception, Pixar draws autonomous, self-directed labor as far more appealing than other types of work. It is less degrading than Lightning's temporary service work with Radiator Springs' paving machine, Bessie; less foolish than the mindless, assembly-line-style mechanical production blindly performed by the population of Ant Island; less heartless than Mr. Huph's white-collar middle management at Insuracare. In consideration of the contrast between hero and villain, moreover, it becomes even plainer that physical labor is also more ethical than more intellectual types of work, particularly the relatively abstracted pursuits of engineering and management. The inventive efforts of engineers like Randall, Syndrome, and Axlerod carry the clear and present potential to hurt; the administrative work of corporate managers like Axlerod and Waternoose allows them to heartlessly sacrifice individuals in pursuit of financial gain. Across its oeuvre, Pixar often doubly condemns its gifted engineers by linking them to aggressive entrepreneurial capitalism, portraying an inventor who stands to profit from his inventions as wholly untrustworthy, even dangerous.

Working outside the norms of consumption—inventing and marketing rather than buying and honoring the product—the intellectually and creatively talented nerd becomes a potentially dangerous, even Machiavellian manipulator of the marketplace. Guys who build are bad enough, in Pixar: Flik is the only builder in any of the Pixar films who is not drawn as evil (possibly because his inventions publicly fail). Even Charles Muntz, alone in a South American jungle, invents the technology to empower his entire canine service staff with speech, and then he turns bad, his speaking dogs menacing and dangerous. Guys who invent and sell for profit, though, are unequivocally untrustworthy: nowhere across the films is a brilliant inventor who markets his products while still retaining a scrap of integrity. Infiltrators of the consumer market like Randall, Syndrome, and Axlerod lie, kidnap, even kill, as they manufacture products and artificially create (or inflate) demand. Nor are the markets they seek to enter those superficial arenas of fashion and trend. In all these cases, the narrative tension that mounts as inventor geniuses seek entrepreneurial success is augmented by a notion of need. Not content to make and sell traditional products that people have always required, not limiting themselves to offering novel innovations that people will enjoy, not even satisfied with using conventional marketing strategies to increase consumers' desire for products they don't yet know they want, Pixar's entrepreneurial villains observe, control, or create what seem like fundamental needs and then sell an unsuspecting but desperate population their necessities. The technology these inventors wield has the potential to seriously impact members of their respective publics on a level from which no one can simply opt out: safety, energy, fuel.

Since the villains perform their work through intricately convoluted machinations, since they express themselves with contradiction and deceit, and since their multiple motives include not only financial greed but also complex emotions like the resentment and anger born of betrayal or shame, Pixar's rendering of villainy is overwhelming, even incomprehensible to its child viewers. What is clear is just that the entrepreneurial inventor is to be seen in an overwhelmingly negative light. Syndrome, for instance, has already succeeded on the international weapons market, but dissatisfied with simply making and selling commodities for profit, he personally yearns for the respect of the people. By killing off the Supers, and then devising a gravely dangerous situation in Municiberg, he aims not only to earn acclaim by showing off his own ability but also to generate business by fabricating a context in which his super gadgets seem necessary to regular people. He doesn't intend to be forever on-call: he tells Mr. Incredible that after his display of "heroics," when he's "had [his] fun," he'll sell his inventions "so that everyone can be superheroes. Everyone can be super." Syndrome's multi-step plan—from inventing to building to scaring to rescuing to selling—combined with his multiple motives—from anger to revenge to greed to a desire for social homogeneity (or at least, through such homogeneity, the ultimate degradation of the remaining Supers)—must be hopelessly confusing to the film's youngest target demographic. The film does not intend for its child viewers to sift through it all, surely, trusting that the difficulty itself will contribute to the necessary negative readings of the character and his actions. *Monsters, Inc.* works similarly. Randall, inextricably linked to the equally villainous C.E.O., Waternoose, has figured out how to halt the impending energy shortage with a new technology, the Scream Extractor, designed to suck scream energy out of children too jaded to be easily frightened. With a scheme nearly as convoluted as Syndrome's, involving kidnapping, double-crossing, and travel by portal across alternate universes, *Monsters, Inc.* assumes that Monstropolis's unsuspecting citizens will buy the differently extracted scream energy in total ignorance of the truly terrifying, criminal, and apparently painful way it's being generated ("silence" being one of Waternoose's stated goals). What children know is perhaps just that Randall is scary, dishonest, and willing to hurt children. Axlerod's plan in *Cars 2* involves creating and then thwarting consumers' desire for biofuel in the hopes of driving everyone back to oil-based fuel products, since his real asset is an enormous oil reserve under the ocean floor. His tangled plot, wedding technology to a need-based consumer vulnerability, woven through with personal ambition and emotional pain, and presented with deceitfulness, undoubtedly leaves its young audiences unclear on the specifics. (We're not even quite sure how to think about Allinol, since Professor Zundapp tells his captured spy that it is a good product except for its susceptibility to electromagnetic pulse, but Holly later informs everyone that it was just reengineered gasoline and never a biofuel at all.) Erecting these sinister but nearly unnavigable criminal plots, these films construct entrepreneurial engineering as a hopelessly complicated (but nonetheless terrifying) villainous specter hovering over the protagonists and other supposed innocents.

The vilification of inventors seems like the most ironic of all observations about Pixar, given the studio's reputation as the "fraternity of geeks" who revolutionized animation with their technological innovations, but associating said villainous inventors with commerce is more ironic still, given the vast merchandising universe of Disney/Pixar. If, as Henry Giroux says, Disney "works hard to transform every child into a lifetime consumer of [its] product ideas,"[2] how could films that consistently associate manufacture and marketing with villainy—and even terror—possibly work in Pixar's best corporate interest?

The flip side of the evil manufacturer narrative, consumer helplessness, does more than augment the villain's threat level. Indirectly but compellingly it inspires viewer sympathy for those entirely dependent on the entrepreneur for the continuation of life as they know it, those consumers thus entirely vulnerable to the market forces inflicted on them: the citizens of Municiberg under attack, the monsters in Monstropolis poised to unwittingly contribute to the torture of children, and the rest of us, waiting perhaps too eagerly to be duped by hucksters of biofuel. The construct of consumer helplessness as a device to channel viewer sympathy is most obvious in the dystopian *WALL-E*. Among adults at least, the depiction of future humans likely elicits initial negative responses ranging from pity to disgust. Overstuffed and under-worked to the point of physical impairment, the Axiom's residents represent consumerism at its worst. Entirely uncritical of the advertising messages around them, they have lost all capacity to resist banal messages like "Time for lunch—in a cup!" and "Try blue—it's the new red!" Separated from one another by just a few feet, they still communicate through electronic devices, all the while in motion to nowhere. They are not just fat (their fingers hardly able to bend enough to press the control buttons on the arms of their hover-chairs); they have physically regressed to an infantile state: in their chairs, their legs bounce restlessly like the babies whose literal indoctrination is complementarily demonstrated in the Buy n Large montage. When he tumbles to the floor, John can't even roll over from his back, like a baby who has not yet begun to crawl. To wrest power away from AUTO, the captain takes a toddler's first steps, arms outstretched, seeking something to hold onto for balance and support.

Almost entirely undifferentiated from one another in the film's motion and sound—their movement seems to be governed by common tracks, or at least the flow of heavy traffic, and their speech overlaps to the point of meaningless cacophony—the bodies aboard the Axiom foretell of a horrific devolution of the human species, away from familiar muscular and skeletal systems as well as intellectual discernment, and the perceptible changes across the gallery of captains' portraits illustrate this process even more conspicuously. For all that, though, the film renders these human characters more sympathetic than despicable. When John's and Mary's otherwise auto-mated lives are momentarily disrupted by WALL-E on his search for EVE, their faces look surprised but friendly, even warm: John somewhat sadly calls goodbye after WALL-E rushes off, in a familiarly poignant shot; Mary helps WALL-E by moving her chair, then watches as he tries to connect with Eva. When they all get dumped out of their chairs, during the climactic showdown between Captain McCrea and AUTO, several of them grab hands in attempts to help one another, and if that gesture is not enough to rehuman-ize the lot of them, John and Mary together embrace a gaggle of preschool-ers, protecting and guiding the children to a soft landing.

WALL-E seems to differ from the other films by the absence of a villain-ous engineer to blame, the designer of the Axiom presumably long dead, and the current captain as helpless as the captives. Technology itself, though, presents a clear villain and market manipulator in the world of *WALL-E*. AUTO's near-total control of the ship, coupled with the robotic advertising voice that makes up the soundtrack for life in perpetual drift, casts even the most pathetic of the people in sharp relief. This contrast affords viewers another opportunity to identify with the humans, seeing kinship in our distinction from the terrifying other. It also absolves ignorant consumers from their complicity in the market forces that have literally decimated the planet by the time of the film's present. The Buy n Large logos littered across the trashy global landscape hold the manufacturer primarily responsible for the damage done, and the people far too young to have been the actual consumers that contributed to the mess—those people whose youth is underscored by their infantile characteristics even as adults—can emerge unscathed from the film's social critique and start anew on the blighted planet. Indeed, sympathy for the humans is necessary to the film's very structure. It is the people going home, after all, reawakening to apparently fundamental human experiences, on which the film stakes its pleasurable and satisfying conclusion.

Viewers' sympathy for the Axiom's human passengers comes in small part from familiarity—they are humans, after all, and the use of fond gazes and small, friendly gestures recall our common ground—but also, in true Disney fashion, from a healthy dose of nostalgia. Like most of the other Pixar films, *WALL-E* remembers the past fondly: the past earth, its former natural food offerings, the kind of authentic interpersonal connection lamentably diminished even in the early twenty-first century. In the other films too, a hearkening back to an idea of the innocent or the authentic, as Keith Booker has said is a common feature of the Disney fairy tale, mitigates an oppressive sense of aggressive, disingenuous, and technology-based capitalism. The tender green sprout planted in the wasteland of the ruined Earth at the end of *WALL-E* is akin to *The Incredibles*' restored supremacy of the "old school" Supers and, in *Monsters, Inc.*, the young child's genuine emotional expression, rather than extracted fear. Even in *Ratatouille*, the least structurally typical of all the Pixar films, it is film critic Anton Ego's nostalgia for the true, simple peasant food that stands symbolically in quiet opposition to Skinner's corporatized low-brow, microwaveable frozen foods, which he plans to market under Gaston's great reputation.

That the Pixar films' lovable, nostalgic stories would further the corporate interests of the giant marketing machine that has produced them, and that they could do this by the counterintuitive vilification of marketing and manufacture like that they will themselves perpetuate in the merchandising campaign of the film, is a paradox foundational to the ideology of Disney Inc. Henry Giroux says that Disney's long history of "contradictory messages" has regularly provided pleasurable tributes to innocence and authenticity while furthering its corporate success.[3] Disney's need to create a worldview consistent with its commercial interests means that its "cutthroat commercial ethos" may find itself in strange juxtaposition to a narrative culture "which presents itself as a paragon of virtue and childlike innocence."[4] But, as Giroux demonstrates, such a contradiction seldom invites deconstruction; Disney, rather, "does both."[5] In Pixar, vilifying the capitalist inventor calls attention away from the manipulative power of the film itself, blocking the view with a comforting narrative of the at-risk consumer being protected from manipulative capitalists, and thus nurtures a pleasurable identification with those who buy.

More insidiously, though, Pixar's narratives influence the very relationship between self and stuff. Giroux explains that as consumerist discourse increasingly replaces the productive language of democratic citizenship, and as the "good life is constructed in terms of what we buy," contemporary culture teaches children to develop "a market-based notion of identity."[6] The work of the Pixar films is to inspire affinity not only with fellow consumers but also with products themselves, sowing the seeds of nostalgia, fondness, and even love within the very purchasable, mass-marketed commodity.

HE TORTURES TOYS! SID AND COMMODITY CULTURE

Sid Philips, even as a gifted, creative builder feared and vilified by everyone around him, may seem like a strange fit in the catalogue of entrepreneurial inventor villains, being a rowdy ten-year-old rather than a billionaire capitalist poised to take over the world. From what little we see of them, Sid's family appears to be far from wealthy. Their dark, modest home boasts a broken television old enough that a pair of pliers can stand in for a channel selection knob; a snoring man napping in front of it in the afternoon might be Sid's unemployed or swing-shift father, suggesting that the family economy is based on blue-collar labor if any labor at all. Nowhere does the Philips family conspicuously consume or obviously display wealth. In any case, Sid is a child. He has no apparent designs on patenting or marketing his one-of-a-kind creations; on the contrary, he seems bent on their destruction. Still, even without representing him as an imminent threat of manipulation or corporate control of the marketplace, in the likeness of Syndrome and his ilk, *Toy Story* sets Sid apart from the typical machinery of consumer capitalism, depicting him as a different but equally worrisome threat to it.

If, as Charles Baudelaire said in 1853, the pre-modern relationship between child and plaything hinged on the childlike faith in the toy's having a soul, then the entire *Toy Story* trilogy might appear as the imagined fulfillment of a nostalgic wish.[7] Even in the twenty-first century, that is, the three films afford viewers the opportunity to temporarily suspend postmodern cynicism and disbelief in the magic of childhood, the reality of pure and unconditional love, or the existence of the unique individual soul. Through their narratives of social fulfillment, the three films valorize friendship and love as the most important facets of the human experience and may thus momentarily inspire even the most jaded of us to acknowledge the value of communal emotional reciprocity, despite our otherwise relentless commodity culture, even as we are aware of the film's self-promotion and available branded merchandise. The toy, rather than being the soulless, mass-marketed item, manufactured in China and overpriced at the big box stores, for which our children will be clamoring as soon as we leave the theater, is temporarily a venerated totem, representing true, unselfish love and the discovery of one's inner value.

Amid this nostalgic pre-modern dream of the toy, Sid plays wrong. Failing to even wonder about the soul within, bypassing what Baudelaire sees as a child's "first metaphysical stirring," the cynical Sid destroys rather than loves his playthings. In Baudelaire's terms, he is the "puzzling" child who breaks the toy without regard for the relationship it posits. It is not that Sid lacks imagination, that ability Baudelaire sees as evidence of the child's spirituality; it's that he imagines himself as a fictional character, playing against and with equally fictional entities. When Sid sees himself in his toys, it is a pretend self, not an authentic one seeking metaphysical self-knowledge or emotional reciprocity. Imagining himself a commander in the midst of a military operation, for instance, he blows up a Combat Carl; portraying a world-famous neurosurgeon, he performs a "double bypass brain transplant" to replace his sister's doll head with that of a pterodactyl. As a C.I.A. operative of some sort, he bends sunlight through a magnifying glass to torture Woody, now imagined as a prisoner of war or enemy spy, into spilling the beans on some covert operation. If his roles are relative to the toys—NASA commander to astronaut, military captain to private, doctor to patient—they are still not relational, assuming neither the child's authentic self nor the essential identity of the toy. Indeed, Sid seldom appears in the film in a non-performative way: even Menacing Older Brother seems like an act. In one possibly poignant split-second, we see the vulnerable child frustrated even in his dreams ("I wanna ride the pony!" he says, just before stirring awake), but that version of the child never emerges through his play or, until the climactic sandbox showdown, interacts with toys.

This very fluidity of individual performance and the consequent absence of an apparently "true" self may be part of why to many viewers Sid seems sociopathic. Who is the *true* kid under all that pretending, and what comprises the integral self when the only common denominator of all his apparent performances seems to be destructiveness? Andy's play, by contrast, assumes individual integrity, evoking that nostalgic, pre-modern sense of the child's discovering his own metaphysical soul through imaginative interchange with the beloved toy. Unlike Sid with his many imagined personalities, even if Andy's toys play different roles in his various play scripts, the child himself stays generally the same, a coherent integral self whose identity does not fluctuate from game to game (or even, much, as he matures over the trilogy). This unchanging Andy loves his toys; he marks their relationship—and his own coherent presence—by writing his name on their boots.

From this faith in and assertion of the integral self, Andy's play honors supposedly authentic relationships, another aspect of child's play that the sociopathic Sid seems to miss. Woody, Buzz, and the gang are Andy's toys, and they love him back. They accompany him, like friends, to the pizza arcade and elsewhere, riding in cars and sleeping in beds like children themselves. To Andy, the relationship goes both ways: he does not just have toys, but he *is*, in part, in relation to his toys. Woody is not only an extension of his imagination, in other words, a pretend companion and friend, but also a source for his own identity. Not a cowboy or a sheriff, Andy nonetheless wears his own cowboy hat and attends his own cowboy camp, as if he is an extension of his favorite toy. When he forges a new relationship with Buzz and his room changes to reflect the shift in (or broadening of) his affection, even this slight outward change reinforces the sense that the child's identity is deeply rooted in his relationships with his playthings.

For Andy, the toys too have integral coherence, relatively unchanging selves. Even in his imaginings, they all basically stay in character. Mr. Potato Head is the one exception, having to role-play as "One-Eyed Bart," but Bo Peep, the delicate female, is always the (stereotypical) delicate female; Sheriff Woody is always the sheriff; Rex is always a dinosaur (even though, in actuality, he's kind of a nebbish); and Slinkey Dog, though occasionally granted superheroic powers, is always a dog and always a pet. In this way, Andy's games may be less pre-modern than post. If not quite the "puerile" imitative play that Baudelaire condemns, Andy's play certainly approximates the "theatrical" mimicry that he observed even in the middle of the nineteenth century, a type of play that, of course, has grown exponentially—perhaps uncontrollably—with the rise of animation and other media forms across the twentieth and twenty-first centuries. David Elkind sees this mimicry as a negative trend in postmodern play and the marketing that shapes it, a feature of contemporary youth culture that diminishes the creative agility of children.[8] Today's toys, he says, "serve to instill the psychology of consumerism . . . transform[ing children] from net producers of their own toy and play culture to net consumers of a play culture imposed by adults."[9] Recounting the marketing history of Barbie, who was originally introduced with clothes and props but not imbued with a particular personality, just so girls *could* "project whatever personalities they want" onto their dolls, as her original maker Ruth Handler insisted, Elkind explains how, when Mattel found itself losing market share in the early 1980s, the company decided Barbie needed a TV show and a salable personality so that they could compete with toys that were already being marketed within these "consumption nets." Over the objections of Handler, he notes, Barbie became "geared mainly to selling associated products in the consumption net and reinforcing brand loyalties."[10] Even though Andy is far too young to have watched original episodes of "Woody's Roundup," his understanding of Woody's personality is entirely in keeping with the toy's branded identity, as we learn even more clearly in the second film. Buzz Lightyear, also defined and marketed within a consumption net of television shows and video games, as well as just advertising, comes with a soul preordained by narrative marketing strategies. Even Buzz believes that his character is his real identity, and Andy certainly buys in.

Sid doesn't. Viewers' sense of Sid's villainy may in fact arise in part from his failure to engage with a branded consumerist culture. In a universe of prepackaged stories (*Toy Story* itself is one), Sid tells different ones, the wrong ones. Rather than reciting the plots that came virtually built in to Buzz, Woody, and the others, he creates bizarre fragments and incomprehensible scenes—scenes of surgery and astrophysics—calling Buzz "a spaceman," and apparently ignorant of Woody's name at all. Though he nominally recognizes the "Buzz Lightyear" in the claw machine as a branded toy with a trademarked name, when he actually plays with him, he values him not for any connection to the Emperor Zurg and the missions of the Galactic Alliance but for the thinnest connection to "space" that gives him an excuse to launch an explosive. Sid maintains a steadfast resistance against marketing, its brand identities, manufactured desire, and marketed narrative play. The television is on, blaring advertisements and cartoons, as "the products sold on the market become the very content of the media image,"[11] but Sid is not watching it.

From a slightly different vantage point on *Toy Story* than is typical, even Sid's most destructive play is admirably inventive and utterly unfettered by manufactured, market-driven desire. Since he sees stuff as mere props for his wildly imaginative play, he doesn't need to buy much, and certainly he doesn't feel the need to buy because of media or peer pressure. Anything will do—Sid uses tools, hardware, magnifying glasses, and broken pieces of toys probably never even his—for the hands-on, kinetic play once a hallmark of boyhood. Disney's promotional materials are bluntly disapproving: "Deep within the inner sanctum of . . . Sid's room," one of the company's web pages declares, "lies a collection of toys that *no boy should have created*."[12] Andy's example, on the other hand, teaches kids how to want particular toys and how to play with them according to story scripts, not unlike the one that viewers of *Toy Story* are in the very act of watching.

At a glance, *Toy Story* seems to display the very opposite of this glorification of the commodity, resisting branded-identity marketing culture and openly critiquing the equation of self and commodity. The entire plot involves Woody teaching Buzz to value himself as an individual with the integral character necessary to love another rather than seeing himself as a television character. "You are not a space ranger," Woody insists. *"You are a toy,"* distinguishing between the branded, mass-marketed commodity and the relational "child's plaything," and thus allowing Buzz to be the sort of receptacle for the child's metaphysical projection that Baudelaire described. But the fact that the characters are toys that can be purchased is not lost on kids, nor do the films let it be. Barbie's chipper reminder to the parents in the audience of *Toy Story 2*, that once before "short-sighted retailers did not order enough [Buzz dolls] to meet demand" pointedly promotes its characters as merchandise and encourages viewers to hurry in to Al's Toy Barn or its real-world equivalent before all the Buzzes are sold. As Karen Brooks notes, Disney "focus[es] more on teaching our children how to be good little materialists in this corporate, consumer-driven world than they do anything else."[13]

Elsewhere, Pixar also resists—and then affirms—this cynical post-modern reading of its own merchandise. In *Cars*, Lightning McQueen initially identifies himself as *"the* Lightning McQueen," a "precision instrument of speed an aerodynamics." Conspicuously lonely, he is not a son or a brother or a friend, only a machine. His hiatus in Radiator Springs leads him to the discovery of himself as an integral being, an authentic self beneath the celebrated, commodity persona whose very body is available as ad space. Turning down the Dinoco sponsorship he has long desired—a source of financial support that would also, perhaps more obviously to children, change his paint color to blue and associate him with a more successful branded product than Rust-eze—Lightning performs his new, coherent metaphysical identity, no longer for sale to the highest bidder. Having surrounded Lightning with bobblehead figurines of himself, though *Cars* also demonstrates to viewers that its main character comes in a variety of purchasable forms. In the very same breath as it uses to mock marketing as disingenuous ("Rust-eze—look like me! Ka-chow!" Lightning says to a room full of rusty, old cars who will never, ever look like him), the film portrays merchandise as desirable and shopping as an ethical, relationship-building act. *Cars* further weds buying with loving and both with being, as shopping reveals the supposedly authentic self to which the film's narrative arcs. Buying stuff is how Lightning builds relationships with the Radiator Springs crowd, who have suffered economically and emotionally because of the interstate highway system that choked off many small American towns in the second half of the twentieth century. He buys new tires from Luigi, organic fuel from Fillmore, and a new paint job from Ramone, giving his patronage to each of the businesses in town, receiving their gratitude and affection in the process. Thus earning his new friendships by shopping, rewarded with personal good will and emotional reciprocity with each purchase, Lightning illustrates the process of triangulating human relationships onto the marketplace. The discovery of his authentic self, that fundamental Disney quest Booker sees throughout the classic films, is inextricably linked to his newfound role of consumer. This reinterpretation of the commodity and its value changes Lightning body and soul: surrounded by friends in a revitalized town, the spark of romance just beginning, his new body paint design visually marks him as a new man. Watching Lightning's example, kids are taught not just to shop—teased into wanting the toys they see on the screen—but also to understand "commodification [as] a defining principle of children's culture."[14]

With modern culture thus defined, Sid's play behaviors may be sociopathic, by definition, or at least they are anti-social. They do indeed challenge the norms of commodity culture; they are in fact detrimental to this particular type of social order. His destructive play may threaten to expose the emptiness of pre-modern metaphysics, to reveal nostalgia as inherently fraudulent in its remembrances. Baudelaire saw the child's failure to find the soul of the toy as the beginning of mature melancholy, but Sid may represent a far more cynical, even nihilistic, postmodern doubt. At very least, Sid disrespects the commodity, that fundamental building block of modern life. Eleanor Byrne and Martin McQuillan explain that Sid's "interference with the commodity . . . is a challenge to the chain of production and is figured as a psychosis."[15] Sid's behaviors render him invulnerable and counterproductive to Disney's consumerist messages, so obviously he must be crazy, and swiftly he must be punished.

A RARE SHERIFF WOODY

Eric Smoodin claims that "Disney constructs childhood so as to make it entirely compatible with consumerism,"[16] its "pretense of innocence," in Giroux's words, "little more than a promotional mask that covers its aggressive marketing techniques and its influence in educating children to become active consumers."[17] In Pixar's entrepreneurial villain plots, the paradox between the search for (and celebration of) an innocent, authentic self and the embrace of crass consumerism emerges in part through the construct of consumer helplessness and nostalgia for a safe and aboveboard marketplace. In the more overt merchandise plots like *Toy Story* and *Cars*, commodities are themselves imbued with spiritual value as the very self is conflated with the marketed commodity. In the first *Cars* movie, Lightning uncovers the authentic self beneath the flash of the brand identity but is never called on to replace one with the other. His newfound authenticity is both: flashy, popular commodity and loving, ethical citizen. In the first *Toy Story*, Buzz similarly learns to value himself for something more than the identity built into his branded body, but he also doesn't have to reject one to embrace the other.

Despite Woody's effort to divide the two, Buzz is *both* a "space ranger" and a "t-o-y." On the other side of the coin, though sociopathic Sid doesn't injure small animals or children, he nevertheless hurts items whose value is not simply utilitarian but vital, emotional, and spiritual.

In a system of industrial capitalism, as Karl Marx explains, commodities have their own kind of mystical spirits, which we imagine so as to veil the labor relations their presence otherwise indicates. "A commodity," says Marx, "is a very strange thing, abounding in metaphysical subtleties and theological niceties."[18] Unlike an object valued primarily for its utility or one valued because it reflects the human effort that went into making it, a "commodity" emerges when "the social character of [labor] . . . takes the form of a social relation between the products."[19] We come to believe that there is an internal, essential value to things, says Marx, just as we might believe in the existence of ghosts or deities; "in that [mist-enveloped region of the religious world], the productions of the human brain appear as independent beings endowed with life, and entering into relation both with one another and the human race."[20] In the *Toy Story* trilogy, the nostalgic notion of the metaphysical value of the beloved toy, itself a reflection of the spirituality of the child, is superimposed onto this sense of the commodity's mystical essence, in Booker's words a "virtual dramatization of the . . . commodity fetish."[21] Retaining both types of spiritual value and eliding the distinction between them, these films model a kind of personal identity whose worth is nevertheless based on a system of market exchange. Since the things themselves appear as persons—characters, at least—they exemplify the commodification of the very self. Graham Huggan, albeit in a different context, describes this tendency as quintessentially postmodern. Citing Fredric Jameson and others, he notes that "commodity fetish is not just rampant, [but] it is the spirit of the age," and one of its chief aspects in the postmodern world is the "reification of people and things into exchangeable . . . objects."[22] Despite their narratives of supposedly authentic self-discovery, Pixar's characters instead demonstrate how individuals may unproblematically view themselves as commodities.

If the first *Toy Story* purports to reverse this very postmodern tendency, as Buzz must learn to devalue himself as a mass-marketed commodity in order to find a different and more authentic identity as "Andy's" toy, then the ostensibly parallel narrative of *Toy Story 2* would seem to incline the same way. Woody, thrust into the marketplace by the greedy fingers of a thieving toy dealer, must navigate his own consumption net to get back to his true self on the other side. But *Toy Story 2*, a film almost entirely about buying and selling, more clearly than ever exposes—and then masks—the commodified essence of its characters, blending the commodity and the authentic to a satisfying but inherently paradoxical resolution. With pivotal scenes set in a toy store's aisles and managerial offices, the film explicitly advertises its own merchandise, reminding viewers to shop early and often for their Buzz toys, and gives Woody his own dollar value and merchandising campaign. It gestures to the dread of obsolescence that will cast its pall over the third film, but it relishes in modern marketing techniques and creates a joyful nostalgia for the consumer product.

In this film, both main characters' narrative arcs take them through notions of selfhood and commodification that are muddled to the point of internal contradiction but nonetheless emblematize this postmodern "spirit of the age."[23] The pastiche of the Buzz Lightyear aisle in Al's Toy Barn, for instance, visually recalls the 1978 horror film *Coma*, the pod prison for the pre-criminals in 2002's *Minority Report*, the final scene of *The Prestige* (2006), and any of a number of science-fiction literary and cinematic accounts of cloning, all uncannily suspending inanimate bodies in perpetuity. Row upon row of Buzz Lightyears in "hypersleep" stare blankly from their packages as the "real" Buzz gazes upward, a tiny toy on the floor, dwarfed by the enormously tall and seemingly endless display. The reiteration of the mechanically reproduced original is visually overwhelming, occupying the entire frame from multiple angles, and judging from the shots' science-fiction kin, it might easily be read as horrifying. Such an image is fundamentally dehumanizing. To make matters worse, Buzz's interaction with an actual clone—a hypermasculine and violent altercation, if cheekily so—poses the potentially serious problem of replacing Buzz, stripping him of his identity so completely that even his friends can't tell whether he or his clone is "real." In the "blank parody" that is the postmodern pastiche, the Buzz Lightyear aisle cheerfully plays its horrific elements for humor and to embrace—not resist—commercial production. Buzz's shock quickly turns to bemused self-critique ("Am I really that fat?" he wonders aloud), and his perusal of his own endlessly reiterated body merely fuels his consumer desire for a new accessory belt.

Even more obviously, but in a much more radical departure from the first film, *Toy Story 2*'s Woody teaches that consumerist conformity is a path to, not a denial of, comprehensive identity formation. From the beginning of the trilogy, the integrity of Woody's metaphysical identity has gone unchallenged. The clarity he has about his individual worth and purpose establishes the backbone of the first film; his total fulfillment in his love- and service-oriented self, in relation both to Andy and to his fellow citizens in the community of the play room, is not only enviable but also the very end to which the film's narrative trajectory leads Buzz. With exceptions made for occasional childish fits of jealousy and pique, Woody is the archetypal wise old man, the lesson-giver, the storyteller who convinces Buzz to reject other ways of being—both the allure of celebrity and the futility of mass-produced, consumption-net branded product—and to value himself instead as "Andy's toy," that projection of the child's soul and facilitator of those most essential human values. As a toy, in Marxist terms, Woody's value might be said to arise from his utility rather than from the marketplace: he is a product without being a commodity. Furthermore, since in his other role his self-directed, autonomous work contributes to the civil harmony of the playroom community, he can be seen as a pre-modern, "self-made" laborer himself, enriching the film's nostalgia with a representation of pre-industrial labor practices.

Ignorant of his former celebrity status, and beloved by the child who uses him and the citizens who depend on his work, Woody remains even into the beginning of the sequel, "not for sale." From this pre-modern utopia, though, Woody is plunged into a market economy: two, actually, as he simultaneously enters both the contemporary rare-toy trade and the historical merchandising campaign that made him a "star." As he moves from the playroom toward the Konishi Toy Museum in Japan, he also goes from seeing himself as the cherished toy valued exclusively—and sufficiently—by his utility as a "child's plaything" to seeing himself as "a rare Sheriff Woody doll."

From the very beginning of *Toy Story 2*, Woody's worth is discussed in terms of market value. Though he ends up in the garage sale by happenstance, attempting to save Wheezy, his friends immediately begin to evaluate his material worth in the context of the sale. Unaware of his rescue plan but seeing him climb into a box, Hamm exclaims, "He's selling himself for $0.25!" and Slinkey Dog laments, "Aw, Woody, you're worth more than that!" The conversation is humorous, of course, but nevertheless odd, one of the film's moments of almost-metafictional self-awareness when we are all reminded that the toys are toys and not really people. When Al offers Andy's mom $50, though, the conversation turns a little more serious. Al insists that "everything is for sale," while Hamm acknowledges that "$50 is not bad," as if suddenly persuadable that selling Woody could be reasonable rather than tragic. Indeed, $50 may seem to young viewers like a lot of money, even at the very same moment as they love Woody and believe he belongs at home in the playroom. Later, when he meets the rest of the "Roundup Gang" in Al's office, Woody too becomes convinced that he's "valuable property," confronted with the whole market context of his celebrity identity. Al ups the price for the benefit of any viewers who might still cling to the notion of a "not-for-sale" Woody: on the phone with his buyer in Japan, Al suggests "adding another zero to that price," and then yells at the airport baggage handler that the collection is worth "more than you make in a year." Thus we all find ourselves with ample evidence to muse, with Hamm, that Woody's price is "not bad!" When Buzz comes to rescue him, Woody is wholly on board with being sold for public display, earnestly and proudly explaining to his friends, "You see, I'm a rare Sheriff Woody doll, and these guys are my Roundup Gang!" Viewers' acceptance of Woody as "valuable property" is a necessary condition to our comprehending this moment: in order to understand the dilemma that Woody faces about whether to go home or to Japan, we have to believe that he has two separate but equal claims to value.

Nor is it just a price tag that Woody embraces: he becomes the commodity. The mass-marketed product appears as his original, authentic self, even amid dozens of other mass-marketed products, and even to him. Jessie begins this process of identification, gushing, "It's you, it's you, it's you," and then, after pulling his string to confirm, gleefully responds to his artificial, manufactured voice, with "It *is* you!" The Prospector similarly labels him with the personal pronoun, albeit observing his confusion: "Why, you don't know who you are, do you?" After a few moments to let it sink in, Woody concurs with Jessie and the Prospector: mouth agape, he says, "That's me," easily conflating the "me" he knows himself to be, from relationships and memories, with the "you" they all understand as a fictional entity and a merchandised character. The ontological structure alone is bizarrely postmodern: if Woody has memories at all, which he must in order to maintain his loyalties to his friends and to Andy, he must also know that he was never the star of any show, being only a doll version of the television show's puppet. The reality he's faced with here is that of being a facsimile, a mass-produced replica of someone or something else. If marginally more rooted in reality than Buzz, who is essentially a mass-marketed simulacrum, his "real" original not even being an object but an endless stream of drawn images, Woody's sense of himself as the television show's Woody is ridiculous. Nonetheless, as Bullseye raises the lights on the mountain of *Roundup* merchandise, the supposed truth of the commodity identity dawns on Woody, whose face is slowly illuminated as if by the rising sun. The film presents the discovery of who he "is" as if he is recovering from amnesia, learning his true identity as new friends are introduced as old friends, as his supposedly former pet horse (whom he has actually never met before) recognizes him and treats him with affection. He learns of his past by watching fictional narratives enacted by the puppet original. Soon, he even echoes the linguistic patterns of the original to render this identification more complete: "Hey howdy hey, that's me. I'm on a yo-yo!," he says, using the catch phrase written on the merchandise despite never having uttered it before, in either film.

"How do you know my name?" Woody asks Jessie, and indeed, Woody's name alone says something about the film's faith in the integrity of the commodified toy. Despite his own ignorance of his televised consumption net, the fact that Woody identifies as "Woody," the name Jessie also knows to call him by, and Andy never calls him anything else either, suggests that even over decades, not one of his owners has ever repurposed or otherwise differently interpreted him. "Everyone knows your name," says Jessie. This detail contributes to viewers' unquestioning acceptance of the conflation of Andy's toy with the celebrity source of all that merchandise. The fetishized spirit of the commodity envelops the pre-modern spirit of the beloved toy (whose loving child might have called him Andy Jr. or anything else), even inside the playroom, just as that internal essence of the commodity gives him value on the marketplace. This is configured as a spiritual development by the often overtly mystical or mythical language of the film: Jessie's "Prospector said one day you'd come" casts him as a reincarnated legend—Jesus or King Arthur—his arrival being prophetically foretold; a few seconds later the Prospector actually calls him "the Prodigal Son." Standing before the smorgasbord of *Woody's Roundup* merchandise, the camera eye focuses tight on a starburst behind a picture of his head, making a halo of sorts to set off the moment at which he accepts the soul inherent in all that stuff.

In a way, then, the makeover montage that follows visually signifies Woody's becoming at last himself, his authentic self restored as he embraces the television character's identity as his own. Barking insistently into the phone, Al arranges for the toy restorer to fix Woody up, airbrushing color back into his cheeks and hair, mending his torn shirtsleeve, and painting over Andy's name on the bottom of his boot. The makeover is presented not as inauthentic, like Mater's disguise sequence in *Cars 2*; on the contrary, the newly painted self is truer than the old, the makeover a graphic disclosure of the discovered real, like Lightning's Radiator Springs paint job in *Cars*. Woody's makeover is a pleasurable scene: slow, richly musical, full of close-ups on Woody's inanimate but smiling face, a visual celebration of the methodical, meticulous art of the toy restorer. The film dwells on the very light gleaming off Woody's newly polished eyes as he becomes perfect, clean, beautiful. If Al has verbally mistreated the old man, the film nonetheless honors him, the ancient artisan of yore whose palsied hands nevertheless can still create beauty.

Immediately after the makeover, Woody's identity shifts into an ambiguous space: restored to "mint," he is both delighted to be new/authentic and still clinging to the old/false. Delighted at his appearance, he still plans to return to Andy, who he thinks "is going to have a hard time ripping" his newly repaired shirt. Soon, however, with the recollection of his fear of toys' inevitable obsolescence, which he has feared since another horror-film visual allusion early in the movie (the lid of a trashcan evoking the cover of the well in 2002's *The Ring)*, he becomes newly persuaded to go to Japan. Newly restored to his authentic self, according to the Propsector, he stands on the brink of immortality, poised to "last forever."

The film is temporarily ambiguous, too, about what Woody should choose—it does not clearly and decisively reject one identity for the other. His close friends, already familiar to child viewers, will be sad if he stays with the Roundup Gang and becomes a museum piece in Japan; Jessie and Bullseye will be sad (and worse) if he goes back to the playroom. Especially following the tear-jerking "When She Loved Me," their position is sympathetic despite their relative newness to the *Toy Story* scene. It is a genuine dilemma: friends will be hurt either way, and neither path is certain to ensure Woody's happy future. Ultimately, as we all listen to the last strains of Woody's theme song, "You've Got a Friend in Me," the sheriff decides to return home to Andy and, as a lucky afterthought, he decides to bring Jessie and Bullseye along. Finally, he has it both ways: the knowledge of his material worth is never rejected or critiqued, though he carries it with him to a different economy. Though Andy's primitive sewing job undoubtedly rates him far below mint condition on the collectible toy market, no one ever mentions his monetary value as having dropped and viewers never unlearn the fact that Woody *is* a rare and valuable commodity.

Finally, it doesn't matter what choice Woody makes: what's irreversible is his acceptance of the value of his commodity identity *as an identity* and that the film authorizes this identification with a parade of fun stuff, a television show, and a literally incomprehensible dollar amount being thrown around in half-heard phone conversations. Woody's choosing to resume his communal role instead of cashing in on his commodity status is belied by Disney's marketing department: the critique of the commodity is the commodity itself. Whether he goes back to the playroom or not, his value has been determined. This is an existential lesson for children that reiterates the relentless consumerism of postmodernism: everyone has value as a commodity.

It is the Prospector, after all, who's the real villain of this film. Al may be a blowhard, and he stands as a structural antagonist to the forward progress of the heroes, but the Prospector is the one with complex motives—including resentment and jealousy toward the protagonists, just like Syndrome and Axlerod and Randall Boggs—who deliberately manipulates and tells outright lies. The Prospector is literally worthless in the film, never having been bought (and thus never having proved his market value), and this, the film seems to say, is the worst thing. Not having been loved by a child, he's never been able to pretend to the metaphysical soul within; always cognizant of his branded identity, he's painfully aware of not having commodity value enough to get sold to the museum on his own, even in mint condition. Al steals from Andy's mom's garage sale, which is bad, and he's definitely loud, annoying, and in the way, but it's the Prospector who hates Woody and acts against him with forethought and maliciousness. The villain is the toy rendered soulless by never having been bought, or loved, which is basically the same thing.

The unscrupulous Al McWhiggin (whose name might suggest that he has descended from the Whigs Marx claimed were just as exploitative of the working classes as the bourgeoisie[24]) cannot be unforgiveable, since he owns a toy store just like the one where, presumably, we'll all go buy our own Buzz Lightyear dolls after the film concludes. He fully appreciates—and reveres, and perpetuates—the consumerist economy; he knows how to recognize value, how to honor and restore the commodity, and how to maintain faith in the branded identity without excessive creativity or other disruption. In Marxist terms, it may be easy enough to see Al as bourgeois because he stands to profit from the sale of the Roundup Gang although he neither made nor restored Woody himself, and it's possible to consider Al's apparent disrespect for the toy restorer as exploitative of the individual laborer. But he's not Axlerod or Randall or the rest, using entrepreneurship to separate himself from "normal" consumption practices. And at the end of the day Al is not treated like the other villains: he's tricked and frustrated but not terrorized (Sid), physically abused (Randall, the Lemons), or killed (Syndrome, Muntz). He's not shipped off to live with the female artist equivalent of Sid Philips, like the Prospector is, riding in the backpack of a child who's tattooed her Barbie almost past the point of brand recognition. At the end of the day, Al is *right*: Woody *is* for sale, in every toy store and Disney store and Wal-Mart in the Western world, and the film wants you to buy one. Even if we condemn Al for not valuing Woody as a friend, we don't—we can't—condemn him for seeing Woody as a product, as we also unquestioningly see him thus. It is just after the hour mark when Woody chooses to return to the playroom, but only sixteen minutes in, the film told us what it needed us to know: "Everything is for sale."

A GATEWAY TO NOWHERE

This apparent paradox between authenticity and consumerism has a particularly interesting analogy in the films' representations of masculinities. Nostalgically celebrating masculine archetypes from across a long American history, the films nonetheless perpetuate a much-lamented postmodern masculine self. For boys in the bully society, the passivity of the postmodern "consuming subject" paradoxically blends with relentlessly hypermasculine standards; a supposedly essentialist masculinity rooted in traditional assumptions of authenticity coexists with its apparent postmodern opposite, a masculine performance enacted through displays of the consumer product. Pixar's simultaneous endorsement of both mirrors the contradictions powerfully present in contemporary boy culture.

Buzz's and Woody's stories (and the toy purchases they likely inspire) carry with them powerful ideological lessons. What Susan Linn says about toys echoes Giroux's observations about Disney: child culture is full of tacit lessons, cultural pedagogies that strengthen a child's understanding of society's values. Our society's values, as Brooks notes, elide the notion of uniqueness with consumerism, forming "good little consumers persuaded to believe we're somehow unique and that through our purchasing power we can proclaim this to the world."[25] That our children want what they watch is both more obvious and less disturbing than the fact of our collective willingness to accept the limits that narrative-based consumption nets tacitly impose on their play. In the very moment we are rooting for WALL-E (and, learning his story, preparing ourselves to buy and play with the *WALL-E* toy), we are becoming John, the uncritical consumer increasingly divorced from his own humanity. The notion of a person as "valuable property" in relation to the material value of others is yet more troubling. As Buzz and Woody learn to accept themselves as both selves and stuff, embracing the idea of their metaphysical souls while accepting that they also have market value and will always be potentially "for sale," the films teach a distinctly postmodern consumerist mentality. What you own holds not only its own mystical value but also yours; you are, yourself, worth something of marketplace exchange value, indicated in part by the commodities that speak your identity for you. Our "ornamental culture" of "marketing and consumerism," Susan Faludi says, "is a ceremonial gateway to nowhere. Its essence is not just the selling act but the act of selling the self."[26]

What this means for boys might be a valid question simply because the Pixar characters are nearly all male. If the protagonists of *Toy Story* were girls, objectified, made over, and faced with the threat of being sold on the market for the voyeuristic pleasure of the masses, critics probably would have asked it by now. As the "invisible" gender, masculinity does not typically command such attention. But across the Pixar boys and men, we can see traces of this conflation of self and stuff even where we might least expect it, suggesting that it is at least a common mechanism of identity formation and expression, and that of course piques our interest in its possible ramifications. Film after film, a male character navigates what it means to be an authentic and/or a commodified self, "the *real* Buzz," "*the* Lightning McQueen," an original, celebrity, or secret identity; this navigation commonly coincides with one's sense of symbolic, commodity-exchange value. Even the dystopian critique of corporate culture that is *WALL-E* introduces the authentic and ethical male by displaying his beloved things, offering up for the consideration of his new friend and love interest the various artifacts he has fancied and collected.

The films' associations between authentic identity and commodities seem to align with what Faludi and others see as characteristic of postmodern masculinity. In the context of the history that leads us to this moment, postmodern consumerist culture has been disruptive to conventional masculine ideals and, according to Faludi, Michael Kimmel, and Giroux, has "disturbed" hegemonic masculinity, and not in an obviously productive way.[27] The gradual supplanting of a manufacturing-based economy by an information-based one, explains Faludi, and the subsequent shift for workers from "industry to service," have removed meaningful social and professional contexts for men.[28] The resultant transformation of the male body "from an agent of production to a receptacle for consumption," says Giroux, coincides with what Faludi calls "ornamental culture," "the ultimate expression of the American Century."[29] Replacing the social institutions that once gave men social purpose, membership, and meaning with "visual spectacles," Faludi says, ornamental culture has reshaped the "most basic sense of manhood by telling [ordinary men] as much as it tells the celebrity that masculinity is something to drape over the body, not draw from inner resources."[30] This transition, in Giroux's words, has contributed to "an identity crisis of unparalleled proportions" for white American men.[31]

Though viewed as deeply problematic by thinkers like Faludi, this version of postmodern masculinity has become almost a cultural commonplace, and in other contemporary cultural texts, like Chuck Palahniuk's novel *Fight Club* and the 1999 film version thereof, it is sharply (if imperfectly) criticized. Palahniuk's protagonist is painfully aware of his hollowed-out, IKEA-catalogue existence; indeed, from this consumerist emptiness arise the entire sadomasochistic enterprise of Fight Club and the megalomaniac Project Mayhem. Lynn M. Ta sees that novel as "a cinematic tirade against this ornamental culture . . . by locating the cause of Jack's seeming loss of masculinity in the proliferation of consumer culture, [which has made] masculinity only available in retail stores."[32] But in Pixar postmodern, ornamental masculinity seems just fine. Like *Fight Club*, the films create a nostalgic longing for an essential type of masculinity that supposedly prevailed before the proliferation of consumerism, but Pixar does so less to critique consumer culture and bemoan this superficial, "market-based" masculinity than to reinforce it.

A culture of aggressively competitive capitalism supports consumerist constructions of identity whereby people's consumer behaviors and commercial possessions appear as clear indications of their personal value. Jesse Klein argues that the bully society so harmful to American adolescent males is just one manifestation of these ideological foundations common across our entire "bully economy." The association between self-worth and the ownership of high-status commodities, just as rampant in adult culture as in high school, has been observed even under experimental conditions; "we are seduced into purchasing products and persuaded that these items or services will boost our confidence and social standing. Then we end up viewing these commodities as essential to our identities."[33] This market-based identity formation—the commodification of people themselves—reinforces the hierarchies according to which we mistreat one another beyond the social world of high school just as much as within it, if not in direct interpersonal ways, through legislative policies and institutional practices that privilege the money-making corporation over the individual person. In the bully economy, Klein argues, "human relationships are reduced to instruments for maximizing profits and status,"[34] and these reductions are used to justify our society's rankings of various people's worth.

Some of the harms that this ubiquitous consumerist ideology poses for boys are equally threatening for everyone: the "groupthink" and "indoctrination" Elkind sees as resulting from postmodern, market-based play are far from desirable for any children,[35] stripping the personal and educational value of play in favor of the uncritical acceptance of the commercial message and replacing personal introspection with the adoption of a simple consumer identity. Certainly, the generic truism that some people are more valuable than others—Woody is clearly *worth* more than Wheezy, who really could go for $0.25 in the garage sale—is a dangerous message for all. More urgent for boys, though, is the fact that the aggressive, competitive, market-based valuation of self and others has not separated from the other ways we value *men*, making "ornamental masculinity" just another contest by which boys must prove their manhood. "By the end of the American century," Faludi says, "every outlet of the consumer world—magazines, ads, movies, sports, music videos—would deliver the message that manhood had become a performative game to be won in the marketplace."[36] Similarly, though he is critical of the way Palahniuk's characters go about addressing these problems (with Neanderthal violence stemming from a presumably essentialist source), Giroux sees *Fight Club* as an illustration of the "crisis of capitalism . . . reduced to the crisis of masculinity," and masculinity a site on which "the violence of capitalism" becomes enacted.[37] Not just emptying the idea of masculinity of its traditional sources of social purpose and personal satisfaction and leaving it hollow, not rewriting masculine standards in terms of "economic capital" instead of "body capital" and the patriarchal traditions of the past, postmodern masculinity taps into the competitive nature of capitalism and superimposes the impossible standards of consumerism onto the already-impossible (essentialist) standards of hypermasculinity.

The ideological foundations of the adolescent bully society are identically paradoxical: the commodity is a necessary but not sufficient condition to a boy's social access and authority, since the commodified "ornamental" persona "draped over" the body does not hide but, on the contrary, is presumed to reveal its inborn authentic masculine authority. And this paradox, of course, is in the very spirit and image of the Disney formula. Nostalgia for "real man" essentialism coexists with the expectations of "economic capital" that demonstrate a successful male's material worth, just as the nostalgia for a time of American innocence coexists with Disney's corporate machinations.[38] The restrictiveness of gender essentialism and the rigorous policing of the hierarchies based thereon are not dismantled by consumerism but reinforced. What a boy *is* is not separate from the items a boy *displays*, so consumer power alone cannot compensate if who he *is* still doesn't measure up.

The Pixar übervillain is he who challenges the commodity and the ideology that gives it value. However he emerges—as the destructive Sid, the entrepreneurial Syndrome, the resourceful Randall, the Machiavellian Axlerod, or the simply obstructionist and unpopular Prospector—he is clearly the worst of foes to a company dependent on the perpetuation of postmodern consumerist ideologies to sell products and the identities that go along with them. But the ways in which his villainy is drawn—as predictably masculine failure—are telling. He lacks "social," "economic," and "body capital"—three of the crucial currencies of the bully society.[39] Sometimes even explicitly unfashionable (Syndrome's "so last year" cape, Randall's "lame" cupcake and uncool glasses), he lacks friends and allies; he also fails if in conflict with a hypermasculine hero. But he has intelligence and ability, so he represents the potential to circumvent the hierarchy by which he is "naturally" ranked low. Pixar's terrifying geek, in other words, with no natural claim to the upper echelons of the bully society, could yet threaten it by using his talents to manufacture the commodities, manipulate the market, and trick the consumers entirely complicit with an ideology of commodification into respecting him on false pretenses.

We could perhaps extend this one step further and fear the geek villains' potential power over the postmodern self. We might recognize our vulnerability on the level of basic consumption, as we depend on even dishonest (and infiltrated) markets for necessities like fuel, safety, and food. If we are our stuff, moreover, fraudulent and unethically produced products—pushed and twisted into the market by false and dishonest manufacturers—may work their ways into our very self-constructions, threatening us at the very foundation of our identity. Terrifying and uncontrollable—the postmodern face of evil—the enemy of the market must be stopped at all costs, so we can go back to buying the lovable, safe products at the Disney store, the toys that train us all to "play nice."

NOTES

1. Michael Kimmel, *Manhood in America: A Cultural History*, 3rd ed. (New York: Oxford University Press, 2012), chapter 1, "The Birth of the Self-Made Man."

2. Henry A. Giroux, *The Mouse That Roared: Disney and the End of Innocence* (Plymouth, England: Rowman & Littlefield, 1999), 25.

3. Giroux, *The Mouse That Roared,* 91.

4. Giroux, *The Mouse That Roared,* 35, 25.

5. Giroux, *The Mouse That Roared,* 91.

6. Giroux, *The Mouse That Roared,* 24, 23.

7. Charles Baudelaire, "A Philosophy of Toys" [1853], in *The Painter of Modern Life and Other Essays*, trans. J. Wayne (New York: Da Capo Press, 1964), 197.

8. David Elkind, *The Power of Play: Learning What Comes Naturally* (Cambridge, MA: Da Capo Press, 2007), 18; Susan Linn, *Consuming Kids: Protecting Our Children from the Onslaught of Marketing & Advertising* (New York: Anchor Books, 2005), 72.

9. Elkind, *The Power of Play* 24, 27.

10. Elkind, *The Power of Play*, 30.

11. Fredric Jameson, *Postmodernism, or, The Cultural Logic of Late Capitalism* (Durham, NC: Duke University Press, 1991), 275.

12. "Mutant Toys," n.p. Quoted also in Alan Ackerman, "The Spirit of Toys: Resurrection and Redemption in *Toy Story* and *Toy Story 2*," *University of Toronto Quarterly* 74, no 4 (2005): 896.

13. Brooks, *Consuming Innocence: Popular Culture and Our Children* (Brisbane: University of Queensland Press, 2010), 177.

14. Giroux, *The Mouse That Roared*, 94.

15. Eleanor Byrne and Martin McQuillan, *Deconstructing Disney* (Sterling, VA: Pluto Press, 2000), 127.

16. Eric Smoodin, *Disney Discourse: Producing the Magic Kingdom* (New York: Routledge, 1994), 18.

17. Giroux, *The Mouse That Roared*, 89.

18. Karl Marx, "The Fetishism of Commodities and the Secret Thereof," from *Capital* (1867), in *Marx and Engels Reader*, ed. Robert C. Tucker (New York: W. W. Norton), 319.

19. Marx, "The Fetishism of Commodities," 320.

20. Marx, "The Fetishism of Commodities," 321.

21. Keith Booker, *Disney, Pixar, and the Hidden Messages of Children's Films* (Westport, CT: Greenwood, 2010), 80.

22. Graham Huggan, *The Postcolonial Exotic: Marketing the Margins* (New York: Routledge, 2001), 18–19.

23. Huggan, *The Postcolonial Exotic*, 18.

24. In 1852, Marx argued that the Whigs were no better than the bourgeoisie, having assumed the exploitative position also held by the Tories. "The oldest, richest, and most arrogant portion of English landed property," he claims, "is the very nucleus of the Whig party," the party in practice standing for something quite opposite to their liberal principles. *New York Daily Tribune*, 21 August 1852, www.marxists.org/archive/marx/works/1852/08/06.htm. See also Jonathan Sperber, *Karl Marx: A Nineteenth-Century Life* (London; New York: W. W. Norton, 2013), 310. As a "McWhiggin," Al may certainly be seen as a descendent of the Whigs.

25. Linn, *Consuming Kids*, 66–68; Brooks, *Consuming Innocence*, 241.

26. Susan Faludi, *Stiffed: The Betrayal of the American Man* (New York: Harper Perennial, 2000), 34–35.

27. Henry A. Giroux, "Private Satisfactions and Public Disorders: *Fight Club*, Patriarchy, and the Politics of Masculine Violence," *Public Spaces and Private Lives: Democracy Beyond 9/11* (Lanham, MD: Rowman & Littlefield), 61.

28. Faludi, *Stiffed*, 34–35.

29. Giroux, "Private Satisfactions and Public Disorders," 61.

30. Faludi, *Stiffed*, 35.

31. Giroux, "Private Satisfactions and Public Disorders," 62.

32. Lynn M. Ta, "Hurt So Good: *Fight Club*, Masculine Violence, and the Crisis of Capitalism," *Journal of American Culture* 29, no. 3, (September 2006): 273–74.

33. Jessie Klein, *The Bully Society: School Shootings and the Crisis of Bullying in America's Schools* (New York: New York University Press, 2012), 163, 171.

34. Klein, *The Bully Society*, 171.

35. Elkind, *The Power of Play*, 28.

36. Faludi, *Stiffed*, 37.

37. Giroux, "Private Satisfactions and Public Disorders," 59.

38. Giroux, *The Mouse That Roared*, 23, 34–35.

39. Klein, *The Bully Society*, 25.

Chapter Six

"She don't love you no more"

Bad Boys and Worse Parents

Throughout this book we've discussed how the Pixar films speak one truth to their child viewers even as they perform another to the close reader of narrative and cinematic images. Be a progressive, caring man, they exhort, but with the "old school" traits of hypermasculinity and emotional restraint; be yourself, but you'll probably fail if you're too different from the norm. Know that you're Super but don't let anyone else see you behave in a manner outside the ordinary. Above all, be kind to the people around you, unless, of course, a lesser boy richly deserves to be forcibly returned to his place. Cultural critics and parents, we believe, need to look closely at these messages and frankly address the various messages they teach children, especially those entrenched ideological elements of American culture that persist though outdated, counterproductive, and even harmful to today's youth. As we've insisted throughout, along with numerous critics of culture and its trappings, Disney and other mainstream media corporations have enormous culture-shaping power, comprising a "public school" that, with or without our consent, teaches our children how to think about gender as well as other social codes and truisms.

But the films speak to adults, too. On one level, that fact is obvious, given the tongue-in-cheek jokes and allusions that have become a staple of modern children's film, those references that float almost imperceptibly over the heads of children too young to understand. Woody's "laser envy" invariably elicits at least a smirk. What's more troubling is that the subtextual cues we've pointed out as potentially significant to boy culture are often invisible to parents, who receive from them different but compatible messages to those absorbed by kids, tacit instructions on how to believe and behave as supportive adults. The films' insidious ideological messages to children, in other words, cloaked in pleasures that transcend generational divides, shape the same belief systems that inform contemporary American parenting: what successful, "good" boys look like, for instance, and what constitute appropriate responses to the supposed outliers. The paradoxical blend of nostalgia and commodification that we discussed in chapter 5 not only normalizes for kids a set of postmodern play behaviors, honoring a type of imaginative work that perpetuates commodity culture, but also teaches parents how to evaluate play, how to encourage certain acts and restrict others. In the contrast between Sid and Andy, the film shows us how to interpret and judge our own and others' children by their use of toys, even at the level of goodness and evil, and to see their engagement with commodities as indicative of their potential success or failure. The films unambiguously reinforce one type of play over another and silently encourage adults to promote it, possibly by buying the brand products that seem necessary to facilitate the desirable behaviors. In Buzz's delight at his own body's new model and Woody's unquestioned acceptance of his monetary value when mint, we are further taught how to satisfy our children's consumerist needs and how to determine their (and their peers') social value.

In many ways, the films are overt in their evaluation (and celebration) of parenting behaviors: Andy's very excellent mother can throw a birthday party in the middle of a move; Marlin earnestly endeavors to do right by his child while keeping him safe from the vast and terrifying sea; Mr. Frederickson is rejuvenated through the surrogate parenting of the child he was never lucky enough to have with his beloved Ellie. Even Sulley finds joy in the fulfillment of a fatherly duty to protect the young Boo. But on the flip side of these frequent and conspicuous homages to individual parent figures is a consistent critique of parenting at the turn of the twenty-first century. If not missing or dead, like Nemo's mom (and the other mothers in *Finding Nemo*), Pixar's parents may be absent presences, with specific gestures to their existence calling attention precisely to what they are not. Missing parents are nothing new in fairy tales—on the contrary, the dead mother trope is nearly uniform across the classic Disney features and its literary forerunners—but rather than using a parent's absence as the impetus to a hero's action or conflict, Pixar seems to critique the absence of "parent*ing*," a particular set of performed behaviors specifically geared toward the nurture of maturing children's emotional and physical wellness. The absence of such behaviors not only hurts individual children but also has a ripple effect on society at large: the children who lack access to an adult performing these behaviors, and performing them in a domestic setting that largely revolves around the child, become dangerous, bullies who pose a great risk to others. The narrative structure of the Pixar bully villain plot allows for a multiplicity of meanings to postmodern parents, but around them all hover contemporary conversations about how an arguably postfeminist world raises its boys. In complex ways and sometimes through apparently progressive gestures, they settle on a narrowly conventional model of domesticity.

PIXAR AND POSTMODERNISM

As we have discussed, the Pixar films are nearly all overtly nostalgic, offering adults the opportunity to fondly recollect their own childhood moments even as they chaperone their children through the films. The visual collage of historical artifacts from Andy's playroom to Radiator Springs' main streets to Monstropolis's fashions may remind parents and grandparents in the audience of their own halcyon childhood days, whenever they took place between the 1950s and the 1980s. As we watch our children watch, we are invited to recall our family's old black-and-white televisions, our small town's drive-in diner, or our very own Speak & Spells and Barbies, or, in true postmodern fashion, those cultural markers we *didn't* have that nonetheless still construct our nostalgic past. Indeed, it may be our own nostalgic pleasures with the texts and their visual pastiche that blind us to their messages about contemporary adulthoods, the way that Elizabeth Bell et al. argue that viewers' "pleasures and participation in Disney film" have often stunted all of our "critical faculties."[1] Lured by the pleasurable pull of the nostalgic, we watch the films as adults recalling childhood, imagining ourselves in times of innocence and ease, sentimentally responding to the icons of our individual and collective past(s).

At the same time, we watch the films as adults who may self-identify in relational and authoritative positions over small children: we are parents, grandparents, aunts, uncles, child care providers. As Thomas de Zengotita describes the midcentury spectatorial position of adult viewers of "family" television shows like *Leave It to Beaver*, we "watch the children from an adult point of view . . . indulging a nostalgic appreciation of childhood."[2] From this position, we may also enjoy the opportunity to identify with Pixar's recurring theme of time's inevitable passage. We're surely not the only parents who got choked up watching Andy prepare to go to college in *Toy Story 3*, and we suspect that more than a few of us reflected on our own perceived losses across a lifetime—losses of social value, of self-esteem, or of important human connections—while watching *The Incredibles* or *Up*. The films not only give adults those tongue-in-cheek jokes that aim conspiratorially over kids' heads to amuse both by their humor and their small moments of harmless departure from that near-constant attention we pay to our children's experiences, but also dwell on feelings and promote values to which we can be counted on to enthusiastically respond as adults—and moreover, as adults who attend children's films. As film after film winds down to its proclamation of the great duty and satisfaction of loving children, Pixar confidently preaches to the choir.

In both of these moments, it should be noted—in the nostalgic recollections of adults' childhoods and, perhaps just as sentimentally, in the poignant homages to the loving responsibilities of adulthood—adult viewers inhabit the same conscious identity. In both cases, we live consciously in the now. But these films are not simply sweet stories decorated with pieces of American popular-cultural history; they're postmodern texts by definition and practice. The anachronistic "history" of artifacts and images, uncritically blending genres and periods, exemplifies the "blank parody" that Fredric Jameson identified as pastiche.[3] The beloved "real" characters across the *Toy Story* trilogy even within their narrative constructs are simulacra, what Jameson describes as the "identical copy for which no original has ever existed."[4] Buzz, after all, is a replica of a cartoon used to market the replicas, and so on; Woody is a doll version of a puppet version of a narrative character, all the while being a narrative character. They appear even less tethered to historical reality when considered alongside the "real" representations that surround them, toys like Barbie and Slinkey Dog who, unlike the protagonists, have actual historical antecedents. The unproblematic coexistence of the represented past and the fictional representation of a past that never was, a feature of many of the films, creates the falsity that Jameson saw as characteristic of the postmodern nostalgia film, "an allusion to a present out of a real history which may as well be a past removed from real history."[5] Nor is it inadvertent, this effacement and repackaging of the historical to manipulate audience's sense of the real, often to the delight of the postmodern audience: most egregious, certainly, were the faux-"vintage" television ads for Lotso Huggin Bear Pixar circulated in advance of the 2010 release of *Toy Story 3*, complete with squiggles to approximate VHS tracking problems. The public response—from the ad world, from consumers—was incredulous delight at the "clever," "cool," and accurate creation of a history that 1980s kids could "kinda sorta" remember.[6]

As postmodern texts, these films speak to adults in the way that postmodern texts do, with what de Zengotita calls "identificational child-centeredness." While children's tales have exercised the ability to speak to both adult and child for as long as we've had literary fairy tales, it is a quintessentially postmodern tendency of the text to construct the adult as an adult and child simultaneously.[7] As "the distinction between child and adult begins to blur," across the second half of the twentieth-century, de Zengotita says, adults increasingly engage with children's texts as the children they still are, coincident with their adult identities, reading not as nostalgic adults but becoming "kids again" in the consumption of the texts.[8] Rather than (simply) reconstructing *Leave it to Beaver*'s wise, amused, and fondly condescending adult position, using de Zengotita's examples, we all become Bart and Lisa Simpson, seeing adults as absurd, deeply flawed, and unable to convey meaningful messages about a fundamentally meaningless world.[9] Contemporary children's media situates parents in a multifaceted position, replete with "options," as de Zengotita notes, and broadcasting messages to the specifically postmodern parent across multiple channels at the same time. In the Pixar tales, nostalgia and celebration and instruction—and this dual spectatorial position of adult and child—combine to shape the way we see the world and our role in it.

THE CHANGING ROLE OF THE ADULT IN TALES FOR CHILDREN

Pixar's tales, though perhaps not "fairy tales" in the strictest structural sense of the term, follow in a long tradition of tales told for the edification and entertainment of children; most conspicuously, they are connected to traditional stories by their immediate ancestor, the classic Disney films that so famously remade fairy tales for a twentieth-century audience. Just as Disney parted ways with Grimm, however, and as the Grimm brothers changed the source material from which they drew, so too is the postmodern children's tale fundamentally changed in social role and function from older folktales. The character of the villain—the quantity and nature of his or her development—has also evolved over time. Furthermore, and significant though less often noted, the rhetorical and psychic position of the postmodern adult in the storytelling situation concurrently shifted, with complementary consequences on the social function of the tale.

Originally orally and communally presented, the earliest folktales were shared with an audience of peers by a physically present storyteller, the narrator of the stories an actual person known and trusted as a member of the community to which he was speaking.[10] This teller's audience included adult listeners who themselves could participate in the rhetorical exchange. According to Maria Tatar, the folkloric audience shared in the story— "work[ing] in concert" with the teller, collaboratively revising the stories that grew to become their community's "unique oral narrative traditions . . . imbu[ed] with their own particular mores and values."[11] The narratives themselves were told by a narrator speaking with the voice of the community, as it were, adult auditors being not passive recipients of the tale but participants in the telling. In these early tales, villains often served as markers of the community's mores and typically functioned as narrative obstacles to the hero's progress, adversaries to the heroes in fairly simple binary relationships.[12] As folktales celebrated the rites and traditions of the community, established its mores and values, and explained natural phenomena, villains often took the form of hyper-natural creatures (wolves and monsters) or metaphysical entities (evil witches), signifying primarily as the personification of an exception that proved the community's rules, primarily by contrast to the tale's hero and his or her journey.

When fairy tales began to be written down and published, becoming part of an "institutionalized" literary tradition in the late-seventeenth and early eighteenth centuries, Jack Zipes notes, they were written for adults, who, as readers, were displaced from a position of meaningful participation in the development of the story or the social extension of the storytelling. The inked-in narrative voice, rather than being a peer in the community and open to collaboration, became increasingly authoritative, both by being inscribed and by being bought, sold, and enjoyed among the literate classes, rather than commonly rehearsed.[13] The very act of reading, fundamentally more private and passive than collaborative participation in a public audience of a storyteller, separated the tales from their earlier community function. "Loss of live contact with the storyteller," says Zipes, eroded the "sense of community" traditionally inherent in the folk tale.[14]

The norming function of the literary fairy tale remained, if gradually more superficially, as the subject matter of the tales written for adult readers still endorsed particular social beliefs and practices, but the society they informed narrowed to that of court civility and manners. By the nineteenth century, as literary fairy tales became more and more tailored to audiences of children,[15] they focused these messages of civilized life onto the experiences of children. Sanitized, overtly moralistic, they became an "institution in middle class societies," says Zipes,[16] designed to domesticate infantile wildness. The Grimm brothers, who Tatar sees as occupying a liminal space between the folktale and the truly "literary" fairy tale, saw themselves as publishing a "manual of manners."[17] The fairy tales themselves became more obviously satisfying to children, happy endings providing closure and optimism, but they remained rigidly patriarchal and largely faithful to hegemonic class notions like the moral progression from rags to riches. In these adult-delivered tales for kids, children were often the heroes, while villains became archetypal exaggerations of adults. If still metaphysical—magic, evil, or monstrously animalistic—and still structural antagonists by and large, villains of the nineteenth-century literary tales often came in the form of evil adults and unnatural parents, as the "nuclear family furnishes the fairy tale's main cast of characters just as family conflict constitutes its most common subject."[18]

The reading experience of the adult thus shifted again, as the adult was further displaced: no longer collaborator with the oral storyteller, and no longer intended audience for the inscribed narrator, the adult's rhetorical function shifted to a kind of spokesperson or mediator. The adult delivered the story. By the twentieth century, as de Zengotita notes, the tale had adapted to accommodate its "bifurcated" audience, offering separate pleasures for children and the "loving but jaded" adults presumed to be reading to them.[19] *Peter Pan*, in de Zengotita's example, "break[s] down the fourth wall in a way calculated to amuse the adult without alienating the child," acutely but good-naturedly exposing childhood for its utter self-absorption and accidental cruelties.[20] Early twentieth-century children's literature, he notes, features "a continuum of possibilities for responding and understanding from the sophisticated adult for whom the whole apparatus is laid bare, to the very youngest listener, innocently involved in the story."[21] Certainly, children's literature and film still speaks directly, and often wittily, to adults in ways that children don't (or shouldn't) understand: the favorite joke of Lightning's Rust-Eze sponsors, for example, voiced by the Magliozzi brothers from NPR's "Car Talk," prompts Lightning to admit that he doesn't have headlights, "because the track is always lit," so that one brother can laughingly call the other a drunk: "So's my brother, but he still needs headlights!"

Still, none of these forms of fairy tales "made any concession to what it was like to be a child," the gesture de Zengotita notes as the defining feature of postmodern children's literature like Maurice Sendak's *Where the Wild Things Are*. In an increasingly "child-centered" postmodern world, he argues, rather than serving as vessels for meanings that originate from adult perspectives, providing socially valuable lessons narrated by and delivered through the hands of adults, for the chief purpose of instructing the child in the norms of his or her society, texts become mirrors, reflecting children's perspectives back to them.[22] Sendak's classic, as de Zengotita reads it, validates Max's unreasonable anger and potential for aggression, walking him through his temper to the point of exhaustion rather than toward some lesson, as in the older tales. Once his fit has subsided, Max may return home to his dinner, but no particular social behavior is enforced by the threat of real danger. No voice speaks conspiratorially to the adult reader about how difficult children can be. On the contrary, says de Zengotita, the book invites us all to recognize the unrepentant id within, those extreme feelings that "burst upon us when we get angry or upset, that explode, that assault us from within," those feelings that, while universal, can be "a very scary fact of life for all of us."[23] He calls this shift in perspective "identificational child-centeredness," signifying the absorption of the child's thoughts and feelings into the adult's mind.[24] As children's media becomes a "fusion of sensibilities," de Zengotita explains, adult readers simply "get to be kids again if [they] feel like it."[25]

Animated film versions of fairy tales and other children's stories, clearly monopolized by Disney at the onset of the "fusion" de Zengotita observes, changed the rhetorical situation of storytelling further by its conversion to a visual medium. The narrative presence of the cinematic tale, such as it is, remains authoritative and even further displaces the adult reader of the literary fairy tale who, after all, is no longer even required to deliver the words of a written narrative. As Zipes explains, "The voice in fairy-tale films is at first effaced so that the image totally dominates the screen, and the words or narrative voice can only speak through the designs of the animator."[26] As the private experience of reading gives way to "pleasurable viewing in an impersonal cinema," the tales may seem to return to a public sphere but do so without reclaiming their former communal characteristics; stories are shared again but without being in any way participatory.[27] Early animators, says Zipes, "appropriated literary and oral fairy tales to subsume the word, to have the final word.[28] As a result, animated fairy tales represent less a community's collective moral voice, informing its shared norms and codes, than a showplace for artists, less a medium for "social edification" than "diversion."[29]

Of course, tales didn't stop teaching when they were converted to film. de Zengotita asserts that "anything a modern adult produces for children is going to teach a lesson of some kind," and cultural texts are now frequently examined for their "pedagogical" impact.[30] But the authoritative voice of the narrative, which through cinema circumvents its former adult intermediary, may speak now for its artists and the corporations who employ them. Rather than asking the community what values should be taught, the corporation teaches the community those lessons that work in its favor. Animated films, while progressing through amazing technological innovations to become spectacular artistic utterances, have also become big-budget commodities that must serve corporate interests in order to survive. The mechanical reproduction of the animated film—all its pleasures projected onto collective but relatively passive audiences—also requires (or enables) an aestheticization of politics that Henry Giroux and others have critiqued: to keep mainstream audiences happy, Giroux says, Disney has beautified historical ugliness, glossed over important social controversies, and exaggerated or elided differences as needed to maintain the generally uncritical enjoyment of its viewership.[31]

Perhaps parents' conscious roles and responsibilities should have changed alongside this shift in the delivery of our stories. Evolving from the ones who participated to the ones who read, we probably ought to have then evolved to the ones critically discerning enough to see the embedded social messages and complicate them if necessary: the "adult advocates" that Tatar maintains we could be if we returned collaboration to the storytelling situation.[32] As countless scholars have noted, we haven't. We persist under the films' "spell," the pleasures that blind us.[33]

Where are the adult readers of cinematic tales, if we neither create nor read nor advocate? The villains have become increasingly three-dimensional, partly, no doubt, from Disney's extension of short stories to feature-length films, and, as we've discussed, much of this growth has been from villainy's metaphysical and archetypal roots to exaggerations of adult values like jealousy, ambition, greed, and vengeance. It's possible, then, that postmodern adult viewers simply identify with the villains. The branding of the Disney villains, complete with a "My Side of the Story" line of children's books that afford the villains rival narratives to their cinematic counterparts', suggests that some viewers have indeed chosen this ironic posture. de Zengotita's notion of "identificational child-centeredness," however, offers us a more comprehensive way of seeing adult viewers' multifaceted spectatorial positions. As *Where the Wild Things Are* speaks to readers of all ages about the terrors of our barely containable emotions, these films too situate parents alongside their children. Edged out of a distinct role in the storytelling process—neither collaborators, nor intended audience, nor readers complicit with an adult narrative voice—postmodern adult viewers occupy the vantage point of the child, instead of, or while, also reflecting on the film from an adult perspective. "The kid and the grownup are simultaneously addressed," says de Zengotita. "You are the one they are for."[34] In Disney films, with their foundations in "innocence" and their frequent domestic and familial plots, we may especially conflate childhood with adulthood. Indeed, adults' tendency to do so may be revealed by the commercial life of the corporation beyond the films, as lifelong brand loyalty spawns things like Disney-themed weddings and honeymoons, events that fuse the branded icons of childhood with ancient social rites of passage into adulthood (rites customarily intended for people who don't have children yet).

Moreover, and more importantly, parents viewing from the vantage points of children are uncritical readers of film. With its many nostalgic pleasures and its many overt concessions to parents, the position of the postmodern adult viewer in Pixar is yet complicated by this tendency to read as child and adult simultaneously. With messages about parents and children firing on multiple levels, the films create a unique critique of postmodern parenting.

THE BULLY PLOT AND POSTMODERN PARENTING

In Pixar, as we've noted earlier, villains have evolved yet further, creating occasions for multiple meaningful messages, varying according to the identificational position of the viewer. Many of the films lack a clear villain, offering structural obstacles in the form of relatively harmless characters: it is the Honorable Doc Hudson, not the trash-talking Chick Hicks, who impedes Lightning's forward movement in the first *Cars* film, for example, but while he makes no bones about his prejudice against upstart race cars, it is his obligation to the law that precipitates his obstructionist narrative role. More often, these antagonistic characters are superficially marked as negative for easier legibility to children, even if they remain relatively innocuous. Al McWhiggin, while dishonest at a sort of shoplifting level, might seem to an adult as suffering more from poor impulse control than pure evil but is easily enough read by kids as bad; Nemo's dentist, blissfully ignorant that his capture of the young fish was anything but a favor, is nonetheless the path to the terrifying "fish-killer," his niece. Charles Muntz, though far scarier than these, being more capable and more blinded by ambition and resentment, still would never have harmed anyone (save Kevin the bird, perhaps) if left to himself in the jungle. Only occasionally is a Pixar villain comparable to classic Disney's exaggeratedly adult evil figures—*Monsters, Inc.*'s Water-noose is half-greed, half-pride, though far more shadowy a figure than Cruel-la or the others, letting his minions do the dirty work of cinematic villainy. In the films that do feature a character widely understood as villainous, though, the construction of villainy is less frequently the personification of adult wickedness than a hurt, smart child defying the hegemonic social order: a damaged kid turned bully. This too gestures toward postmodern values as de Zengotita describes them, illustrating our cultural conviction in the blameless "inner life" of the child and our subsequent tendency to judge "inappropri-ate" behavior or reactions instead of moral character.[35] But as we've dis-cussed elsewhere, Pixar's bully villains all go unforgiven, despite their very apparent inner lives and their unsurprising, if not justifiable, acting out.

Pixar's failure to deconstruct the hierarchy that informs the bully society, and the quiet glorification of bully behaviors and attitudes when performed by the protagonists of films like *Cars 2*, reveal the films' awareness of how bullies behave. The films accurately depict their villains' behavior as bully-ing—in *Toy Story 3*, even identifying it as such by name—and the social tensions that often give rise to bullying situations. Though there is not a legal definition of bullying that extends nationwide, most experts see it as repeated aggressive behavior characterized by an imbalance of power. In schools, kids called bullies are those who use their social and/or physical power to control or harm those of lower status and, by doing so, to elevate their own. "In other words," according to Emily Bazelon, author of *Sticks and Stones: Defeating the Culture of Bullying and Rediscovering the Power of Character and Em-pathy*, "it's about one person with more social status lording it over another person, over and over again, to make him miserable."[36]

Sid Phillips, though frequently read as a bully, doesn't actually fit this definition by virtue of the strange ontological structure of his film—in the reality he can perceive, he doesn't seem to strive for social status or threaten anyone at all—but the hierarchal position he holds over the films' toy protag-onists, and the fear he uses it to inspire, might reasonably enough suggest bullying. Better examples are Syndrome, who is desperate to advance his status and hurts many others in his endeavors to do so, and Hopper, whose threatening if occasional presence controls the lives and livelihoods of every-one in Ant Island. The scariest bully in the Pixar filmography is surely Lotso Huggin' Bear, the lord of the daycare whom Jessie actually calls "bully" for his reign of tyranny and terror. In what may be the ultimate Pixar pastiche—*Toy Story 3* an homage to many a prison-break film—Lotso's ruthless control over Sunnyside is that of a mob boss or a wicked warden. One expects any moment he's going to make someone an offer he or she can't refuse. Determined to stay in power and to secure the cushiest jobs for his cronies, he forces or coerces others into serving his interests and performs the violent acts permissible in a children's film: he rips off Mrs. Potato Head's mouth, confines and surveils the daycare's toy residents, and insists on strict adherence to his rules, punishing offenses with a night "in the [sand]box."

As well as understanding how bullies act, Pixar also seems to have a strong and clear opinion on how bullies are made. The Pixar films are different from the older tales, even through the classic Disney films across the twentieth century, in that the bully villain is himself a narrative product, a constructed self rather than an essentialist personification of evil traits. Syndrome, the Prospector, Lotso—even, very subtly, Hopper—are literal or figurative orphans, their lives navigated on their own after deeply felt losses. Hopper's mother is dead, and he resents the role he's forced to play with regard to his brother. The Prospector has never had a parent at all, living his life in the figurative orphanage of a dime store watching all the other toy/children be bought/adopted. Buddy's mother may still exist as her boy matures into the faux-Super Syndrome, if she ever existed at all (Mr. Incredible tells a policeman to "make sure [she] knows what he's been up to," but she never appears in the film and it's unlikely that Mr. Incredible knows much about the child's home life), but he has asked explicitly for the nurture and care of his idol (and father figure) Mr. Incredible and has been summarily rebuffed. He expresses his anger in specifically family-oriented rhetoric years later when he has the chance to confront Mr. Incredible. Delighting in hurting his now-nemesis by (apparently) killing his real family, then taunting the couple for "[getting] busy" and having children of their own, he finally resorts to kidnapping the baby Jack-Jack, proposing to nurture the child himself: "You took away my future," he tells Mr. Incredible. "I'm simply returning the favor. Oh, don't worry—I'll be a good mentor—supportive, encouraging, everything you weren't." His bullying behavior is unambiguously linked to his lack of parental support.

In the real world, too, bullying has been tied to parenting: kids at risk for becoming bullies may lack parental involvement, parental warmth, and parental supervision.[37] Compared with their fairy tale roots, then, Pixar's villains are realistic and timely. Neither monstrous, metaphysical antagonists setting parameters for socially appropriate attitudes and behaviors nor hyperbolic personifications of sinful adult transgressions, Pixar's bad guys reflect a specific—and pressing—social issue of their time. As they draw their clear causality between an unhappy childhood and a bully villain, they construct the urgent problem of bullying as a largely familial error.

Once the beloved toy of the very young Daisy, Lotso Huggin' Bear's life has changed irreparably by the time we encounter him at the Sunnyside Daycare. In a flashback narrated by Chuckles the Clown, we see Daisy, having fallen asleep at a family picnic, being carried back to her parents' car, as Lotso, Chuckles, and Big Baby are left behind. By the time the toys find their way back to their child, her parents have bought her a replacement Lotso. Immediately enraged at this discovery, our Lotso just as immediately enacts bullying behaviors. Ripping off Big Baby's Daisy pendant, he figuratively renders the (cognitively much younger, if larger) toy an orphan too and projects his own feelings of abandonment on the baby doll, sneering, "She don't love you no more." He doesn't perform physical violence, but it is clear enough that he is trying to lower his victim's status in an effort to feel less worthless himself, to establish a power differential by which he can feel superiority and exercise control. His behavior is awful, obviously: deliberately hurting the younger child's feelings because his own feelings are hurt is thoughtless and cruel. It's also not incomprehensible, and maybe not unforgivable, given the suddenness and depth of his pain and the lack of other obvious avenues for expressing it. No one is there to help Lotso navigate the complex feelings of abandonment, distrust, and fear for the future, perhaps even responsibility to the other toys as Woody no doubt would have felt, as the favorite toy and thus authority figure in the playroom. Dan Kindlon and Michael Thompson have well documented the difficulty that many boys and men have finding emotional outlets other than anger and withdrawal, given the masculine norms by which they are socialized.[38] If Lotso had been taught a healthier way of working through his emotions, he might not have instantaneously and irrevocably turned bully before our eyes. But then he wouldn't be an unparented child in the first place, left alone to find his way.

Lotso's early life would seem to hold the capacity to undermine viewers' hatred and fear by introducing sympathy. Indeed, there is no other cause for his wickedness and no confusion whatsoever about the causality between his childhood hurt and his mistreatment of others. Yet even the sympathetic back story of the failed parent doesn't allow Lotso to be forgiven, any more than such a story helped Syndrome or Axlerod to be understood, as we have described earlier. Like the other bully villain films, *Toy Story 3* allows the villain's sad narrative to be told and then largely ignored, the back story remaining just present enough to explain the villain's behavior but not to materially affect the outcome of the plot or even the consciousness (or consciences) of any of the characters. "Something snapped," says Chuckles, "[and] he wasn't anyone's friend [anymore]." "Inside he's a monster," echoes Buttercup (who, incidentally, has never met him). When Woody, the undeniable moral compass of the entire trilogy, has the opportunity to reason with Lotso, he begins gently enough by correcting the very interpretation of events that seems to cause Lotso the greatest pain: she didn't reject him,

Woody clarifies, "she lost [him]." But when Lotso retorts, swapping Woody's verb with the more cutting *replaced*, Woody quickly switches back into simplistic antagonism. Instead of explaining how a small child's parents might have replaced her beloved but absent toy in order to help alleviate her sadness, encouraging Lotso to practice empathy, to forgive Daisy, to reassess his own damaged sense of self-worth, and to move on with his life, Woody gets personally insulting, adding to the bear's sense of worthlessness and isolating him even from the cronies with whom he shares his tragic past. Daisy didn't replace all of them, Woody insists: "She replaced *you*." This exchange reminds viewers of Lotso's painful past, but the primary rhetorical effects of Woody's remark are to expose his deceit and to get Big Baby on their side, not to reach out to Lotso as a fellow toy in pain. Later, when he chooses to rescue Lotso from the trash heap, any sympathy Woody might have for the lonely bear does not factor in. He seems motivated only by the kind of generic goodness displayed in weekly installments of *Woody's Roundup* and the inability to sit by while another toy—any toy—dies a horrible death. No one—not even Jessie, who has her own version of this narrative from *Toy Story 2*—reads Lotso's back story toward a productive empathy for the abandoned child.

Nor is the audience encouraged toward such an empathic reading. The narrative turn that seems to disallow forgiveness is augmented by the bully's immediate threat level to others. Woody reminds viewers less how Lotso was hurt than how he hurt Big Baby, so that we can substitute our remaining pity for unadulterated contempt. All of Pixar's bully villains cross a similarly visible line, as if to obliterate any remaining sentimentality. Whatever their past pains and crimes, in a crucial present moment they publicly threaten or harm others, often the most vulnerable of the characters. Syndrome's "termination" of many of the remaining Supers has happened between the acts and is coolly enough presented to Mr. Incredible and the audience via database field, but he goes too far when he jeopardizes the Parr baby right in front of his family and everyone. Axlerod's deceit and plotting has gone on for years, and the nameless, faceless racers destroyed in wide-angle shots and television clips demonstrate his badness, but a ticking bomb right on Mater's wide-eyed, guileless face means that our dear Radiator Springs familiar could explode before our very eyes. Similarly, Lotso has been controlling everyone around him for some time, but when we see Big Baby's sadness at the exposure of his years-long betrayal—"Mama," he whimpers, his only line in the film—his visible pain marks a decisive moment. By turning his force on the youngest of the crew, Lotso lets his present behaviors drown out his sad past.

That Pixar refuses to forgive or reform its bullies, even as the films provide narrative evidence of their being made and not born, even as the films make visible their childhood pain and isolation, is a problem in its own right, lending support to an unproductive tendency to discard so-called "bullies" as lost causes. Bazelon sees the "stigma" of the label as a counterproductive feature of the current rhetoric surrounding bullying, and not just because its overuse flattens out the distinctions between a variety of children's interactions. Such a reduction from child to label, and sometimes from deeply suffering child to simplistically negative label, she says, "makes a child seem permanently heartless, rather than capable of feeling empathy."[39] If we wish to solve the problem of bullying, the answer is more empathy, not just more discipline, and more systemic critique, not scapegoating. "If you zero in only on the personal flaws of the kids caught up in bullying . . . you miss the way they respond to the environments they find themselves in," Bazelon claims, and then challenges: "How can families and schools dismantle . . . [this] system?"[40] The Pixar films capitalize on current anxieties about bullying, but rather than contribute to this project of dismantling the structures that enable it, they perform the very counterproductive oversimplification and scapegoating that Bazelon warns against. There is a terrible irony in our collective withholding of caring feelings for one child while reiterating the myth that it is he who is unfeeling.

PIXAR'S POSTFEMINIST ANTIFEMINISM

The narrative construct of the bully villain works for something, though, just not dismantling the structures that perpetuate bullying. The films' refusal to forgive their badly parented (former) children for bullying not only exiles and punishes the bullies but ensures that parents can't be let off the hook either. If bullying behavior is both the unpardonable sin of the child and the responsibility of the parent who failed him, then both parties pose a risk to society and its innocent children. Thoughtless moms like Daisy, selfish father figures like Mr. Incredible, and absent-present parents like Sid Phillips's, napping and toasting fatty snacks but providing no emotional support or supervision, are only one step removed from doing harm to other, innocent children: ours. Though "family" is constructed in a number of unconventional ways across the Pixar canon, particularly with the presence of single and surrogate fathers like Mr. Frederickson, it appears as the one necessary condition to bully prevention. In keeping with what Giroux notes about Disney's tendency to sanitize controversy for the conservative maintenance of "innocence" and its pedagogical power, the structure of the bully narrative privileges a conventional, middle-class ideology of parenting over any productive critique of educational and social meaning-making institutions. Bullies come from bad homes, the films demonstrate, displacing the problem and dodging the complexity of the issue, leaving untroubled the ideological underpinnings of Jesse Klein's "bully economy" and other contributing factors.

In *Toy Story 3*, bully culture is explicitly opposed to family, after Lotso invites Andy's toys to consider returning to the Sunnyside "family": "This isn't a family," retorts Jessie. "It's a prison." Familial roles may be performed by people with no natural relation—Andy's toys see themselves as a family, for which identification Buzz is mocked as a "family man"—but the work of a family can only be done at home. Unlike countless fairy-tale heroes whose missing moms compel a journey to self-sufficiency, honor, or rescue, Pixar's children simply cannot thrive without active and attentive parent figures. No late-in-life redemption is possible; no school system or peer group affords another path to peace and successful maturation. Even a high-quality daycare full of teachers, children, and toys can never help the irreversibly "snapped" Lotso to grow into a healthy adult mindset. Nothing but good parenting can ever diminish the risk that a potential bully poses to others. As Klein and numerous others have demonstrated, though, bullying is not the problem of a few bad families; it ideologically underpins the central social institution of American children's lives. In view of their function as sites of socialization as well as individual growth, schools recognize that they are the default location for bully prevention efforts, but they cannot do it alone and certainly not without widespread support and reinforcement. In truth, as Bazelon notes, any widely successful response to the systemic problem(s) of bullying will have to be far more complex than this, involving "teenagers, parents, teachers, counselors, principals, police, lawmakers, Internet entrepreneurs, and engineers."[41] The view from Pixar, though, indicating that bullying is a narrative entirely enclosed within the family structure, sees no hope for children of bad parents and, perhaps more importantly, no possible solution other than good parenting.

Those endangered others—those from "good" homes—are just as unproblematically drawn as innocent, separate from any larger system in which bully behaviors thrive. This binary oversimplification is why it is so easy to see Woody as being purely defensive against Lotso and not spiteful to the already-suffering toy, why Mater and the rest of the Radiator Springs crowd are justified, not vicious, in their correction of the Lemons, why Sulley's treatment of the young Mike Wazowski reveals his personal pain even more than that he inflicts. Giroux likens Disney's sanitization of history to an "affirmation of a Norman Rockwell painting," arguing that its "manage[ment] [of] exoticism" has worked to "cancel out diversity," and its reinforcement of a comfortable consumerist culture legitimates the beliefs and tendencies of "the relatively affluent middle class who are their patrons."[42] Similarly, Pixar spins boy culture to comfort the comfortable. Exteriorizing and simplifying the bully villain to the product of bad parents, we are rewarded with a singular model of safe and happy American childhood.

Parental anxieties are compounded by the postmodern structure of the cinematic experience for adult viewers of children's tales. The multiple messages absorbed by the adult in the passive and fluid spectatorial position de Zengotita describes yield numerous simultaneous interpretations. As caretakers ourselves, adult viewers may accept blame or at least acknowledge the enormous responsibility for raising happy and well-socialized children, seeing ourselves as materially contributing to youth culture. (Any internet-savvy mom knows how postmodern discourses of parenting traffic in guilt.) Parent viewers may also unconsciously convert this guilt or responsibility into blame directed toward other parents: we are the ones, after all, taking our children to the movies and/or buying them DVDs. Since we can blame bully children in the same breath as we blame their bad parents, we may be disinclined to feel accountable to them, leading to a denial of civic responsibility beyond our homes. This resistance may be enhanced by the fact that, watching as child viewers ourselves, we too fear the bully villain—and, moreover, watching as parents and children simultaneously, we fear them on behalf of our children. The films encourage the sense that our primary—indeed, our exclusive—duty is protecting our own. Unredeemable anyway, other people's children are certainly not worth any risk to us, if those chiefly responsible for them (as we are our own kids) have failed in their sacred duties.

Our other concern about Pixar's bully plots has to do with their reinforcement of a traditionally gendered family shape, even among makeshift or surrogate families. In a world where parenting duties are being assigned to—and enjoyed by—fathers, these family values plots still often task mothers and fathers with quite different roles, and these traditional tendencies quietly contribute to contemporary conversations about how our arguably postfeminist age is failing its boys. How necessary are fathers to raising boys? Can women succeed on their own? Do career women selfishly sacrifice their children's well-being for professional success and personal satisfaction? Is feminism itself the reason for crises in masculine identities of all ages? Books, articles, blogs, and a wide range of other media, from conservative advice manuals to scholarly analyses of sociological and educational data, argue vehemently on every aspect of these questions, invoking religion, politics, and/or socioeconomic information to situate the problems of boyhood in relation to current trends in parenting. Some of the most stridently antifeminist groups doggedly argue that women simply can't raise boys to be good men, for the simple fact that they are not men themselves and thus cannot set the examples of masculinity that good men will follow; from the same end of the political spectrum comes the paradoxical claim that women ought not leave the home either, as if women are necessary but insufficient to raising strong and successful men. Nonprofit organizations cite evidence from educational research to promote fatherhood, encouraging men to embrace domestic responsibilities by measuring their necessity while delicately avoiding any comment on mothers' abilities; advocates for single mothers challenge any and all data that suggest women cannot compensate if circumstances so dictate. Writers steeped in the philosophies of feminism cite yet more data to suggest that the quality of a child's parenting matters more than the gender of the parents, carving out space for adoptive single mothers and lesbian families. Each and all of these positions, unsurprisingly, inspire public outrage from one quarter or another. The one thing we do know is that the questions seem timely and significant. [43]

Pixar's endorsement of a spectrum of dads makes a resounding affirmative contribution to one current conversation, at least. From the figurative adoption of Russell to the single parenting of Nemo to the homosocial co-parenting of Andy, fathers are crucial to the successful raising of boys. In the opening chapter of this book, we argued that a midcentury homesteader model of masculinity—Daniel Boone and Sheriff Woody himself—showcases the satisfactions of fatherhood, and throughout the entire Pixar canon, fatherhood is similarly championed. Sulley, Doc Hudson, Mr. Frederickson, Crush, Gil, even the Emperor Zurg demonstrate fathering behaviors and its many pleasures. If biological fathers aren't strictly necessary, no happy and successful boy lacks a loving father figure.

Unhappy, delinquent boys do. Mothers alone, it seems, can't do the job. Buddy's mother is invoked in Mr. Incredible's instructions to the cops, but never makes an appearance as one who parents, and the absence of his (never-mentioned) father leaves the boy to go looking for a father-figure on his own. When his Super idol rejects him, his mother can't compensate. Either she isn't there to prevent him from "snapping" when such a search proves fruitless, or her presence is insufficient. Russell lives the same story to a more successful conclusion; with a barely-there mom who can't fill the gap left by his divorced, remarried, and perpetually absent father, he too must find his own surrogate dad. Luckily for him, though, Mr. Frederickson responds in time. Andy's mom seems to be the obvious exception to this rule, but she has the silent help of a masculine playroom staff: Buzz and Woody even talk about their "job" of raising Andy to maturity and whether, in *Toy Story 3*, their "duty" is done when he leaves for college. Mothers, sisters, school—even camp and Scouts—cannot fulfill a boy's need for a caring man and mentor.

If children are to be successfully nurtured, then, mothers must have the help of men; unfortunately, even with it, they must occupy retrograde domestic roles. Even with all these great dads around to share caretaking responsibilities with the strong and capable women Pixar has drawn, there is nothing to alleviate the domestic pressures of traditional at-home mothering. As we discussed in a previous article, Pixar's celebrations of fatherhood might be seen as postfeminist, as they expand traditional masculine roles to include emotionally satisfying homosocialities and kinder, gentler communal and familial orientations for men. Though in the first chapter of this book we consider that, with a longer historical view, Pixar's masculinities may be more old-fashioned than at first they appear, and that the ubiquity of such messages might be restrictive for little boys in an already overly conformist world, we admittedly take pleasure in this glorification of dads. Men stepping up to provide loving presences in boys' lives—and male characters standing as examples of such caretaking to boys who too seldom have male elementary teachers or other childcare providers—meet with our hearty approbation. But if this is a male version of a postfeminist world, it isn't a world where feminism has made much progress for women. Women can be professionally successful spinsters like Edna Mode, but if they don't *both* benefit from the assistance of men *and* assume a primarily domestic orientation to life, they simply cannot raise a child well.

The idealization of an old-fashioned two-parent heteronormative home and the domestic wife and mother who lives there suggests not a postfeminist picture of parenting but an anti-feminist one. As *Toy Story 3* ends, we enjoy the heteronormative coupling of Jessie and her newly Latin lover Buzz, and, in epilogue fashion, see Barbie and Ken as adoptive parents to Big Baby: everybody is happy once paired up and raising a family. More dramatically, successful heteronormative parenting resolves the film's very climactic tension, as Mr. and Mrs. Potato Head's adopted alien triplets save them all from the hellish incinerator. "My boys!" shouts Mr. Potato Head, to which they reply in unison, "Daddy!" These nuclear families depend on mother and father alike, but with or without men, Pixar's good women are those whose primary function is to support their families. Andy's mom is always present in her children's home, even without any visible means of financial support. Though in the third film she knows Bonnie's mom, who works at the day care, there is nothing to suggest that Andy or Molly ever attended there, nor has there ever been any obvious need, and Andy's departure for college is a credit to her efforts. Her only wish is to be "always with [him]," as he moves through life. The other films, too, only cast domestically inclined mothers in a positive light. Helen Parr seems to have happily given up her career for her kids, despite how much she obviously enjoyed crime-fighting before they were born. Having sidelined her own high-powered career, Sally now has time to serve as both mother figure and love interest to Lightning. She still works, not only as the occasional town attorney but also by running the Cozy Cone Motel, where her job by definition provides the comforts of home, but of course, in a harmonious little town with no tourism, she doesn't actually have to perform either job's duties very often. Bonnie's mom, like Sally, works, but in a traditionally feminine job at Sunnyside and, as an added perk, she never even needs to leave her child to perform it.

This lovely rendering of the domestic woman is further underscored by contrast: mothers who aren't fully present in the home fail, and fail spectacularly, with dramatic repercussions for the greater society. This too, if subtly, participates in the rhetorical clamor of late feminism about successful childrearing, wherein working moms have been "besieged" by judgment and criticism.[44] Buddy's absent-present mother has indirectly caused havoc on Municiberg and the death of countless Supers; Sid's mother, known only by a voice ("Your pop tart is ready!" she bellows, while her unsupervised son "tortures toys" in his multiply padlocked lair at the top of the stairs), has similarly put untold numbers of toys at risk. While the young Daisy clearly couldn't help losing Lotso any more than Nemo's mom could help getting eaten by a barracuda, she seems to bear responsibility for the "monster" Lotso grows up to be: even Woody's syntactical construction blames her for hurting Lotso, not her parents' indulgence or Lotso's codependence or the commodity culture that made Lotso an infinitely replaceable brand product in the first place. Jessie's "mom," Emily, also had other things to do—like grow up—and thus caused unspeakable heartache, undiluted even over the years between *Toy Story 2* and the end of the trilogy.

Good parenting is required in these films, and parenting behaviors are honored. But while this creates what seems like a postfeminist opportunity for men, it depicts a familiar dilemma for contemporary women. The films give men license to enjoy parenting, in other words, but women can't enjoy anything else without accepting the social and personal responsibility of unleashing miserable, dangerous boys on the world. Without expressly vilifying working moms and alienating half its fan base, Pixar manages to reiterate the idyllic world of the stay-at-home mother, the attentive father, and the healthy child entirely isolated from the dangers and inequities of the world. After all, just about the worst thing imaginable in Pixar is daycare, that "sad, lonely place for washed-up old toys who have no owners."

Toy Story 3 is unequivocal in its condemnation of Sunnyside, not just under the reign of Lotso and the horror-film shot in which he first arrives but because of the brutality and chaos of the children's play. With no apparent curriculum or engaged supervisory adults, day care is a frightening anarchic space where kids are singularly destructive. Andy's toys, even before Lotso becomes a threat, see themselves in a dangerous place from which they must escape. What self-respecting mother could blithely enroll her child there? Even Bonnie's mom, who works there, doesn't send her daughter into one of the classrooms. Though in the closing credits, Bonnie seems to have a student cubby, so that her backpack can serve as the means for transmitting messages between the friends, we never see her interact with either the Butterfly or the Caterpillar room children. Indeed, the sweet little girl's entering that dystopian universe would add a whole new level of tension to the film: who would rescue her? Instead, while the frenzied students are at recess, she sits quietly on the counter, close to her mom. The almost ridiculously exaggerated visible contrast to daycare is Bonnie's perfect yard, with a white picket fence and two parents engaged in the very act of nurturing, attending to gardening tasks while the child plays contentedly on the meticulous lawn.

The film rewards Bonnie's family by selecting them as a good new home for Andy's toys, which not only provides the perfect, happy resolution to the beloved objects terrified of their obsolescence, but also in so doing, also teaches viewers what family models reap the social and personal rewards of happy and healthy children.

One effect of this quiet traditionalism is to safely contain the problems of today's "boy crisis" in the domestic space, allowing us to blame one another—and, indirectly, feminism—for any and all problems boys face, rather than addressing the structural, systemic problems in contemporary boy culture. In a postfeminist age of complex mommy guilt, social and institutional panic about bullying, and mass confusion about how to raise boys, the postmodern antifeminism of Pixar's culturally powerful catalog is worth a second glance, not just because it's not fair, but because, enhanced with all the enchanting nostalgic pleasures for which Disney is so beloved, it keeps us from asking the questions necessary to identifying and solving the problems being faced daily by American boys. Coupled with the other traditional masculinities endorsed by the entire Pixar catalog, this old-fashioned view does more than entertain us with pleasurable nostalgia, and as parents and critics, we need to pay close attention. As much as anything we do or say, these cultural pedagogies are teaching our boys what it means to be men.

NOTES

1. Elizabeth Bell, Lynda Haas, and Laura Sells, eds., *From Mouse to Mermaid: The Politics of Film, Gender, and Culture* (Bloomington: Indiana University Press, 2008), 4.

2. Thomas de Zengotita, *Mediated: How the Media Shapes Your World and the Way You Live In It* (New York: Bloomsbury, 2005), 61–62.

3. Fredric Jameson, *Postmodernism, or, the Cultural Logic of Late Capitalism*, reprint ed. (Durham, NC: Duke University Press, 1990), 17.

4. Jameson, *Postmodernism*, 18.

5. Jameson, *Postmodernism*, 118.

6. The "kinda sorta" language comes from MaryAnn Johanson ("Retro Ad: 1980s Lots-o'-Huggin' Bear Commercial," 28 July 2011, www.flickfilosopher.com/2011/07/retro-ad-1980s-lots-o-huggin-bear-commercial.html), but similar comments are easy to find from fans and bloggers. Blogger Justin Kirkwood accuses Pixar of "implanting false childhood memories to virally promote" the film (www.notarealthing.com/2010/04/lots-o-huggin-bear).

7. de Zengotita, *Mediated*, 67.

8. de Zengotita, *Mediated*, 58.

9. de Zengotita, *Mediated*, 62–63.

10. Jack Zipes, "Breaking the Disney Spell," in *From Mouse to Mermaid: The Politics of Film, Gender, and Culture*, ed. Elizabeth Bell, Lynda Haas, and Laura Sells (Bloomington: Indiana University Press, 2008), 22.

11. Tatar, *The Hard Facts of the Grimms' Fairy Tales* (Princeton, NJ: Princeton University Press, 2003), 25.

12. Tatar, *The Hard Facts*, 71.

13. Zipes, "Breaking the Disney Spell," 25.

14. Zipes, "Breaking the Disney Spell," 30.

15. Tatar, *The Hard Facts*, 24.

16. Zipes, "Breaking the Disney Spell," 26.

17. Tatar, *The Hard Facts,* 32, 19.

18. Tatar, *The Hard Facts,* 10.

19. de Zengotita, *Mediated*, 50.

20. de Zengotita, *Mediated*, 49

21. de Zengotita, *Mediated*, 53.

22. de Zengotita, *Mediated*, 56.

23. de Zengotita, *Mediated*, 67.

24. de Zengotita, *Mediated*, 55.

25. de Zengotita, *Mediated*, 58.

26. Zipes, "Breaking the Disney Spell," 30.

27. Zipes, "Breaking the Disney Spell," 40.

28. Zipes, "Breaking the Disney Spell," 30–31.

29. Zipes, "Breaking the Disney Spell," 40.

30. de Zengotita, *Mediated*, 45; Paulo Friere and Henry A. Giroux, "Pedagogy, Popular Culture, and Public Life: An Introduction," in *Popular Culture, Schooling and Everyday Life,* ed. Henry A. Giroux and Roger Simon (New York: Bergin & Garvey, 1989).

31. Henry A. Giroux claims that our "enchantment comes at a high price, however, if the audience is meant to suspend judgment of the films' ideological messages" (*The Mouse That Roared: Disney and the End of Innocence* [Plymouth, England: Rowman & Littlefield, 1999], 96).

32. Maria Tatar, "Is Anybody Out There Listening? Fairy Tales and the Voice of the Child," in *Infant Tongues: The Voice of the Child In Literature*, ed. Elizabeth Goodenough, Mark A. Heberle, and Naomi B. Sokoloff (Detroit, MI: Wayne State University Press, 1994), 275.

33. Zipes, "Breaking the Disney Spell."

34. de Zengotita, *Mediated*, 67, 70.

35. de Zengotita, *Mediated*, 65.

36. Emily Bazelon, "Defining Bullying Down," *New York Times*, 12 March 2013, A23, www.nytimes.com/2013/03/12/opinion/defining-bullying-down.html. Other information comes from www.stopbullying.gov, and Joan Littlefield Cook and Greg Cook, *Child Development Principles and Perspectives* (Boston: Pearson, 2009), excerpted on www.education.com.

37. Renae D. Duncan offers a thorough review of the research. Among the many findings she cites are those that connect bullying to families with low cohesion and disharmony, including children being ignored and receiving very few positive emotional responses ("Family Relationships of Bullies and Victims," in *Bullying in North American Schools*, ed. Dorothy L. Espelage and Susan M. Swearer [New York: Routledge, 2011], 194).

38. Dan Kindlon and Michael Thompson, *Raising Cain: Protecting the Emotional Life of Boys* (New York: Ballantine Books, 1999), 5.

39. Emily Bazelon, "Defining Bully Down," *New York Times*, 12 March 2013, www.nytimes.com/2013/03/12/opinion/defining-bullying-down.htm (30 October 2013).

40. Emily Bazelon, *Sticks and Stones: Defeating the Culture of Bullying and Rediscovering the Power of Character and Empathy* (New York: Random House, 2013), 15.

41. Bazelon, *Sticks and Stones,* 18.

42. Giroux, *The Mouse That Roared,* 42, 124.

43. The range of attitudes might be sketched from James Dobson's *Bringing Up Boys* (Wheaton, IL: Tyndale House Publishers, 2001) to Peggy Drexler's *Raising Boys Without Men* (Emmaus, PA: Rodale, 2005), with the National Fatherhood Initiative in between (www.fatherhood.org), but countless other books, blogs, talk radio programs, websites, and articles are weighing in on these questions. See also Kenneth B. Kidd, *Making American Boys: Boyology and the Feral Tale* (Minneapolis: University of Minnesota Press, 2004), 180–81.

44. Susan Chira, *A Mother's Place: Choosing Work and Family Without Guilt or Blame* (New York: Harper Perennial, 1998), 3.

Bibliography

Ackerman, Alan. "The Spirit of Toys: Resurrection and Redemption in *Toy Story* and *Toy Story 2.*" *University of Toronto Quarterly* 74, no 4 (2005): 895–912.

Allen, Henry. "An Inexplicable Gift for Fame." *Wall Street Journal*, 28 May 2011. http://online.wsj.com/news/articles/SB10001424052748703730804576319112014330104 (1 November 2013).

Aronowitz, Stanley. *The Politics of Identity.* New York: Routledge, 1992.

Aronson, Eliot. *Nobody Left to Hate: Teaching Compassion After Columbine.* New York: Henry Holt, 2001.

Attebery, Brian. "Beyond Captain Nemo: Disney's Science Fiction." Pp. 148–60 in *From Mouse to Mermaid: The Politics of Film, Gender, and Culture,* edited by Elizabeth Bell, Lynda Haas, and Laura Sells. Bloomington: Indiana University Press, 2008.

Baudelaire, Charles. "A Philosophy of Toys" [1853]. Pp. 197–203 in *The Painter of Modern Life and Other Essays,* translated by J. Wayne. New York: Da Capo Press, 1964.

Bazelon, Emily. "Defining Bully Down." *New York Times.* 12 March 2013. www.nytimes.com/2013/03/12/opinion/defining-bullying-down.htm (30 October 2013).

———. *Sticks and Stones: Defeating the Culture of Bullying and Rediscovering the Power of Character and Empathy.* New York: Random House, 2013.

Bell, Elizabeth, Lynda Haas, and Laura Sells, eds. *From Mouse to Mermaid: The Politics of Film, Gender, and Culture.* Bloomington: Indiana University Press, 2008.

Booker, Keith. *Disney, Pixar, and the Hidden Messages of Children's Films.* Westport, CT: Greenwood, 2010.

Bronski, Michael. "High School Hell." *Z Net—The Spirit Of Resistance Lives.* 1999. www.zcommunications.org/high-school-hell-by-michael-bronski (30 October 2013).

Brooks, David. "Honor Code." *New York Times*, 5 July 2012, A23. www.nytimes.com/2012/07/06/opinion/honor-code.html (30 October 2013).

Brooks, Karen. *Consuming Innocence: Popular Culture and Our Children.* Brisbane: University of Queensland Press, 2010.

Brown, Brooks, and Rob Merritt. *No Easy Answers: The Truth Behind Death at Columbine.* New York: Lantern Books, 2002.

Brown, Lyn, Sharon Lamb, and Mark Tappan. *Packaging Boyhood: Saving Our Sons from Superheroes, Slackers, and Other Media Stereotypes.* New York: St. Martin's Press, 2009.

Brydon, Suzan. "Men at the Heart of Mothering: Finding Mother in *Finding Nemo.*" *Journal of Gender Studies* 18, no. 2 (June 2009): 131–46.

Butler, Judith. *Gender Trouble: Feminism and the Subversion of Identity.* 2nd ed. New York: Routledge, 1990.

————. "Performative Acts and Gender Constitution: an Essay in Phenomenology and Feminist Theory." *Theatre Journal* 40, no. 4 (December 1988): 519–31.

Byrne, Eleanor, and Martin McQuillan. *Deconstructing Disney*. Sterling, VA: Pluto Press, 2000.

Card, Claudia. "Pinocchio." Pp. 62–71 in *From Mouse to Mermaid: The Politics of Film, Gender, and Culture,* edited by Elizabeth Bell, Lynda Haas, and Laura Sells. Bloomington: Indiana University Press, 2008.

Carroll, Noel. *The Philosophy of Horror: Or, Paradoxes of the Heart*. New York: Routledge, 1990.

Chalmers, Phil. *Inside the Mind of a Teen Killer*. Nashville, TN: Thomas Nelson, 2009.

Chemaly, Soraya. "'Boy Crisis' in Education Is a Microcosm of Women's Lives." *Huffington Post*, 9 July 2012. www.huffingtonpost.com/soraya-chemaly/boy-crisis-in-education_b_1655282.html (30 October 2013).

Chira, Susan. *A Mother's Place: Choosing Work and Family Without Guilt or Blame*. New York: Harper Perennial, 1998.

Connell, R. W. *Masculinities*. Berkeley: University of California Press, 1995.

Connell, R. W., and James Messerschmidt. "Hegemonic Masculinity: Rethinking the Concept." *Gender & Society* 19, no. 6 (December 2005): 829–59.

Cook, Joan Littlefield, and Greg Cook. *Child Development Principles and Perspectives.* Boston: Pearson, 2009.

Corbett, Ken. *Boyhoods: Rethinking Masculinities*. New Haven, CT: Yale University Press, 2009.

Cornwell, Christopher, David B. Mustard, and Jessica Van Parys. "Noncognitive Skills and the Gender Disparities in Test Scores and Teacher Assessments: Evidence from Primary School." *Journal of Human Resources* 48, no. 1 (Winter 2013): 236–64.

Cullen, Dave. "The Rumor That Won't Go Away." *Salon*, 24 April 1999, www.salon.com/1999/04/24/rumors (1 November 2013).

Daniels, Susan, and Michael M. Piechowski, eds. *Living with Intensity: Understanding the Sensitivity, Excitability, and the Emotional Development of Gifted Children, Adolescents, and Adults*. Scottsdale, AZ: Great Potential Press, 2008.

de Zengotita, Thomas. *Mediated: How the Media Shapes Your World and the Way You Live in It*. New York: Bloomsbury, 2005.

Duncan, Ranae D. "Family Relationships of Bullies and Victims." Pp. 191–204 in *Bullying in North American Schools*, edited by Dorothy L. Espelage and Susan M. Swearer. New York: Routledge, 2011.

Dyer, Richard. *White: Essays on Race and Culture*. London: Routledge, 1997.

Elkind, David. *The Power of Play: Learning What Comes Naturally*. Reprint edition. Cambridge, MA: Da Capo Press, 2007.

Epstein, Jennifer. "Male Studies vs. Men's Studies." *Inside Higher Ed*, April 2010. www.insidehighered.com/news/2010/04/08/males (30 October 2013).

Faludi, Susan. *Stiffed: The Betrayal of the American Man*. New York: Harper Perennial, 2000.

Faragher, John M. *Daniel Boone: The Life and Legend of an American Pioneer*. New York: Henry Holt, 1992.

Farrell, Warren. *The Myth of Male Power: Why Men Are the Disposable Sex*. New York: Simon and Schuster, 1993.

Friere, Paulo, and Henry A. Giroux. "Pedagogy, Popular Culture, and Public Life: An Introduction." Pp. vii–xii in *Popular Culture, Schooling and Everyday Life,* edited by Henry A. Giroux and Roger Simon. New York: Bergin & Garvey, 1989.

Genz, Stèphanie, and Benjamin A. Brabon. *Postfeminism: Cultural Texts and Theories*. Edinburgh: Edinburgh University Press, 2009.

Gilbert, Susan. "A Conversation with Elliot Aronson; No One Left to Hate: Averting Columbines." *New York Times*, 27 March 2001, www.nytimes.com/2001/03/27/health/a-conversation-with-elliot-aronson-no-one-left-to-hate-averting-columbines.html (1 November 2013).

Gillam, Ken, and Shannon R. Wooden. "Post Princess Models of Gender: The New Man in Disney/Pixar." *Journal of Popular Film and Television* 36, no. 1 (2008): 2–8.

Giroux, Henry A. "Memory and Pedagogy in the 'Wonderful World of Disney': Beyond the Politics of Innocence." Pp. 43–61 in *From Mouse to Mermaid: The Politics of Film, Gender, and Culture,* edited by Elizabeth Bell, Lynda Haas, and Laura Sells. Bloomington: Indiana University Press, 2008.

———. "Private Satisfactions and Public Disorders: *Fight Club,* Patriarchy, and the Politics of Masculine Violence." *Public Spaces and Private Lives: Democracy Beyond 9/11.* Lanham, MD: Rowman & Littlefield, 2003.

———. *The Mouse That Roared: Disney and the End of Innocence.* Plymouth, England: Rowman & Littlefield, 1999.

———. "Animating Youth: The Disnification of Children's Culture." *Socialist Review* 24, no. 3 (1995): 23–55.

Giroux, Henry A., and Roger Simon, eds. *Popular Culture: Schooling and Everyday Life.* New York: Bergin & Garvey, 1989.

Grose, Jessica. "Omega Males and the Women Who Hate Them." *Slate,* 18 March 2010. www.slate.com/articles/double_x/doublex/2010/03/omega_males_and_the_women _who_hate_them.html. (1 November 2013).

Halberstam, Judith. *The Queer Art of Failure.* Durham, NC: Duke University Press, 2011.

Huggan, Graham. *The Postcolonial Exotic: Marketing the Margins.* New York: Routledge, 2001.

Jameson, Fredric. *Postmodernism, or, the Cultural Logic of Late Capitalism.* Reprint edition. Durham, NC: Duke University Press, 1990.

Jeffords, Susan. "The Curse of Masculinity: Disney's *Beauty and the Beast.*" Pp. 161–72 in *From Mouse to Mermaid: The Politics of Film, Gender, and Culture,* edited by Elizabeth Bell, Lynda Haas, and Laura Sells. Bloomington: Indiana University Press, 2008.

———. *Hard Bodies: Hollywood Masculinity in the Reagan Era.* New Brunswick, NJ: Rutgers University Press, 1993.

Kerr, Barbara A., and Sanford J. Cohn. *Smart Boys: Talent, Manhood, and the Search for Meaning.* Scottsdale, AZ: Great Potential Press, 2001.

Kidd, Kenneth B. *Making American Boys: Boyology and the Feral Tale.* Minneapolis: University of Minnesota Press, 2004.

Kimmel, Michael. "Solving the 'Boy Crisis' in Schools." *Huffington Post,* 30 April 2013.

———. *Manhood in America: A Cultural History.* 3rd edition. New York: Oxford University Press, 2012.

———. *Guyland: The Perilous World Where Boys Become Men.* New York: HarperCollins, 2008.

———. "Masculinity as Homophobia: Fear, Shame, and Silence in the Construction of Gender Identity." Pp. 266–87 in *The Masculinities Reader,* edited by Stephen Whitehead and Frank Barrett. Cambridge, UK: Polity, 2001.

———. "A War Against Boys?" *Tikkun,* November–December 2000. www.tikkun.org/next-gen/a-war-against-boys (30 October 2012).

Kimmel, Michael, and Christina Sommers. "Do Boys Face More Sexism Than Girls?" *Huffington Post,* 20 February 2013, www.huffingtonpost.com/michael-kimmel/lets-talk-boys_b_2645801.html (30 October 2013).

Kindlon, Dan, and Michael Thompson. *Raising Cain: Protecting the Emotional Life of Boys.* New York: Ballantine Books, 1999.

Kinney, D. A. "From Nerds to Normals: The Recovery of Identity among Adolescents from Middle School to High School. *Sociology of Education* 66, no. 1 (1993): 21–40.

Klein, Jessie. *The Bully Society: School Shootings and the Crisis of Bullying in America's Schools.* New York: New York University Press, 2012.

Kline, Stephen. *Out of the Garden: Toys and Children's Culture in the Age of TV Marketing.* New York: Verso, 1995.

LaPierre, Wayne. National Rifle Association press conference. 21 December 2012. http:// home.nra.org/pdf/Transcript_PDF.pdf (30 October 2013).

Lewin, Tamar. "Math Scores Show No Gap for Girls, Study Finds." *New York Times,* 25 July 2008. www.nytimes.com/2008/07/25/education/25math.html (30 October 2013).

————. "At Colleges, Women Are Leaving Men in the Dust." *New York Times*, July 9, 2006, A1. www.nytimes.com/2006/07/09/education/09college.html (30 October 2013).

Lewis, Gail. "The Need to Create: Constructive and Destructive Behavior in Creatively Gifted Children." *Gifted Education International* 7, no. 2 (January 1991): 62–68.

Linn, Susan. *Consuming Kids: Protecting Our Children from the Onslaught of Marketing & Advertising*. New York: Anchor Books, 2005.

Marx, Karl. "The Fetishism of Commodities and the Secret Thereof." From *Capital* (1867). Pp. 320–21 in *The Marx and Engels Reader*, 2nd edition, edited by Robert C. Tucker. New York: W. W. Norton, 1978.

————. "The Elections in England: Tories and Whigs." *New York Daily Tribune*, 21 August 1852. www.marxists.org/archive/marx/works/1852/08/06.htm (1 November 2013).

Matthews, Jay. "Study Casts Doubt on the 'Boy Crisis.'" *Washington Post*, 26 June 2006. www.washingtonpost.com/wp-dyn/content/article/2006/06/25/AR2006062501047.html (30 October 2013).

Mead, Sara. "The Evidence Suggests Otherwise: The Truth about Boys and Girls." *Education Sector, American Institute for Research*, June 2006. www.educationsector.org/sites/default/files/publications/ESO_BoysAndGirls.pdf (30 October 2013).

Messner, Michael A. "The Masculinity of the Governator: Muscle and Compassion in American Politics." *Gender & Society* 21, no. 4 (August 2007): 461–80.

————. "The Limits of 'The Male Sex Role': An Analysis of the Men's Liberation and Men's Rights Movements' Discourse." *Gender & Society* 12, no. 3 (June 1998): 255–76.

————. *Power at Play: Sports and the Problem of Masculinity*. Boston: Beacon Press, 1992.

Millett, Ann. "'Other' Fish in the Sea: *Finding Nemo* as an Epic Representation of Disability." *Disability Studies Quarterly* 24, no. 1 (Winter 2004). http://dsq-sds.org/article/view/873/1048 (1 November 2013)

Mundy, Liza. *The Richer Sex: How the New Majority of Female Breadwinners Is Transforming Our Culture*. New York: Free Press, 2013.

Murphy Patrick D. "'The Whole Wide World Was Scrubbed Clean': The Androcentric Animation of Denatured Disney." Pp. 125–36 in *From Mouse to Mermaid: The Politics of Film, Gender, and Culture*, edited by Elizabeth Bell, Lynda Haas, and Laura Sells. Bloomington: Indiana University Press, 2008.

"Mutant Toys." *Disney.com*. n.d. www.disney.go.com/disneyvideos/animatedfilms/toystory/characters/mutant.htm (1 November 2013).

Newman, Katherine S. "Roots of a Rampage." *The Nation*, December 19, 2012. www.thenation.com/article/171866/roots-rampage (1 November 2013).

————. "School Shootings: Why They Do It." *Baltimore Sun*, August 28, 2012. http://articles.baltimoresun.com/2012-08-28/news/bs-ed-school-shootings-20120828_1_random-shootings-rampage-social-media (1 November 2013).

Oldenziel, Ruth. *Making Technology Masculine: Men, Women, and Modern Machines in America, 1870–1945*. Amsterdam: Amsterdam University Press, 1999.

Orenstein, Peggy. *Cinderella Ate My Daughter: Dispatches from the Frontlines of the New Girlie-Girl Culture*. New York: HarperCollins, 2011.

Pollack, William. *Real Boys: Rescuing Our Sons from the Myths of Boyhood*. New York: Henry Holt, 1998.

Price, David A. *The Pixar Touch*. New York: Vintage Books, 2008.

Propp, Vladmir. *Morphology of the Folktale*. 2nd ed. Edited by Louis A. Wagner. Austin: University of Texas Press, 1968 [1928].

Rosin, Hanna. *The End of Men and the Rise of Women*. New York: Riverhead Books, 2012.

————. "The End of Men." *Atlantic*, 8 June 2010. www.theatlantic.com/magazine/archive/2010/07/the-end-of-men/308135/ (1 November 2013).

Sax, Leonard. *Boys Adrift: The Five Factors Driving the Growing Epidemic of Unmotivated Boys and Underachieving Young Men*. New York: Basic Books, 2007.

Schwarz, Alan, and Sarah Cohen. "A.D.H.D. Seen in 11% of U.S. Children as Diagnoses Rise." *New York Times*, 1 April 2013. www.nytimes.com/services/xml/rss/yahoo/myyahoo/2013/04/01/health/more-diagnoses-of-hyperactivity-causing-concern.xml (26 September 2013).

Smoodin, Eric, ed. *Disney Discourse: Producing the Magic Kingdom.* New York: Routledge, 1994.

Sommers, Christina Hoff. "The Boys at the Back." *New York Times*, 2 February 2013, SR1. http://opinionator.blogs.nytimes.com/2013/02/02/the-boys-at-the-back (30 October 2013).

———. *The War Against Boys: How Misguided Policies Are Harming Our Young Men.* New York: Simon & Schuster, 2000.

Sparks, Sarah D. "Report Points to Widening Gap in Boys' Educational Attainment." *Education Week*, 17 May 2011, http://blogs.edweek.org/edweek/inside-school-research/2011/05/report_boys_college_readiness.html (30 October 2013).

Stokes, Colin. "How Movies Teach Manhood." *TED: Ideas Worth Spreading*, November 2012. www.ted.com/talks/colin_stokes_how_movies_teach_manhood.html (30 October 2013).

Stroud, Angela. "Good Guys with Guns: Hegemonic Masculinity and Concealed Handguns." *Gender & Society* 26, no. 2 (April 2012): 216–38.

Ta, Lynn M. "Hurt So Good: *Fight Club*, Masculine Violence, and the Crisis of Capitalism." *Journal of American Culture* 29, no. 3 (September 2006): 265–77.

Tatar, Maria. *The Hard Facts of the Grimms' Fairy Tales.* Princeton, NJ: Princeton University Press, 2003.

———. "Is Anybody Out There Listening? Fairy Tales and the Voice of the Child." Pp. 275–83 in *Infant Tongues: The Voice of the Child In Literature*, edited by Elizabeth Goodenough, Mark A. Heberle, and Naomi B. Sokoloff. Detroit, MI: Wayne State University Press, 1994.

Think Tank. "Is There a War Against Boys?" *PBS*, 29 July 2000. www.pbs.org/thinktank/transcript893.html (30 October 2013).

Vary, Adam B. "The Monsters University Character Who Changed Gender at the Last Minute." *Buzzfeed Entertainment*, 22 June 2013. www.buzzfeed.com/adambvary/monsters-university-dean-hardscrabble-change-gender (1 November 2013).

Webb, James T., Janet L. Gore, Edward R. Amend, and Arlene R. DeVries. *A Parent's Guide to Gifted Children.* Scottsdale, AZ: Great Potential Press, 2007.

Wilgoren, Jodi. "Terror in Littleton: The Group." *New York Times*, 25 April 1999. www.nytimes.com/1999/04/25/us/terror-in-littleton-the-group-society-of-outcasts-began-with-a-99-black-coat.html (1 November 2013).

Zipes, Jack. "Breaking the Disney Spell." Pp. 21–42 in *From Mouse to Mermaid: The Politics of Film, Gender, and Culture*, edited by Elizabeth Bell, Lynda Haas, and Laura Sells. Bloomington: Indiana University Press, 2008.

Index

About the Authors

Shannon R. Wooden is associate professor of English at Missouri State University, where she teaches British literature, literary theory, and narrative medicine. Long interested in gender studies and feminist theory, she has previously published on representations of women in film and on strategies for teaching the work of women writers outside of gender-studies frameworks. More recently, theorizing the role(s) of ethics in literary pedagogy, she has examined narrative medicine as a pedagogical paradigm for reading literature as empathic practice. Currently, she is studying popular representations of illness, particularly as it may affect hegemonic gender identity.

Ken Gillam, director of composition at Missouri State University, teaches composition theory and writing pedagogy. His research interests lie in exploring writers' ideological foundations, particularly those rooted in the cultural constructions of gender and class. In previous publications, he has applied ecological theories of composition to open-access and online pedagogical environments, carving out a place in academic writing to acknowledge the numerous rhetorical paradigms that contribute to student writers' meaning-making efforts. Currently, he is developing curricula to improve general education students' critical literacy with popular culture and its various rhetorical forms.

When they began collaborating on the larger project of raising their two sons, Oscar and Archie, the authors realized that their professional interests had direct bearing on their personal lives. Decades of thinking like critics and teachers disrupted the easy pleasures of watching children's media, and this book arose from numerous productive conversations with the boys about their beloved films.